THE PRUDENT CHEF

Eat Well for Less

---

150 Recipes
Ten Chapters

Darius Redmond

The Prudent Chef: Eat Well for Less

Copyright © 2026 Darius Redmond
All rights reserved.

ISBN 979-8-9958963-0-2

Published by Parchment House Publishing

The information in this book is provided for educational and practical preparedness purposes. The author makes no warranties regarding the completeness or accuracy of the information and accepts no liability for any loss or damage arising from its use. Always use common sense and consult appropriate authorities when making decisions about food safety, particularly in emergency situations.

Parchment House Publishing
ParchmentHousePublishing.com

First Edition, 2026

To my wife, Anthea.

For everything.

For the people who prepare not out of fear,
but out of love for the ones beside them.

For anyone who has ever gone hungry and had nothing.
Now you do.

Why This Book Exists

As of April 2026, the United States carries nearly $40 trillion in national debt, a number so large it has ceased to feel real to most people. It is real. It cannot be repaid. Inflation has driven the cost of groceries, housing, fuel, and basic necessities to levels that were unimaginable five years ago. Geopolitical fractures that were once theoretical are now daily headlines: a war in the Middle East with no clear end, allied nations negotiating trade arrangements that deliberately exclude the United States, and the slow but measurable erosion of the US dollar as the world's reserve currency.

These are not opinions. They are documented, observable facts. And the honest assessment of where these trends lead is not reassuring.

This book was written for the person who has never had to think about any of this before. Not for hardened preppers who already have a plan, they know most of what is in these pages. This book is for John Q. Public. The person who has always been able to go to the grocery store. The person whose emergency plan has never been tested. The person who does not know what to cook when the power is out, the store shelves are thin, money is tight, and the cell phone signal is gone.

That person needs to know. And the window to learn and prepare is now, not after.

The recipes in this book are not exotic or complicated. They are the recipes that kept families alive through two World Wars, through the Great Depression of the 1930s, through droughts and famines and every other disaster that has tested human endurance. They were developed by people who had no margin for error, who could not afford to waste a potato peel, who made bread from three ingredients, who knew that a ham bone and a bag of dried beans was a week of meals. These people fed their families under conditions that most modern Americans cannot imagine.

You do not have to wait for a crisis to use this book. Many of these recipes will save you money right now, today, regardless of what happens next. But if harder times come, and the weight of evidence suggests they will, you will be fed. Your family will be fed. That is what this book is for.

Prepare now. While you still can.

How to Use This Book

The book is organized by food type, not by occasion.

If you need bread and you have flour, go to Chapter I. If you need protein from inexpensive cuts, go to Chapter III. If your food reserves are running critically low and you need to know what to do right now, go directly to Chapter IX. If you want to know which foods in your pantry are safe to eat after nuclear fallout, go to Chapter X. You do not need to read this book cover to cover. Use it as a reference.

Chapter VIII: Preservation & Emergency Rations. Read this before you need it.

Chapter VIII is not just about canning and jerky. It contains two complete food production systems you can run indoors with no electricity, no garden, and no special equipment: bean sprouts grown in mason jars that produce fresh living food in four days from dried beans you already have, and oyster mushrooms grown on cardboard and coffee grounds in any cool dark space. It also contains purpose-built emergency ration recipes developed by the United States government during the Cold War. This chapter was designed for the situation where the grocery store is not an option. Read it now, while you have time to prepare, not after.

Chapter IX: What To Do When Your Reserves Have Almost Run Out. If that moment is now, go there immediately.

Chapter IX is the most important chapter in this book for the person in genuine crisis. It is not reference material. It is not footnotes. It is a complete step-by-step plan written specifically for someone who has looked at what they have left and realized it is running out. It tells you exactly what to do starting today: how to inventory and ration what remains, how to start growing fresh food from your existing stores within the week, how to stretch everything as far as it will go, how to protect your seed supply so you do not run out permanently, and what a realistic day of food looks like when reserves are critically low. If you are reading this book because that situation is already here, close this page and go directly to Chapter IX now. Everything else in this book will still be here when you come back.

The Field Notes.

Every recipe ends with a Field Note, a practical tip about technique, substitution, or storage that did not fit in the method. Read the field note before you start cooking. It often contains the one thing that makes the difference between a recipe that works and one that does not.

About the ingredients.

Every recipe in this book is built from ingredients available at any grocery store, dollar store, or big-box retailer. No specialty items are required. Where a recipe calls for something that might not be in your pantry, a substitute is documented.

Baking soda and baking powder are not the same thing. This matters.

These two ingredients sit next to each other on the grocery store shelf, cost about the same, and look nearly identical in a recipe. They are not interchangeable. Using the wrong one produces flat, dense, or bitter baked goods. Here is the distinction.

Baking soda is pure sodium bicarbonate. The most common brand is Arm & Hammer, the orange box with the yellow logo that has been in American kitchens since the 1860s. Baking soda is a base. On its own it does nothing. It needs an acid already present in the recipe to activate it and produce the bubbles that make baked goods rise. That acid can be buttermilk, vinegar, lemon juice, molasses, brown sugar, honey, or yogurt. When baking soda meets the acid, the reaction is immediate, batter using baking soda needs to go into the pan or oven quickly before the bubbles escape. It is approximately four times stronger than baking powder, which is why recipes call for much smaller amounts, typically a quarter to half a teaspoon.

Baking powder already contains baking soda plus a dry acid, plus a small amount of cornstarch to keep it stable. Common brands include Rumford, Calumet, and Davis, the small cans in the baking aisle. Baking powder is self-contained. It does not need an acid in the recipe because the acid is already mixed in. Most baking powder sold today is double-acting, meaning it produces bubbles twice: once when the batter gets wet and again when it hits heat in the oven. This gives more rise and allows a longer window between mixing and baking. Baking powder is used when a recipe has no acidic ingredients.

Many recipes use both together: the baking soda reacts with whatever acid is in the recipe for immediate lift, and the baking powder provides a second rise in the oven. If a recipe calls for both, use both.

> *Field Note: If you run out of baking powder and a recipe calls for it: substitute one quarter teaspoon baking soda plus half a teaspoon cream of tartar for every one teaspoon of baking powder required. This works because you are recreating the baking soda plus acid combination that baking powder already contains. If you have neither, a sourdough starter handles all leavening on its own. See Recipe 8-1.*

About serving sizes.

Serving sizes in this book are based on genuine hunger, not the modest portions printed on commercial packaging or served in restaurants. A recipe that serves four means four people who have not eaten recently will be satisfied. It does not mean four small polite portions. If your household is doing physical work, hauling, building, farming, walking long distances, dealing with the physical demands that come with a crisis situation, caloric needs increase significantly. A person doing hard manual labor in cold weather may need 3,000 to 4,000 calories per day, twice the standard desk-job baseline. Serve accordingly. In difficult circumstances, underfeeding the people doing the work is a costly mistake. When in doubt, make more.

About cooking without power.

Many recipes include both oven and open-fire or stovetop-only instructions. If you own one cast iron skillet and one cast iron Dutch oven, you can make almost everything in this book over a camp stove, a wood fire, or a charcoal grill. That combination of two pieces of cookware is the single most valuable kitchen investment for preparedness purposes.

Recipe 5-10: The Wish Sandwich.

One recipe in this book, Recipe 5-10, is two slices of bread with nothing between them. It is included not as a recipe but as a record. Millions of families during the worst years of the Depression fed their children exactly this for lunch because there was nothing else. It is in this book so it is not forgotten. Every other recipe exists so that one does not have to be made. Build your pantry before you need it.

Contents

CHAPTER I   Breads, Grains, & Gravies
Recipes 1-1 through 1-16 (16 recipes) Hardtack, biscuits, cornbreads, flatbreads, and gravies. If you can make bread, you can feed people.

CHAPTER II   Soups & Broths
Recipes 2-1 through 2-17 (17 recipes) From water soup to bone broth. How to turn almost nothing into something hot and filling.

CHAPTER III   Protein: Meat, Fish & Eggs
Recipes 3-1 through 3-26 (26 recipes) Jerky, pemmican, organ meats, canned fish, eggs, and the cheap cuts worth knowing. PLUS FIVE RECIPES FOR WHEN THERE IS NO MEAT AT ALL.

CHAPTER IV   Beans, Grains & Vegetables
Recipes 4-1 through 4-19 (19 recipes) Dried beans, cornmeal, grits, sweet potatoes, and wild greens. Ends with the meal that feeds the world.

CHAPTER V   Sandwiches & Quick Meals
Recipes 5-1 through 5-19 (19 recipes) From peanut butter and pickle to the wish sandwich. Everything from a full lunch to two slices of bread with nothing between them.

CHAPTER VI   Snacks & Staples
Recipes 6-1 through 6-15 (15 recipes) Sardines on crackers, cornbread in cold milk, stovetop popcorn, and the case for never pouring bacon drippings down the drain.

CHAPTER VII   Desserts & Sweet Table
Recipes 7-1 through 7-24 (24 recipes) Twenty-four cheap desserts. Morale matters. A dollar can of pineapple makes a cake that feeds ten.

CHAPTER VIII   Preservation & Emergency Rations
Recipes 8-1 through 8-14 (14 recipes) How to make food last without refrigeration. Salt cures, drying, pickling, purpose-built survival rations, how to grow fresh food from almost nothing, and emergency food for your pets.

CHAPTER IX   What To Do When Your Reserves Have Almost Run Out
READ THIS NOW Not footnotes. Not reference material. A complete step-by-step survival plan for when your food supply is critically low. If that moment is now, start here.

CHAPTER X   Protecting Your Food Supply in Nuclear Fallout
Reference chapter, no recipe numbers What actually contaminates food, what does not, and exactly what to do about it. Sources: FEMA, CDC, WHO.

The Survival Pantry

What to stock before you need it

The following list is not aspirational. It is the practical minimum, the ingredients that appear most frequently across this book, that store the longest, and that deliver the most calories and nutrition per dollar. You do not need all of it at once. Buy what you can, when you can, and rotate it. A pantry built over six months costs almost nothing per week. A pantry assembled in a panic costs a great deal and is often wrong.

Everything here is available at any grocery store, big-box retailer, or online. No specialty suppliers required.

A note on prices: this book does not list specific prices for any item. Food costs are volatile, subject to inflation, supply disruptions, and regional variation that makes any printed price outdated almost immediately. For every item on this list, source from the lowest-cost option available to you, store brands, bulk bins, discount grocers, big-box warehouse stores, and dollar stores all carry most of these items and frequently at significantly lower prices than name-brand grocery shelves. The calories are identical regardless of the label.

Start Here: The Core Five

Before anything else on this list, stock these five things. They are the calorie backbone of this entire book and the foundation that every other item builds on. They are also the cheapest, most widely available, and longest-storing foods that exist. If money is tight and you can only do one thing, do this.

• White rice, 25 lbs (11.3 kg), approximately 41,000 calories. Shelf life of 25+ years sealed. Feeds people at every meal in every culture on earth.

• Dried beans, assorted, 25 lbs (11.3 kg) total, approximately 40,000 calories. Combined with rice, forms a complete protein. Six months of protein for one person in a single sealed bucket.

• Rolled oats, 25 lbs (11.3 kg), approximately 43,000 calories. Breakfast, supper, baking, and emergency ration bars. 25-30 year shelf life sealed.

• All-purpose flour, 25 lbs (11.3 kg), approximately 41,000 calories. Bread, biscuits, gravy, pasta, and thickening for soups and stews.

• Peanut butter, 10 lbs (4.5 kg), approximately 37,000 calories. The most calorie-dense shelf-stable food on this list at 3,700 calories per pound. Complete protein when paired with any grain.

Those five items together represent approximately 202,000 calories. At 2,000 calories per day that is 101 days, over three months of food for one person. For two people eating normally it is six weeks. All five are available at any grocery store or big-box retailer. That is the entry point. Everything else on this list extends your reserve further, adds variety, and improves nutrition. But those five items, in a cool dark location, are the foundation nothing else works without.

Add canned goods and the picture improves further. Twenty-four cans of beans, twenty-four cans of tuna or salmon, and twelve cans of condensed soup add roughly 30,000 more calories and significant protein, another two weeks per person on top of the dry goods base. Canned goods require no cooking equipment and no water beyond what is already in the can, which matters when infrastructure is uncertain. Stock them alongside the dry goods, not instead of them.

> *Field Note: The single most important thing to understand about food storage: the food you store must be food your household will actually eat. A can of sardines that sits untouched because nobody in the house will eat sardines is not part of your reserve. Stock what your family eats. Rotate it. Eat from it and replace it. A living pantry you use every week is more valuable than a sealed vault nobody opens.*

GRAINS & STARCHES

• All-purpose flour, 25 lbs (11.3 kg). Sealed in Mylar bags with oxygen absorbers: 10+ years shelf life.

• Stone-ground cornmeal, 10 lbs (4.5 kg). Sealed: 5+ years. The base of more recipes in this book than any other single ingredient.

• Old-fashioned rolled oats, 25 lbs (11.3 kg). Sealed in Mylar: 25-30 years. Breakfast, supper, baking, and emergency bars.

• Long-grain white rice, 25 lbs (11.3 kg). Sealed: 25+ years. Brown rice has more nutrition but shorter shelf life, white rice stores longer.

• Dried pasta, 10 lbs (4.5 kg) assorted shapes. 2+ years sealed.

• Baking powder, 2 lbs (905 g). Test it: 1 tsp (5 ml) in 1/4 cup (60 ml) hot water should bubble vigorously. Replace if it does not.

• Baking soda, 2 lbs (905 g). Leavening, cleaning, and dozens of other uses.

• Active dry yeast, sealed packets. Keeps 2+ years past the best-by date in a cool location. Or maintain a potato starter (Recipe 8-1) as a permanent free alternative that never runs out and never expires.

DRIED BEANS & LEGUMES

Dried beans are the most cost-effective protein and calorie source available to anyone with a pot and a heat source. A 5-gallon (18.9 L) bucket of mixed dried beans, sealed, stored in a cool basement, is six months of protein for one person.

• Pinto beans, 10 lbs (4.5 kg).

• Navy or great northern beans, 5 lbs (2.3 kg).

• Split peas, 5 lbs (2.3 kg). No soaking required. Ready in 90 minutes.

• Red lentils, 5 lbs (2.3 kg). No soaking. Ready in 12 minutes. The fastest protein you can cook from dry.

• Dried lentils (green or brown), 5 lbs (2.3 kg). Ready in 25 minutes.

• Black-eyed peas, 5 lbs (2.3 kg).

COOKING FAT

• Vegetable shortening (Crisco), 6 lbs (2.7 kg). 2+ years shelf life. Works in every recipe in this book that calls for lard or fat.

• Lard, 4 lbs (1.8 kg). Longer shelf life than butter. Better for biscuits and pie crust than shortening.

• Olive oil or vegetable oil, 2 liters. 18 months.

• Save every tablespoon of bacon drippings in a sealed jar. Free cooking fat that keeps 2 weeks at room temperature, months refrigerated.

CANNED GOODS

• Canned salmon, 24 cans (14.75 oz, 420 g). Complete protein, omega-3s, and calcium from edible bones. 3-5 year shelf life.

• Canned sardines, 48 tins. The most nutritionally complete and cheapest canned protein available.

• Canned tuna, 24 cans.

• Spam, 12 cans. Shelf-stable 3+ years. Fries well. Reliable when other protein is unavailable.

• Canned tomatoes, 24 cans crushed or whole. Appear in more recipes than almost anything else on this list.

• Canned beans, 24 cans assorted. For when there is no time to soak dried beans.

• Condensed soups, 12 cans. Tomato soup is a baking ingredient (see Recipe 7-21).

SALT, SUGAR & SWEETENERS

• Iodized table salt, 10 lbs (4.5 kg). Indefinite shelf life. Iodized specifically, iodine deficiency is a real risk in prolonged disruption.

• Non-iodized pickling salt, 5 lbs (2.3 kg). For preservation recipes. Iodine interferes with curing and fermentation.

• Granulated white sugar, 25 lbs (11.3 kg). Sealed: indefinite shelf life.

• Brown sugar, 5 lbs (2.3 kg). Store airtight.

• Honey, 3 lbs (1.4 kg). Genuine indefinite shelf life when sealed. Natural antimicrobial properties.

• Blackstrap molasses, 1 quart (945 ml). Iron, calcium, potassium. Cheap. Shelf-stable.

• Peanut butter, 10 lbs (4.5 kg). Natural only (peanuts and salt). 3,700 calories per pound. One of the most calorie-dense shelf-stable foods available. Appears in Recipe 2-13 (Peanut Butter Soup), Recipe 5-6 (Peanut Butter and Pickle Sandwich), Recipe 7-1 (No-Bake Chocolate Oatmeal Cookies), Recipe 7-23 (Potato Candy), and Recipe 8-3 (2400-Calorie Emergency Bars). Natural peanut butter stores better than sweetened commercial varieties and works in both sweet and savory applications.

• Whole peanuts in shell, 5 lbs (2.3 kg). The long-term backup to jarred peanut butter. Unshelled peanuts store 4-6 months at room temperature and over a year in a cool dry location. When jarred peanut butter runs out, roast shelled peanuts in a dry pan over medium heat until golden and fragrant, add salt, and blend or mash until smooth. That is the complete recipe for scratch peanut butter. No oil needed, the peanuts contain enough natural fat to become smooth with sufficient mashing. A fork and a bowl works if no blender is available. Important: peanut allergies are severe and can be fatal. If you are cooking for others, always ask before using peanuts or peanut butter in any form.

SHELF-STABLE DAIRY

• Powdered whole milk, 10 lbs (4.5 kg). Sealed: 2-10 years depending on packaging. Reconstitutes to full-strength milk. Works in every recipe in this book that calls for milk.

• Canned evaporated milk, 12 cans. Richer than reconstituted powder. 18-24 months.

• Canned sweetened condensed milk, 6 cans. For desserts and emergency calorie bars.

Cheese: What Actually Keeps

Most cheese belongs to the refrigerator and is gone within days if power fails. But two categories are genuine pantry staples that belong in any serious food reserve.

The first is canned grated parmesan, the green Kraft can and its equivalents. This is shelf-stable for 12 months or more unopened and several months after opening in a cool location. It is not the same product as fresh parmesan but it is real cheese with real fat and protein, and a few tablespoons transforms the flavor of almost anything. Add it to pasta, stir it into bean soup, sprinkle it over rice and lentils, fold it into cornbread batter, or use it to finish any dish that needs depth and salt. Stock six to twelve cans. They are inexpensive, take almost no space, and will be among the most useful things on your shelf.

The second is wax-coated hard cheese, aged cheddar, gouda, and edam are the most commonly available. The wax coating is a preservation barrier, not decoration. A wax-coated block stored in a cool dark location keeps for three to six months without refrigeration. A cool basement can extend that further. Check it monthly. Surface mold on hard cheese is not spoilage, cut away a half-inch around and below any mold spot and the interior is safe to eat. This is the same principle that has applied to hard cheese storage for centuries. If the interior smells sour, tastes off, or shows mold throughout rather than on the surface only, discard it.

Powdered cheese is the third option and the longest keeper. Sealed in a can or Mylar bag, powdered cheddar has a shelf life of ten or more years. It reconstitutes into a sauce with water or milk, works stirred into cornbread batter or mashed potatoes, and provides real fat and flavor at a fraction of the cost of fresh cheese. It is available at most farm supply stores, Amazon, and any preparedness supplier.

Recipes where shelf-stable cheese makes a direct improvement:

• Recipe 2-4 (Bread Soup), a tablespoon of grated parmesan stirred in enriches the broth and adds depth.

• Recipe 4-16 (Red Lentil Dal), parmesan or powdered cheddar stirred in off the heat enriches the entire dish.

• Recipe 4-19 (Beans & Rice), hard cheese grated over the top converts a survival meal into something genuinely satisfying.

• Recipe 5-16 (Creamed Chipped Beef on Toast), powdered cheddar stirred into the gravy produces a richer sauce.

• Recipe 6-13 (Velveeta on Crackers), where fresh Velveeta is unavailable, reconstituted powdered cheddar is a direct substitute.

• Any pasta preparation, canned parmesan over pasta with oil and garlic (Recipe 4-16 method applied to pasta) is a complete meal from shelf-stable ingredients.

• Recipe 1-3 (Skillet Cornbread), two tablespoons of powdered cheddar or grated parmesan stirred into the batter adds fat, protein, and flavor at almost no additional cost.

You do not need a full spice rack. You need these:

• Salt and black pepper, already listed above, but worth repeating. These two do more work than everything else combined.

• Cayenne, 1 lb (455 g). Heat, flavor, and mild antimicrobial properties.

• Garlic powder, 1 lb (455 g). Fresh garlic stores 6 months in a cool dry location. Powder is the backup.

• Cinnamon, 1 lb (455 g). Essential for oatmeal, sweet potatoes, desserts, and apple preparations.

• Apple cider vinegar, 1 gallon (3.8 L). Pickling, gravy brightening, bread substitute for buttermilk, and general preservation.

• Soy sauce, 2 bottles. Indefinite shelf life unopened, 1-2 years after opening. Appears in multiple recipes as a flavor base for meat substitutes, jerky marinades, and lentil preparations. One of the most useful flavor-building ingredients in this book.

• Yellow mustard, 4 bottles. Condiment, acid, binding agent. Appears throughout.

• Cocoa powder, 2 lbs (905 g). Wacky Cake, Chocolate Cobbler, No-Bake Cookies, three recipes that require no eggs or refrigerated ingredients.

WHAT THIS PANTRY ACTUALLY GETS YOU

If you stock everything on this list, you have approximately 445,000 calories of shelf-stable food. At 2,000 calories per day, the standard adult maintenance level, that is roughly 222 days of food for one person, or just over seven months. At a leaner 1,500 calories per day, it stretches to nearly ten months. For two people eating normally, plan on three to four months.

Those numbers assume you can and will eat everything on the list. In practice, most households cannot. Dietary restrictions, food allergies, intolerances, and plain personal preference will remove some items for some people. Cayenne and hot spices are on this list, if you or someone in your household cannot tolerate heat, those calories do not count for you. Peanuts and peanut butter are here, a peanut allergy removes nearly 50,000 calories from your reserve. Canned fish appears multiple times, if no one in the household will eat sardines, those 48 tins are not actually part of your food supply. Be honest about what your household will actually eat under stress, and stock accordingly. A pantry full of food nobody will touch is not a reserve. It is storage.

The practical approach: build around the items your household already eats and genuinely likes. Rice, beans, oats, flour, and pasta are the non-negotiable core, almost everyone tolerates all five, they form the calorie backbone of the entire list, and together they represent roughly 175,000 calories before anything else is added. Everything else on this list builds on that core and extends both the duration and the variety. Substitute freely. If cayenne is not tolerable, skip it and add more of what is. If sardines will not be eaten, replace those calories with more canned tuna or salmon. The goal is a reserve your household will actually use. That reserve will keep you fed. A theoretically perfect pantry that goes untouched will not.

A NOTE ON STORAGE

The difference between a pantry that lasts one year and one that lasts ten is packaging, not ingredients. Mylar bags with oxygen absorbers, sealed inside food-grade 5-gallon (18.9 L) buckets, will keep white rice, dried beans, oats, flour, sugar, and salt for a decade or more with no loss of quality. A complete setup, bags, absorbers, bucket sealer, and buckets, costs under $50 and is available on Amazon or at any farm supply store.

Store in the coolest, darkest location available. A basement or interior closet is better than a garage or attic. Heat and light are the enemies of shelf life, not time.

Label everything with the purchase date. Rotate, put new purchases behind older stock and use the oldest first. A pantry that is never rotated is a pantry that fails when you need it most.

Start now. Buy a little extra every week. Within six months you will have a meaningful reserve. Within a year you will have something that could carry your family through a genuine crisis. The cost per week is less than a fast food meal.

IF YOU CANNOT AFFORD MYLAR: THE OLD WAY STILL WORKS

Mylar bags and oxygen absorbers are the modern answer to long-term food storage. They work extremely well. They also cost money, require ordering online or finding a farm supply store, and assume you have the time and resources to set the system up properly.

If you do not have that money or that access right now, understand this: people stored food successfully for thousands of years before Mylar existed. The Amish do it today without any of it. Your great-grandmother did it without any of it. The enemies of stored food have always been the same five things: moisture, oxygen, light, heat, and pests. Every method below addresses those five things using what you likely already have or can get for almost nothing.

Glass jars with tight lids.

Mason jars are genuine long-term storage containers. A quart mason jar filled with dried lentils, sealed tightly, stored in a cool dark cabinet, will last two to five years with no special treatment. You probably already own these. If you do not, they cost about a dollar each at any dollar store or thrift shop. Wide-mouth jars are easier to fill and clean. Fill them completely, less air space means longer storage life.

Clean buckets with tight lids.

Any food-grade bucket with a gasket lid works for dry goods storage. You do not have to buy these. Delis, bakeries, and restaurant kitchens throw them away constantly. Walk into any deli or bakery and ask if they have empty pickle buckets or frosting buckets they are discarding. Most will hand you a stack for free. Wash thoroughly with hot soapy water, rinse completely, dry fully before filling. A clean five-gallon pickle bucket with a tight lid stores 25 pounds (11.3 kg) of rice or beans adequately for two to four years in a cool location.

Bay leaves.

Dried bay leaves repel pantry insects naturally. The Amish have used this for generations. Tuck four or five dried bay leaves into every container of stored grain, rice, flour, or beans. Replace them once a year. A two-dollar jar of bay leaves from any dollar store or grocery store protects a significant quantity of stored food from weevils and beetles. This is not folk medicine. It works because bay leaves contain compounds that interfere with the reproductive cycle of common pantry insects.

Wood ash.

Dry wood ash from any clean fire, wood stove, or fireplace mixed lightly through stored grain or beans repels insects and has been used for this purpose across every continent for thousands of years. Use only ash from clean wood, not treated lumber or charcoal lighter fluid. A thin layer on the bottom of the storage container, the grain on top, and a thin layer on top of the grain before sealing. The grain is rinsed before cooking and the ash rinses away completely. Free if you have any source of wood fire.

Cool and dark is more important than the container.

Temperature is the single biggest factor in how long stored food lasts. A cool basement or interior closet dramatically extends the life of anything you store, regardless of the container. A root cellar, which is simply a hole in the ground or a deeply buried room that stays cool year-round through the earth's natural insulation, is what farming families used for centuries before refrigeration existed. You do not need to build one. You need to find the coolest, darkest place in your home and put your food there. A north-facing interior closet on a lower floor is better than a garage. A basement corner away from the water heater is better than a pantry near the stove. No cost. Just awareness.

What this gets you without spending anything extra.

Clean free buckets from a deli, filled with dried beans and rice, a handful of bay leaves in each, sealed with a tight lid, stored in your coolest interior space: two to four years of shelf-stable food storage. That is not as long as Mylar. It is entirely sufficient for a genuine crisis reserve. When you have more money, upgrade to Mylar bags inside those same buckets and extend your storage life to ten years or more. But do not wait for the perfect system before starting. A bucket of beans in a closet today is worth more than a perfect Mylar setup you cannot afford yet.

> *Field Note: One thing that has not changed in ten thousand years of food storage: dry food stays safe. Wet food spoils. Every method above is aimed at keeping moisture out. If your storage location has any dampness, any condensation, any humidity, address that first. A $5 box of moisture absorber packets placed inside the storage area costs almost nothing and solves the problem that ruins more stored food than any other single factor.*

About Nutrition

Calories alone are not enough for the long term.

The Core Five plus saved cooking fat will keep your household fed and functional through weeks of hard times. For shorter emergencies, that is enough.

For longer periods, these staples need to be supplemented. A diet of grain and beans alone, sustained for months, can lead to nutritional deficiencies that historically caused real harm. They are entirely preventable with very small amounts of the right foods.

Three Deficiency Diseases to Know

SCURVY: Vitamin C deficiency. Develops in roughly 8 to 12 weeks of no intake. Bleeding gums, fatigue, poor wound healing, joint pain. Fully reversible with vitamin C.

BERIBERI: Thiamine (B1) deficiency. Develops in 2 to 3 months on a diet of mostly polished white rice or refined grains. Weakness, nerve pain in arms and legs, swelling, irregular heartbeat. Reversible with thiamine, ideally before nerve damage sets in.

PELLAGRA: Niacin (B3) deficiency. Develops in 2 to 3 months on diets where corn is the dominant grain without supplementation. Skin rash on sun-exposed areas, diarrhea, confusion. Historically deadly in the American South before niacin fortification.

All three are preventable with the foods listed below.

Vitamin C, about 45 mg daily

Any one of these covers it. Combine if you can.

- Raw cabbage, 1 cup (240 ml) shredded daily provides about 25 mg. Cabbage stores for months in a cool place.
- Sauerkraut, half a cup daily provides about 15 mg. A small crock of salted shredded cabbage at room temperature ferments in 2 to 3 weeks and keeps for a year. The vitamin C survives the fermentation.
- Fresh sprouts, 1 cup (240 ml) daily provides about 15 to 20 mg. Recipe 8-10 covers growing them indoors from stored dry beans in about four days, year-round, with no soil and no sunlight.
- Pine needle tea, 1 cup (240 ml) daily provides about 10 to 20 mg. Steep young needles of Eastern white pine or Scots pine in hot but not boiling water for 10 minutes. Identify the species correctly. Avoid during pregnancy.
- Potatoes, 2 to 3 medium daily provide about 30 to 40 mg total.

- Lemons or limes, when available, are excellent. A British naval custom of stocking citrus on long voyages gave English sailors the nickname "limeys" after scurvy stopped killing them in the 1700s. Lemons have slightly more vitamin C than limes, but either works.
- Rose hips, where they grow, are extraordinarily high in vitamin C and dry well for winter tea.

Thiamine, vitamin B1, about 1.2 mg daily

- Whole grain oats, 1 cup (240 ml) cooked: 0.2 mg. Already a staple here.
- Beans or lentils, 1 cup (240 ml) cooked: 0.3 to 0.4 mg. Already a staple here.
- Peanut butter, 2 tablespoons (30 ml): small contribution but helpful daily.
- Nutritional or brewer's yeast, 1 tablespoon (15 ml): over 1 mg, an excellent source if available.

The key rule: avoid building a diet around white rice alone. Brown rice, oats, stone-ground cornmeal, and beans together provide what you need.

Niacin, vitamin B3, about 16 mg daily

- Peanut butter, 2 tablespoons (30 ml): about 4 mg. Already on the pantry list.
- Whole grain bread or oats, daily.
- Beans, daily.
- Cornmeal preparation: when corn is your main staple, traditional preparation matters. Treating corn with a small amount of food-grade lime (calcium hydroxide) before grinding, called nixtamalization, releases the niacin that is otherwise chemically bound in the corn. This is how Mexican and Central American cuisines prevent pellagra despite corn-heavy diets. The American South did not do this historically, which is why pellagra was epidemic there.

Field Note: THE DAILY SURVIVAL TONIC. One cup daily, from pantry staples: 2 tablespoons (30 ml) blackstrap molasses, 1 tablespoon (15 ml) apple cider vinegar, 1 cup (240 ml) hot water. Stir to dissolve and drink warm. Blackstrap molasses (the dark, bitter kind, not light cooking molasses) provides meaningful amounts of iron, calcium, magnesium, potassium, and B6. Apple cider vinegar supports digestion. Together they fill many of the mineral and B-vitamin gaps that grain-and-bean diets miss. Variations: a teaspoon of honey softens the bite. A pinch of salt restores electrolytes if the household is sweating. When lemons or limes are available, substitute the juice for the vinegar; this also adds vitamin C. The tonic does NOT replace vitamin C on its own. For that, eat something fresh, sprouted, or fermented daily.

If blackstrap molasses is unavailable

The same mineral and B-vitamin support can come from one of these:

- Daily bone broth. A cup of bone broth simmered for several hours with a splash of apple cider vinegar (which pulls minerals out of the bones) provides calcium, magnesium, and gelatin. Save bones from any meat the household has access to. The longer the simmer, the better.

- Brewer's yeast or nutritional yeast. One tablespoon daily, stirred into soup, the tonic, or sprinkled on popcorn, provides nearly all the B vitamins an adult needs for the day. Sold cheaply in bulk at health-food stores and keeps for years sealed.
- Eggshell powder. Clean, dried, finely-ground eggshells stirred into soup or the tonic at about half a teaspoon daily provide a large amount of calcium. Free if your household eats eggs.
- A simpler tonic. 1 cup (240 ml) hot water, 1 tablespoon (15 ml) apple cider vinegar, 1 teaspoon (5 ml) honey, a pinch of salt. Less mineral content than the molasses version, but supports digestion and provides trace minerals from the salt.

If a multivitamin is affordable and accessible, take one daily. It is the cheapest insurance against deficiency available. But shelves go bare and budgets run dry, and the foods above were curing scurvy, beriberi, and pellagra for centuries before vitamins came in bottles.

BREADS, GRAINS, & GRAVIES

Hardtack, biscuits, cornbread, flatbreads, and gravies: water gravy, redeye gravy, tomato gravy, and sawmill gravy

Flour and water. Salt and heat. These are the components of every bread in this chapter and the baseline from which all other cooking builds. A person who can reliably produce biscuits from cold lard and flour, cornbread from a cast iron skillet, and hardtack from three ingredients has solved the most fundamental problem in cooking: how to make a calorie-dense, filling base food from nearly nothing. The second half of this chapter is gravies. Water gravy, redeye gravy, tomato gravy, and sawmill gravy each appear on their own page under the Gravies section divider. They are here and not in a separate chapter because they exist for one purpose: to be poured over bread. Bread alone is fuel. Bread with gravy is supper.

✦　✦　✦

HARDTACK

"Three ingredients. Shelf life measured in years. Soldiers carried these into battle for two thousand years for good reason."

Serves: 12 crackers   Time: 75 min

History & Context

Flour, water, and salt baked until completely dry. No fat, no leavening, nothing that can go rancid. A properly baked hardtack cracker will last years in any dry container, this has been verified by Civil War-era crackers found still edible over a century later. It is not pleasant to eat dry. It is not meant to be. It is meant to be in your pantry when everything else runs out.

Ingredients

- 2 cups (480 ml) all-purpose flour
- 1/2 tsp (3 ml) salt
- 1/2 cup (120 ml) water approximately

Method

1. Combine flour and salt. Add water a tablespoon at a time, mixing until a very stiff dough forms, stiffer than bread dough. It should barely hold together.
2. Roll to 1/3-inch (1 cm) thick on a floured surface. Cut into 3x3-inch (7.5x7.5 cm) squares.
3. Use a nail, skewer, or straw to punch a 4x4 grid of holes through each cracker. This lets moisture escape during baking.
4. Place on an ungreased baking sheet. Bake at 375°F (190°C) for 30 minutes.
5. Flip each cracker. Bake another 30 minutes.
6. Turn the oven off. Do not remove the crackers. Leave them in the cooling oven for at least one more hour. This passive drying step removes the moisture that active baking cannot reach.
7. Remove only when completely cool and completely hard. No flex whatsoever. If they bend, they need more time.

Field Note: Moisture is the only thing that kills hardtack. The cooling-oven step is not optional if long-term storage is the goal. Store in an airtight tin or sealed Mylar bag in a cool dry location. To eat: soak in water, broth, or coffee for 5-10 minutes, or fry soaked crackers in fat until the outside crisps again. The ratio is 3:1 flour to water by weight, scale to any quantity you need.

SOURDOUGH BISCUITS

"A maintained sourdough starter produces leavened bread indefinitely from nothing but flour and water. That is the point."

Serves: 8-10   Time: 20 min + starter

History & Context

A sourdough starter is a living culture of wild yeast that costs nothing to maintain and provides leavening permanently as long as it is fed. In any extended situation where commercial yeast becomes unavailable, a starter is the difference between flat bread and risen bread. The starter needs flour and water every day. That is the entire cost.

Ingredients

- Starter: 1 cup (240 ml) flour + 1 cup (240 ml) water + 1 tbsp (15 ml) plain yogurt (maintained 3-5 days before use)
- 2 cups (480 ml) flour
- 1 tsp (5 ml) salt
- 1/4 tsp (1 ml) baking soda
- 2 tbsp (30 ml) cold lard or shortening
- 1/2 cup (120 ml) active sourdough starter
- 1/4 cup (60 ml) water or buttermilk as needed

Method

1. Make starter 3-5 days ahead: combine 1 cup (240 ml) flour, 1 cup (240 ml) water, 1 tbsp (15 ml) plain yogurt. Feed daily by discarding half and adding fresh flour and water. Ready when it bubbles actively within 6-12 hours of feeding.
2. Combine flour, salt, and baking soda. Cut in cold lard until crumbly.
3. Add active starter and mix. Add water only if needed, dough should be slightly tacky but not wet.
4. Pat to 3/4-inch (2 cm) thick on a floured surface, handling minimally. Cut with a floured glass or cutter.
5. Dutch oven method: grease interior, place biscuits touching, lid on. Set on 8-10 coals, place 10-12 coals on lid. Bake 15-20 minutes, rotating every 5 minutes.
6. Oven method: 450°F (230°C) for 12-15 minutes until golden.

> *Field Note: Feed the starter daily: discard half, add equal parts flour and water by weight. A healthy starter bubbles vigorously and smells like mild yogurt. If it develops a gray liquid on top (called hooch), pour it off and feed again, the culture is*

SKILLET CORNBREAD

"Cornmeal, fat, and heat. No yeast, no rising time, no special equipment beyond a pan."

Serves: 6-8   Time: 30 min

History & Context

Cornmeal requires no living culture, no rising time, and no refrigerated ingredients. Stone-ground cornmeal stored in sealed Mylar bags lasts a decade or more. When the sourdough starter fails or there is no time, this is the backup bread, made from shelf-stable ingredients in 30 minutes over any heat source.

Ingredients

- 1.5 cups (360 ml) stone-ground cornmeal
- 1/2 cup (120 ml) all-purpose flour
- 1 tsp (5 ml) salt
- 1 tsp (5 ml) baking soda
- 1 egg
- 1 cup (240 ml) buttermilk or 1 cup (240 ml) water + 1 tbsp (15 ml) vinegar
- 3 tbsp (45 ml) lard or bacon drippings

Method

1. Heat a 10-inch (25 cm) cast iron skillet over medium-high. Add lard and let it get hot until shimmering.
2. Combine cornmeal, flour, salt, and baking soda in a bowl.
3. Beat egg into buttermilk (or water + vinegar). Pour into dry ingredients and stir just until combined, do not overmix.
4. Pour batter into the hot skillet. The edges should sizzle immediately on contact.
5. Camp method: cover with a lid, set on medium coals, place a few coals on the lid. Cook 20-25 minutes.
6. Oven method: 425°F (220°C) for 20-22 minutes until golden and pulling from edges.
7. Rest 5 minutes before turning out. The bottom should be dark golden-brown.

Field Note: Hot fat in the pan before the batter goes in is what creates the crackling bottom crust. A cold pan produces pale, soft-bottomed cornbread with no crust. If you have no egg, omit it, the cornbread will be slightly more crumbly but entirely edible.

PANDAMPO, SIMPLE FLATBREAD

"Flour, salt, lard, water, and a hot pan. Done in 25 minutes with no oven."

Serves: 6-8 flatbreads   Time: 25 min

History & Context

A simple leavened flatbread that needs no oven, just a hot skillet and five minutes per side. The baking powder replaces yeast, meaning zero wait time. When there is no time or no oven, this is the fastest warm bread available from shelf-stable ingredients.

Ingredients

- 2 cups (480 ml) all-purpose flour
- 1 tsp (5 ml) salt
- 1.5 tsp (8 ml) baking powder
- 2 tbsp (30 ml) lard, shortening, or any cooking fat
- 3/4 cup (180 ml) warm water approximately

Method

1. Combine flour, salt, and baking powder. Rub in fat until the mixture resembles coarse sand.
2. Add warm water gradually, mixing until a soft pliable dough forms. It should not be sticky.
3. Divide into 6-8 equal balls. Cover and rest 10 minutes.
4. Flatten each ball with your palm, then roll to about 1/4-inch (0.5 cm) thick.
5. Cook in a dry, very hot cast iron skillet 2-3 minutes per side until brown spots form and the bread puffs slightly.
6. Eat immediately or wrap in a clean cloth to keep warm.

Field Note: Charred spots are correct, they are caramelized starch and add flavor. If the skillet is hot enough, the bread will puff slightly during cooking. Eat within a few hours; this flatbread does not keep well. It is a same-day bread.

POURABLE GARLIC FLATBREAD

"A liquid batter poured into a pan. No kneading, no resting, no yeast. Done in three minutes per round."

Serves: 6 flatbreads   Time: 20 min

History & Context

The simplest possible wheat bread, a thin batter rather than a dough, poured directly into a hot pan. No kneading, no rising time, no oven. Garlic and green onion cost almost nothing and are the difference between a bread you eat willingly every day and one you eat only because you have to.

Ingredients

- 1.5 cups (360 ml) all-purpose flour
- 1 tsp (5 ml) salt
- 1 tsp (5 ml) sugar
- 1 tbsp (15 ml) melted fat (butter, lard, or any cooking oil)
- 1 tbsp (15 ml) minced garlic, fresh, jarred, or 1 tsp (5 ml) garlic powder
- 2-3 tbsp (30 to 45 ml) finely chopped green onion or any available herb
- 1.5 cups (360 ml) water
- A small amount of oil for the pan

Method

1. Combine flour, salt, sugar, garlic, green onion, and melted fat in a bowl.
2. Add water gradually while stirring. Mix until completely smooth with no lumps. The batter should flow easily from a spoon, thinner than pancake batter.
3. Heat a skillet over medium heat. Add a very small amount of oil and wipe it around, the pan should be barely coated, not pooled.
4. Ladle enough batter to cover the pan bottom in a thin layer. Use the back of the ladle to spread it into a wide circle.
5. Cook over medium-low until the surface looks dry and edges are set, about 2 minutes.
6. Flip. When air pockets begin to inflate, increase heat to medium. Press pockets gently with a spatula. Turn frequently.
7. Done when both sides are golden-brown with dark spots and the bread has puffed. Remove and stack.

Field Note: Start medium-low to set the batter without burning, then increase heat when bubbles appear so the steam can puff the bread. Too hot from the start cooks the bottom before the batter can spread. Without garlic or green onion, this is about four cents of ingredients per flatbread.

JOHNNY CAKES & HO CAKES

"Cornmeal, boiling water, salt, and a hot surface. The difference between the two is thickness and fat, both are real bread."

Serves: 4-6   Time: 25 min

History & Context

Cornmeal and boiling water cooked on a hot surface. No eggs, no milk, no leavening. If you have cornmeal and fire you have bread. These two preparations share the same three ingredients and differ in one thing: how much fat is in the pan and how thick the batter runs. A johnny cake is thicker, griddled in a modest amount of fat, with a creamy interior and crispy exterior. A ho cake is thinner, fried in a generous amount of fat, producing something crispier throughout with lacy edges. The distinction is regional tradition as much as technique, New England called them johnny cakes, the South called them ho cakes. Both have been feeding people from nothing for three hundred years. Make whichever your pan and fat supply favor.

Ingredients

- 1 cup (240 ml) stone-ground white or yellow cornmeal
- 1/2 to 1 tsp (3 to 5 ml) salt
- Boiling water, start with 3/4 cup (180 ml), adjust as needed
- Lard or bacon drippings, modest amount for johnny cakes, generous for ho cakes
- Sorghum, molasses, or any sweetener for serving

Method

1. Combine cornmeal and salt in a bowl.
2. Pour boiling water over the cornmeal while stirring immediately. The boiling water is not optional, cold water produces crumbly cakes that fall apart. Add fat and stir in while the mixture is hot enough to melt it.
3. Rest 5 minutes, the cornmeal continues absorbing water. Adjust consistency: for johnny cakes, the batter should be thick but just spreadable. For ho cakes, add a little more water until the batter is thicker than pancake batter but thin enough to spread slightly when it hits the pan.
4. FOR JOHNNY CAKES: heat a cast iron griddle over medium-high with a thin film of lard until very hot. Scoop about 2 tablespoons (30 ml) per cake. Flatten to about 1/3-inch (1 cm) thick with the back of a wet spoon. Cook without moving 4-5 minutes until deeply golden-brown on the bottom and the edges look dry. Flip once. Cook 3-4 more minutes.

5. FOR HO CAKES: heat a cast iron skillet over medium-high with a generous coating of lard, more than you think you need, until shimmering and just beginning to smoke. Pour roughly 3 tablespoons (45 ml) of batter per cake. It should spread to about 4 inches (10 cm) on its own. Cook without touching 3-4 minutes until edges look dry and the bottom is deep golden-brown. Flip once. Cook 2-3 more minutes.

6. Serve hot with sorghum, molasses, or any available sweetener.

Field Note: The griddle or skillet must be fully preheated before the batter goes on, a drop of water should sizzle sharply and evaporate on contact. Too cool and the cakes stick and absorb fat rather than crisping. The key difference in practice: johnny cakes are griddled like a thick pancake, ho cakes are shallow-fried like a fritter. Both are correct. Use whichever technique your fat supply supports.

BUTTERMILK BISCUITS

"The technique is the recipe. Cold fat, minimal handling, high heat. Everything else is flour."

Serves: 8-10 biscuits   Time: 25 min

History & Context

The most useful biscuit recipe to know uses cold lard, cold buttermilk, and as little handling as possible. Lard produces a flakier result than butter and is cheaper. The technique, cutting fat into flour without warming it, handling the dough as few times as possible, is the entire skill. If you have buttermilk, use it. If you do not, substitute whole milk with a tablespoon of vinegar stirred in and rested five minutes, it works identically. If you have only powdered milk, reconstitute it and add the vinegar the same way. The substitution is in the field note. The technique is the same regardless of which liquid you use.

Ingredients

- 2 cups (480 ml) all-purpose flour
- 1 tbsp (15 ml) baking powder
- 1/2 tsp (3 ml) baking soda
- 1 tsp (5 ml) salt
- 1/3 cup (80 ml) cold lard, cut into small pieces
- 3/4 cup (180 ml) cold buttermilk (or 3/4 cup (180 ml) milk + 2 tsp (10 ml) vinegar, rested 5 minutes)
- Sorghum, honey, or any sweetener for serving

Method

1. Preheat oven to 450°F (230°C). The oven must be fully at temperature before biscuits go in.
2. Whisk together flour, baking powder, baking soda, and salt.
3. Add cold lard. Using fingertips, press and smear fat into flour quickly, you want irregular pieces from crumb-size to pea-size still visible. Do not overwork. Work fast to keep fat cold.
4. Pour in cold buttermilk all at once. Stir with a fork from the center out just until dough comes together, stop the moment no dry flour is visible.
5. Turn onto floured surface. Pat to 3/4-inch (2 cm) thick. Fold in half and pat again. Repeat twice. Cut with a sharp glass or cutter pressing straight down, do not twist.
6. Place biscuits touching each other on an ungreased sheet. Bake 12-14 minutes until tops are golden.
7. Split with a fork. Serve with sorghum.

FRIED BREAD DOUGH

"Any yeast dough, dropped in hot fat, puffs into something golden and hollow. The fastest way from raw dough to hot food."

Serves: 8-10 pieces   Time: 90 min including rising

History & Context

A portion of bread dough dropped into hot fat rather than baked. The dough puffs dramatically as it hits the oil, turning hollow and golden in under two minutes. This technique requires yeast dough, active dry yeast, sourdough starter, or any leavened dough, and hot fat. What it does not require is an oven. When the oven is unavailable but a pot of fat and a heat source are, this converts the same dough you were already making into a completely different hot food. It is not a substitute for having yeast in your pantry. It is a technique for when you have yeast but no oven.

Ingredients

- 3 cups (720 ml) flour, 1 packet (2.25 tsp, 11 ml) active dry yeast, 1 cup (240 ml) warm water, 1 tsp (5 ml) sugar, 1 tsp (5 ml) salt, 1 tbsp (15 ml) lard
- Lard or any fat for frying, at least 2 inches (5 cm) deep in a heavy pot
- Granulated sugar, honey, or sorghum for serving

Method

1. Dissolve sugar in warm water (110°F, 45°C). Sprinkle yeast over surface. Let stand 5-10 minutes until foamy.
2. Combine flour and salt. Add lard and rub into flour with fingers. Add yeast mixture, stir until shaggy dough forms.
3. Knead 8-10 minutes until smooth and slightly tacky. Place in a greased bowl, cover, and let rise 1 hour until doubled.
4. Heat fat to 350-375°F (175 to 190°C). Test with a small piece of dough, it should sink briefly, rise to the surface, and sizzle actively.
5. Pinch off golf-ball sized pieces of risen dough. Stretch and flatten gently to about 1/4-inch (0.5 cm) thick.
6. Lower carefully into hot fat. It will puff dramatically. Fry 1-2 minutes per side until deeply golden.
7. Drain briefly. Dust with sugar or drizzle with sweetener while hot.

Field Note: Any yeast dough works, including a batch that failed to rise properly for loaves. Dry active yeast sealed airtight keeps for 2+ years in a cool location. The frying technique converts a baking ingredient into a no-oven hot food, useful when power is out or you are cooking over fire. If commercial yeast is unavailable, the potato starter from recipe 8-1 substitutes directly, use 1/4 cup (60 ml) active starter per packet of yeast called for. Allow extra rising time of 1-3 hours.

GRAVIES

WATER GRAVY

"Flour, fat, water, and salt. The most fundamental thing you can pour over bread."

Serves: 4   Time: 20 min

History & Context

When there is no milk for white gravy and no meat on the pan to produce drippings, water gravy is what remains. It still requires fat, lard, bacon drippings, or any cooking fat from your pantry, but it requires nothing fresh, nothing refrigerated, and nothing from an animal you cooked that day. Flour browned in fat, thinned with water, seasoned with salt and pepper. The browning is everything, flour cooked long enough to turn a rich medium-brown develops a nutty, complex flavor that makes water gravy worth eating rather than merely edible.

Ingredients

- 2 tbsp (30 ml) lard or bacon drippings
- 3 tbsp (45 ml) all-purpose flour
- 1.5 cups (360 ml) water
- 1/2 tsp (3 ml) salt
- 1/2 tsp (3 ml) black pepper
- Optional: pinch of onion powder, garlic powder, or dried sage

Method

1. Heat lard in a cast iron skillet over medium heat until shimmering.
2. Add all the flour at once. Stir constantly with a wooden spoon.
3. Cook the roux for 5-7 minutes, stirring constantly, until the flour turns a rich medium-brown, the color of a paper grocery bag. A nutty, toasted smell should be strong. Do not rush this step. Under-browned roux tastes like raw flour paste.
4. Reduce heat slightly. Add water slowly, about 1/4 cup (60 ml) at a time, while stirring hard. The roux will absorb the water and thicken immediately.
5. Continue adding water until all is incorporated and the gravy is smooth.
6. Bring to a gentle simmer. Cook 3-4 minutes until the gravy is pourable.
7. Season with salt and pepper. Pour over split biscuits, cornbread, or bread.

Field Note: This is the floor of what cooking can be: three shelf-stable ingredients producing something warm and filling. The browning step is the only skill involved. Pale roux tastes like flour glue. Brown roux tastes like something worth eating. That is the entire difference.

REDEYE GRAVY & BISCUITS

"Ham drippings and black coffee. Two ingredients most people have. The result is better than it sounds."

Serves: 4-6   Time: 30 min

History & Context

Ham or bacon drippings left in a hot pan, deglazed with black coffee. The coffee pulls up every caramelized bit of meat from the pan bottom and creates a thin, dark, intensely flavored gravy that costs nothing since you are using what would otherwise be discarded. Serve over biscuits.

Ingredients

- 4-6 slices country ham, heavily cured bacon, or any cured pork
- 1/2 cup (120 ml) strong black coffee, instant works fine
- Biscuits for serving (see 1-7)

Method

1. Fry ham or bacon in a dry cast iron skillet over medium-high heat, 2-3 minutes per side until edges crisp.
2. Remove meat. The pan should have a dark coating of browned fond. Do not wipe it out.
3. Pour black coffee into the hot pan. It will spit and steam. Stir and scrape the bottom constantly for about one minute as the fond dissolves into the liquid.
4. The gravy will be very thin and dark, that is correct. It thickens slightly as it reduces.
5. Pour over split hot biscuits.

Field Note: The browned fond on the pan bottom is the entire recipe. Cleaning the pan between steps eliminates the dish. Use the strongest coffee available, the bitterness balances the salt of the cured meat. Instant coffee dissolved double-strength works perfectly.

TOMATO GRAVY

"When the pantry holds nothing but flour, fat, and canned tomatoes, this is supper."

Serves: 6-8   Time: 20 min

History & Context

A roux made from bacon drippings and flour, thinned with canned tomatoes. Three shelf-stable ingredients that produce something substantially more satisfying than any of them alone. A case of canned tomatoes combined with flour and lard means this meal is available for months.

Ingredients

- 2 tbsp (30 ml) bacon drippings or lard
- 3 tbsp (45 ml) all-purpose flour
- 1 can (14.5 oz, 410 g) crushed or stewed tomatoes
- 1/2 cup (120 ml) water
- 1/2 tsp (3 ml) salt
- 1/4 tsp (1 ml) black pepper
- Pinch of sugar
- Biscuits or cornbread for serving

Method

1. Heat bacon drippings in a cast iron skillet over medium heat until shimmering.
2. Add flour and stir constantly 2-3 minutes until the roux turns light golden and smells nutty.
3. Pour in canned tomatoes and water. The roux will seize, stir hard and fast, it will smooth out within 30 seconds.
4. Mash tomato pieces with the back of a spoon as you stir. Leave some texture.
5. Add salt, pepper, and sugar. Stir and taste. Simmer 5 minutes to thicken and mellow.
6. Ladle generously over split hot biscuits or cornbread.

Field Note: Canned tomatoes are among the most versatile long-term pantry items, long shelf life, genuine nutrition, and useful in a wide range of preparations. A case of 24 cans costs about $20 and represents months of this meal.

SAWMILL GRAVY

"Flour, fat, and milk. The most filling thing you can put on a biscuit."

Serves: 4   Time: 15 min

History & Context

A browned roux thinned with milk and seasoned heavily with black pepper. Poured over biscuits it produces a complete meal from five cheap ingredients. Powdered whole milk reconstituted to normal strength works perfectly and is shelf-stable for years, an important substitution when fresh milk is unavailable.

Ingredients

- 2 tbsp (30 ml) lard or bacon drippings
- 2-3 tbsp (30 to 45 ml) all-purpose flour
- 2 cups (480 ml) whole milk or reconstituted powdered milk
- 1 tsp (5 ml) black pepper, this dish should be noticeably peppery
- Salt to taste
- Optional: 2-3 tbsp (30 to 45 ml) crumbled cooked sausage or bacon

Method

1. Heat lard in a cast iron skillet over medium heat until shimmering.
2. Add flour and stir constantly 2-3 minutes until the roux turns golden-tan.
3. Reduce heat slightly. Pour in about half the milk while whisking hard. Whisk smooth, then add remaining milk gradually.
4. Increase heat to medium and stir constantly as the gravy thickens, about 5 minutes. If too thick, add a splash more milk.
5. Season heavily with black pepper and salt. Fold in sausage or bacon if using.
6. Pour over split hot biscuits.

Field Note: Lump-free gravy comes from adding milk gradually and whisking constantly. Never pour all the liquid at once into a roux. Powdered milk reconstituted to slightly above normal strength produces gravy indistinguishable from fresh milk in this application.

CORN PONE

"Cornmeal, water, and salt. The most elemental bread that exists."

Serves: 4-5 pones   Time: 30 min

History & Context

No leavening, no fat, no eggs. Cornmeal, boiling water, and salt pressed into a patty and cooked directly on a hot surface. This is the floor of what bread can be. Two of these in a coat pocket is a full meal's worth of calories. They keep for several days and improve with a second frying.

Ingredients

- 1 cup (240 ml) stone-ground white or yellow cornmeal
- 1/2 tsp (3 ml) salt
- Boiling water, approximately 1/2 cup (120 ml), added slowly

Method

1. Measure cornmeal and salt into a bowl.
2. Add boiling water a few tablespoons at a time, stirring after each addition. You want a stiff, moldable dough, significantly stiffer than biscuit dough.
3. Rest 5 minutes as the cornmeal continues absorbing water.
4. Wet hands thoroughly. Shape dough into thick oval cakes about 3/4-inch (2 cm) thick and 3 inches (7.5 cm) long.
5. Skillet method: fry in a barely greased cast iron skillet over medium heat 10-12 minutes per side until firm throughout.
6. Campfire method: lay directly on hot flat stones or coals at the fire's edge. Cook 15-20 minutes per side. A hard dark crust will form.
7. Corn pone is a vehicle for liquids, serve with beans, pot liquor, or broth.

Field Note: Boiling water pre-gelatinizes the starch, which is what makes the dough hold together without eggs or fat. Cold water produces a crumbly mess. Store cooked corn pone in a cloth and it keeps 2-3 days. It improves with a second frying.

CRACKLIN CORNBREAD

"Pork rinds or cracklings stirred into cornbread batter. More calories, more flavor, better crust."

Serves: 6-8   Time: 30 min

History & Context

Commercial pork rinds are shelf-stable, cheap, and available everywhere. Folded into cornbread batter before baking, they add fat, protein, and a salty richness to every bite. The fat in the rinds melts during baking and releases into the bread. This is more calorie-dense than plain cornbread and more worth eating.

Ingredients

- 1.5 cups (360 ml) stone-ground cornmeal
- 1/2 cup (120 ml) flour
- 1 tsp (5 ml) salt
- 1 tsp (5 ml) baking powder
- 1/2 tsp (3 ml) baking soda
- 1 egg
- 1 cup (240 ml) buttermilk or 1 cup (240 ml) water + 1 tbsp (15 ml) vinegar
- 3 tbsp (45 ml) rendered lard
- 1/2 cup (120 ml) commercial pork rinds (no artificial flavoring), broken into 1/2-inch (1.5 cm) pieces

Method

1. Preheat oven to 425°F (220°C). Place a 10-inch (25 cm) cast iron skillet in the oven with 2 tbsp (30 ml) lard to heat.
2. Combine cornmeal, flour, salt, baking powder, and baking soda.
3. Whisk egg, buttermilk, and 1 tbsp (15 ml) melted lard. Add to dry ingredients and stir minimally.
4. Fold in broken pork rind pieces gently.
5. Remove hot skillet from oven. Pour in batter, it should sizzle immediately.
6. Bake 20-22 minutes until golden on top and pulling from edges.

__Field Note:__ Break pork rinds into rough 1/2-inch (1.5 cm) pieces before adding, too fine and they disappear, too large and they don't integrate. Plain pork rinds without artificial flavoring are available at any gas station or grocery store and store well at *room temperature for months.*

POTATO WATER BREAD

"The cloudy water left after boiling potatoes produces better bread than plain water. Never pour it down the drain."

Serves: 1 loaf   Time: 3 hours including rising

History & Context

Potato cooking water is starchy and slightly acidic. It feeds yeast more efficiently than plain water, produces a more vigorous rise, and results in a loaf that stays soft for days longer than standard bread. This is free if you are already boiling potatoes, the only cost is not throwing it away.

Ingredients

- 1 cup (240 ml) potato water (reserved from boiling potatoes, cooled to lukewarm)
- 2.25 tsp (11 ml) active dry yeast (1 standard packet)
- 1 tsp (5 ml) sugar
- 3 cups (720 ml) all-purpose flour plus extra for kneading
- 1.5 tsp (8 ml) salt
- 1 tbsp (15 ml) lard, butter, or shortening
- Optional: 1/4 cup (60 ml) leftover mashed potato worked into the dough

Method

1. Cool potato water to about 110°F (45°C), warm but not hot on your wrist. Combine with sugar and yeast. Let stand 5-10 minutes until foamy.
2. Add salt and fat to the yeast mixture.
3. Add flour one cup at a time, stirring after each addition. When too stiff to stir, turn onto a floured surface.
4. Knead 8-10 minutes until smooth, elastic, and slightly tacky. It should spring back when poked.
5. Place in a greased bowl, cover, and let rise in a warm location 1 to 1.5 hours until doubled.
6. Punch down. Shape into a loaf and place in a greased 9x5 inch (23x13 cm) pan. Cover and let rise again 45-60 minutes until domed above the rim.
7. Bake at 375°F (190°C) for 30-35 minutes until golden and hollow-sounding when tapped on the bottom.
8. Cool at least 20 minutes before slicing.

Field Note: Keep a jar in the refrigerator and add potato water to it every time you

FRIED DONUTS FROM DOUGH

"Any yeast dough dropped in hot fat puffs hollow and golden in two minutes. Morale food costs the same as bread."

Serves: 8-10 pieces   Time: 30 min using risen dough

History & Context

A portion of bread dough set aside and fried rather than baked. The dough puffs dramatically in hot fat, turning golden and hollow. Dusted with sugar while hot, it costs the same as a loaf of bread and has a completely different effect on the people eating it. In situations where morale matters, this is a legitimate use of flour.

Ingredients

- Any batch of risen yeast dough, use a portion of whatever bread dough you have made
- Lard or oil for deep frying, at least 2 inches (5 cm) deep in a heavy pot
- Granulated sugar, powdered sugar, honey, or sorghum for serving

Method

1. Heat fat to 350-375°F (175 to 190°C). Test with a small piece of dough, it should sizzle immediately and float to the surface.
2. Pinch off golf-ball sized pieces of risen dough. Stretch and flatten gently to about 1/4-inch (0.5 cm) thick with your hands.
3. Lower carefully into the hot fat. It will puff dramatically within seconds.
4. Fry 1-2 minutes per side until deeply golden.
5. Drain briefly on cloth or paper.
6. Dust with sugar or drizzle with sweetener while still hot.
7. Eat within 30 minutes.

Field Note: Use any yeast dough, including a batch that failed to rise enough for loaves. Failed bread dough fries perfectly. The morale value of hot sweet food in a difficult situation is not trivial and should not be dismissed. If commercial yeast is unavailable, the potato starter from recipe 8-1 substitutes directly at 1/4 cup (60 ml) per packet, allow extra rising time of 1-3 hours.

SOUPS & BROTHS

From water soup to bone broth to the perpetual pot

A pot of water on a fire is the beginning of everything in this chapter. What goes into that water determines whether the result is a light meal or a sustaining one. Water soup is water, an onion, stale bread, and whatever scraps are available. Egg drop soup is one egg in a quart of salted water, done in eight minutes. These are not compromised versions of real soup, they are real soup, produced from the actual contents of a depleted pantry. The perpetual soup pot at the end of this chapter is not a recipe. It is a system. It never runs out as long as you keep adding to it. Bring it to a full rolling boil once every day. That daily boil is the single non-negotiable rule.

❖ ❖ ❖

WATER SOUP

"Boiling water over stale bread with whatever scraps are available. The floor of soup."

Serves: 2   Time: 30 min

History & Context

Water, an onion, any vegetable scraps, salt, and stale bread. This is soup when there is almost nothing. The stale bread in the bowl turns the hot liquid into something with texture and some calories. Every vegetable end, carrot top, potato peel, and herb stem that goes in the trash is a missed opportunity for this.

Ingredients

- 4 cups (960 ml) water
- 1 onion diced
- Any available vegetable scraps: potato peels, celery ends, carrot tops
- Salt and black pepper
- 1 slice stale bread per person, toasted
- Optional: 1 tbsp (15 ml) bacon drippings

Method

1. Bring water to a boil. Add diced onion and all available scraps.
2. Season with salt and pepper. Simmer 20-30 minutes until onion is soft.
3. Strain out solids for a clear broth, or leave in for more substance.
4. Toast the stale bread until very crisp. Place in the bottom of each serving bowl.
5. Ladle hot broth over the toast. The bread will soften into a warm mass with texture.
6. Add bacon drippings directly to the bowl for richness if available.

Field Note: Maintain a scrap bag in the refrigerator, add every onion end, carrot top, potato peel, and vegetable trim as you cook. Make broth from it weekly. This costs nothing and produces something from waste.

POTATO PEEL SOUP

"The part of the potato most people throw away has the highest concentration of nutrients."

Serves: 3-4   Time: 45 min

History & Context

Potato peels simmered with an onion and a bay leaf until the broth turns starchy and faintly creamy. The starch thickens the broth naturally with no added flour. Most of a potato's vitamins and minerals sit immediately under the skin. Peeling aggressively and throwing the peels away is one of the more wasteful things a kitchen regularly does.

Ingredients

- Peels from 4-6 medium potatoes
- 1 onion diced
- 1 bay leaf
- 4 cups (960 ml) water
- Salt and black pepper
- Optional: 1 tbsp (15 ml) butter, splash of milk

Method

1. Save potato peels in cold water as you peel potatoes for another dish.
2. Combine peels, onion, bay leaf, water, and salt in a pot. Bring to a boil.
3. Simmer 30-40 minutes until peels have broken down and broth is slightly starchy.
4. Remove the bay leaf. Strain, pressing peels through to extract maximum starch.
5. Add optional butter and milk. Adjust seasoning.
6. Serve with any available bread.

Field Note: *The starch from the peels thickens the broth naturally. Peel potatoes thinly, a thick peel wastes what you are about to eat.*

EGG DROP SOUP

"One egg in a quart of salted water becomes supper for two."

Serves: 2   Time: 8 min

History & Context

Beaten egg poured in a thin stream into boiling liquid cooks instantly into ribbons. One egg stretched into soup for two people by adding it to a quart of well-seasoned water. When eggs are rationed or scarce, this is how you make them go further.

Ingredients

- 4 cups (960 ml) water or thin broth
- 1-2 eggs
- Salt and black pepper
- Optional: scallion tops, dried parsley, pinch of turmeric for color

Method

1. Bring water or salted broth to a full rolling boil.
2. Beat egg or eggs until completely combined.
3. Create a slow swirl in the boiling liquid by stirring in one direction.
4. Hold a fork over the pot, tines pointing down. Pour beaten egg slowly through the tines in a thin stream.
5. Stop stirring. Let ribbons set 30 seconds without touching.
6. Season with salt and pepper. Serve immediately.

Field Note: The fork controls the pour, breaking the egg stream into fine threads that set instantly rather than clumping. Too fast and you get blobs. Too slow and you get wisps. The fork makes it reliable on the first try.

BREAD SOUP

"Stale bread simmered in milk or water until it dissolves into a thick warm porridge."

Serves: 2   Time: 15 min

History & Context

Stale bread that has gone too hard to eat comfortably becomes the base of a hot soup when simmered in liquid. Pennsylvania Dutch communities called it milk soup and fed it to children as a routine meal. It requires no skill, produces something genuinely comforting, and converts what would have been thrown away into a meal.

Ingredients

- 3-4 slices stale white bread
- 2 cups (480 ml) whole milk or water
- 1 tsp (5 ml) butter
- 1/2 tsp (3 ml) salt
- Optional: 1 beaten egg, 1 tbsp (15 ml) bacon drippings, pinch of sugar

Method

1. Tear stale bread into rough pieces in a heavy saucepan.
2. Pour milk or water over bread. Soak 5 minutes.
3. Add butter and salt. Bring to a gentle simmer over medium-low, stirring frequently.
4. As it heats, the bread dissolves into the liquid. Stir and mash with a spoon until reaching a thick porridge consistency, about 10 minutes.
5. If adding egg: beat separately, then stir into hot but not boiling soup.
6. If adding bacon drippings: stir in at the end for depth.

Field Note: Day-old or older bread works better than very fresh bread, which turns gummy rather than dissolving cleanly. The ratio is flexible, more bread gives a thicker result.

BEAN AND HAM BONE SOUP

"A leftover ham bone costs nothing. Dried beans cost almost nothing. Together they make a week of lunches."

Serves: 6-8   Time: 3 hours

History & Context

Dried beans simmered with a ham bone until the broth becomes thick and dark. The ham bone was the residue of a previous meal, free. Dried beans are the cheapest protein available. The long slow simmer converts both into something that keeps for days and costs under two dollars to make.

Ingredients

- 1 lb (455 g) dried navy, pinto, or great northern beans
- 1 ham bone, smoked ham hock, or 3-4 strips bacon
- 1 large onion diced
- 3 cloves garlic
- 2 carrots diced (optional)
- 8 cups (1.9 L) water
- Salt and black pepper

Method

1. Soak beans overnight in 3x their volume of water, or quick-soak: cover with water, boil 2 minutes, soak 1 hour. Drain.
2. Combine drained beans, ham bone, onion, garlic, and water in a large pot.
3. Bring to a boil, skim any foam.
4. Reduce to a low simmer. Add carrots if using. Cover and cook 2-3 hours until beans are completely soft.
5. Remove ham bone. Strip any meat and return to soup.
6. Season with salt and pepper after tasting, the ham bone contributes significant salt.
7. For thicker soup: mash 2 cups (480 ml) of beans against the pot side and stir back in.

Field Note: Ham bones are frequently free or very cheap from grocery store deli counters after holiday sales. Ask specifically, most stores throw them out. Never discard a ham bone from your own cooking. Freeze it if you are not making soup immediately.

CARAMELIZED ONION SOUP

"Onions cooked low and slow until deeply sweet. Water and stale bread turn them into a complete meal."

Serves: 4   Time: 55 min

History & Context

Onions cost almost nothing and keep for weeks without refrigeration. Cooked slowly in fat for 40-50 minutes, their sugars caramelize into complex flavor compounds that make plain water taste like rich broth. This is one of the cheapest filling meals a kitchen can produce.

Ingredients

- 4-5 large yellow onions, halved and thinly sliced
- 2 tbsp (30 ml) butter or bacon drippings
- 4 cups (960 ml) water or thin broth
- 1 tsp (5 ml) salt
- Black pepper
- 2-3 slices stale bread
- Optional: splash of apple cider vinegar

Method

1. Heat fat in a heavy pot over medium-low. Add all sliced onions and a pinch of salt.
2. Cook over medium-low heat 40-50 minutes, stirring every few minutes, until onions are deeply brown and reduced to a fraction of their original volume. This cannot be rushed.
3. If onions stick, add a splash of water and scrape up the brown bits, this adds depth.
4. Once deeply caramelized, add water, remaining salt, and pepper. Simmer 10 minutes.
5. Tear stale bread into pieces and add. Simmer another 10 minutes until bread dissolves into the broth.
6. Add vinegar for brightness if available.

Field Note: 40-50 minutes at medium-low. This step cannot be shortened. The color change from pale yellow to deep brown is the Maillard reaction, the flavor compounds responsible for the result only form above a certain temperature over sufficient time.

HOMEMADE TOMATO SOUP

"A can of tomatoes, a roux, and a quarter teaspoon of baking soda. Better than anything in a can."

Serves: 4   Time: 25 min

History & Context

The baking soda is the technique: a small amount of alkaline ingredient neutralizes enough of the tomato's natural acidity to produce a round, sweet flavor without adding sugar. This one step is the difference between tart tomato water and a soup worth eating. Canned tomatoes store for years and cost very little.

Ingredients

- 1 can (28 oz, 795 g) crushed or whole tomatoes
- 1 tbsp (15 ml) butter or lard
- 1/2 small onion diced
- 1 clove garlic minced
- 1/4 tsp (1 ml) baking soda
- 1/2 cup (120 ml) whole milk, cream, or reconstituted powdered milk
- Salt and black pepper

Method

1. Melt fat in a saucepan over medium heat. Add onion and cook 5 minutes until softened.
2. Add garlic. Cook 1 minute.
3. Add canned tomatoes, breaking up whole ones. Simmer 10 minutes.
4. Add baking soda. It will foam vigorously, stir through the foam.
5. Simmer 2 more minutes after foam subsides.
6. Blend smooth or mash and strain.
7. Stir in milk over low heat. Do not boil after adding dairy.
8. Season with salt and pepper.

Field Note: 1/4 tsp (1 ml) baking soda per 28 oz (795 g) of tomatoes is the correct amount. Too much tastes soapy. The foam is CO_2 being released as the acid is neutralized, stir through it and it subsides within a minute.

RIBBLE SOUP

"Flour and egg rubbed between your palms into simmering milk. Five minutes of work, a full bowl of food."

Serves: 4   Time: 20 min

History & Context

Egg-and-flour dough rubbed between the palms over a pot of simmering milk until pea-sized dumplings fall in. The simplest possible dumpling, no rolling, no cutting, no equipment beyond your hands. A full pot of filling soup from three ingredients.

Ingredients

- 1 cup (240 ml) flour
- 1 egg
- 1/4 tsp (1 ml) salt
- 1 quart (945 ml) whole milk or broth
- Salt and white pepper
- Optional: 1 tbsp (15 ml) butter

Method

1. Heat milk or broth in a saucepan over medium heat until just below a simmer.
2. Make the ribble dough: combine flour, egg, and salt with a fork until it forms rough crumbly clumps, not a smooth dough.
3. Hold the bowl over the simmering liquid. Take handfuls of dough and rub between your palms over the pot, letting pea-sized pieces fall in.
4. Continue with all the dough, stirring gently.
5. Cook 2-3 minutes until ribbles are tender and the liquid has thickened slightly.
6. Season with salt and white pepper. Add butter if available.

Field Note: The rubbing technique creates irregular pieces that cook evenly. This scales down perfectly for a single person, just use 1/4 cup (60 ml) flour and one small egg.

SPLIT PEA SOUP

"Dried split peas need no soaking. Two hours of simmering and they dissolve into a thick filling meal."

Serves: 6-8   Time: 2 hours

History & Context

Dried split peas are among the cheapest and most nutritionally complete dried legumes available. They require no soaking before cooking, dissolve into a thick soup without blending, and cost almost nothing. A one-pound bag produces six to eight full servings.

Ingredients

- 1 lb (455 g) dried split peas (green or yellow), rinsed
- 1 ham bone, hock, or 4 strips bacon
- 1 large onion diced
- 2 carrots diced
- 3 cloves garlic
- 8 cups (1.9 L) water
- 1 bay leaf
- Salt and black pepper

Method

1. No soaking required. Rinse peas under cold water.
2. Combine all ingredients in a large pot. Bring to a boil and skim any foam.
3. Reduce to a low simmer. Cover and cook 1.5-2 hours, stirring every 20 minutes, until peas have completely dissolved into a thick soup.
4. Remove ham bone and bay leaf. Shred any meat and return to soup.
5. Season with salt and pepper. Add water when reheating, this soup thickens dramatically as it cools.

Field Note: Split peas cook faster than most dried legumes and need no soaking, which makes them one of the most practical dried beans to keep on hand. A 5-lb (2.3 kg) bag stores indefinitely sealed and represents dozens of meals.

GARLIC BROTH

"Forty whole garlic cloves cooked slowly become sweet and mild. The result is both a meal and a useful remedy."

Serves: 4   Time: 40 min

History & Context

Whole garlic cloves cooked gently in oil or fat for ten minutes before being simmered in water become sweet, mild, and almost creamy, nothing like raw garlic. The resulting broth is legitimately useful for respiratory illness and digestive problems, effects that have been documented beyond folk medicine. It costs almost nothing to make.

Ingredients

- 40 garlic cloves (about 3 heads), peeled, kept whole
- 4 cups (960 ml) water
- 2 tbsp (30 ml) olive oil or lard
- 1 bay leaf
- 4 dried sage leaves or 1/2 tsp (3 ml) dried sage
- Salt and pepper
- Optional: splash of apple cider vinegar, stale bread per bowl

Method

1. Heat olive oil in a pot over medium. Add whole garlic cloves. Cook gently 10 minutes until golden but not brown.
2. Add water, bay leaf, sage, and salt.
3. Simmer 25-30 minutes until garlic cloves are completely soft.
4. Strain, pressing garlic through the strainer to extract the softened flesh into the broth.
5. Taste and adjust salt. Add vinegar for brightness.
6. Serve in a bowl over toasted stale bread if available.

Field Note: Forty cloves of slow-cooked garlic produce something sweet and mild. The sharp pungency only develops when garlic cells are crushed, whole cloves cooked gently produce a different compound profile entirely.

BROWN FLOUR SOUP

"Flour toasted in fat until dark and nutty, thinned with water. Government emergency rations were built around this technique."

Serves: 4   Time: 20 min

History & Context

During the Depression, flour sacks included recipes printed on the back for making the flour go as far as possible. Brown flour soup was one of them: flour cooked in fat until deeply brown, then thinned with water into a filling broth. The browning transforms raw flour paste into something with genuine flavor through the same Maillard chemistry that makes seared meat taste better than boiled.

Ingredients

- 3 tbsp (45 ml) all-purpose flour
- 2 tbsp (30 ml) butter or lard
- 4 cups (960 ml) water or thin broth
- Salt and black pepper
- Optional: dried onion flakes, garlic powder, 1 tbsp (15 ml) bacon drippings

Method

1. Heat butter or lard in a saucepan over medium heat until melted.
2. Add flour all at once. Stir constantly with a wooden spoon.
3. Cook the roux over medium to medium-low heat, stirring constantly, for 8-12 minutes until it turns a rich medium-brown with a deep nutty smell. Not burned. Not pale.
4. Reduce heat to low. Add 2 tablespoons (30 ml) of water while whisking hard.
5. Add remaining water gradually, whisking smooth after each addition.
6. Bring to a gentle simmer, whisking constantly, until the soup reaches a pourable consistency.
7. Season with salt, pepper, and any optional spices.

Field Note: *Light-colored roux tastes floury and bland. Properly dark roux develops flavor compounds that are absent from underdone flour. This is the same principle behind dark Cajun roux and water gravy. Time and consistent stirring is the entire technique.*

BONE MARROW BROTH

"Roasted bones simmered for hours produce one of the most nutritionally complete broths possible from near-nothing."

Serves: 8 cups broth   Time: 5-9 hours

History & Context

Marrow bones are frequently free or nearly free from butchers because most customers do not know what to do with them. Roasted first to develop flavor, then simmered for hours with a splash of vinegar to pull minerals from the bone into the liquid, they produce a broth that is dense with collagen, minerals, and fat. Roasting first is the critical step most people skip.

Ingredients

- 2-3 lbs (0.9 to 1.4 kg) beef marrow bones or mixed soup bones
- 1 large onion quartered
- 3 stalks celery
- 2 carrots
- 2 tbsp (30 ml) apple cider vinegar
- 10 peppercorns
- 1 bay leaf
- 8 cups (1.9 L) cold water
- Salt

Method

1. Roast bones first: place on a baking sheet at 400°F (205°C) for 30 minutes until deeply browned. Do not skip this step.
2. Transfer roasted bones to a large pot. Add all vegetables, vinegar, peppercorns, bay leaf, and cold water.
3. Bring to a slow boil. Skim all foam during the first 20 minutes.
4. Reduce to the lowest possible simmer. Cook 4-8 hours.
5. Strain through fine mesh, pressing vegetables to extract all liquid.
6. Cool and skim fat from the top, or leave it for caloric value.
7. Season with salt.

Field Note: The roasting step before simmering is what separates average bone broth from exceptional, the fond on the pan, scraped in with a splash of water,

---

PEANUT BUTTER SOUP

"Peanut butter is 3,700 calories per pound and shelf-stable. It also makes excellent soup."

Serves: 4   Time: 25 min

History & Context

Peanut-based soups have been part of West African and Southern American cooking for centuries. During the Depression, the combination of cheap peanut butter with water and basic aromatics produced a high-protein, high-calorie soup that cost almost nothing to make. Natural peanut butter, peanuts and salt only, is essential. Sweetened commercial peanut butter creates a soup that reads as dessert.

Ingredients

- 3 tbsp (45 ml) natural peanut butter (peanuts and salt only)
- 1 medium onion diced
- 2 stalks celery diced
- 2 cloves garlic
- 4 cups (960 ml) water or broth
- 1/2 tsp (3 ml) cayenne
- Salt
- Optional: 1 small sweet potato diced, 1 can diced tomatoes

Method

1. Sauté onion and celery in 1 tbsp (15 ml) oil or lard over medium heat until softened, about 5 minutes.
2. Add garlic. Cook 1 minute.
3. Add water or broth. Bring to a simmer.
4. In a small bowl, mix peanut butter with a ladleful of hot broth until completely smooth, this prevents clumping.
5. Pour the peanut butter mixture into the pot while stirring constantly.
6. Add cayenne and salt. Add sweet potato and/or tomatoes if using and simmer 15-20 minutes until tender.
7. Taste and adjust salt and heat.

Field Note: *Peanut butter is one of the most calorie-dense and shelf-stable pantry items: 3,700 calories per pound, 2+ year shelf life, and functional as a protein source across a wide range of preparations. Natural peanut butter (no added sugar*

POTATO AND ONION SOUP WITH POACHED EGG

"Fifteen minutes from an empty pan to a complete meal with protein."

Serves: 2   Time: 20 min

History & Context

Diced potatoes and onion simmered in salted water, with an egg cracked directly into the broth for the last three minutes. The poached egg adds protein that would otherwise require meat. The broken yolk enriches every spoonful of broth. Two people can eat from this for under fifty cents.

Ingredients

- 2 medium potatoes, peeled and diced small
- 1 medium onion diced
- 4 cups (960 ml) water
- 1 tsp (5 ml) salt
- Black pepper
- 1-2 eggs
- Optional: 1 tbsp (15 ml) butter, dried parsley

Method

1. Place diced potatoes and onion in a pot with water and salt. Bring to a boil.
2. Reduce to a medium simmer and cook 12-15 minutes until potatoes are fully tender.
3. Reduce heat until the broth is barely simmering, no visible bubbles breaking the surface.
4. Crack each egg into a small cup first, then slide gently into the simmering broth.
5. Cook uncovered 3 minutes for a runny yolk, 4-5 minutes for a set yolk.
6. Ladle carefully into a bowl keeping the egg intact on top.
7. Add butter if available. Season with pepper. Break the yolk at the table.

Field Note: The water must be barely simmering, not boiling, when the eggs go in. Boiling water breaks the white apart into ragged shreds. The surface should barely move.

THE PERPETUAL SOUP POT

"Not a recipe. A system. One pot, one fire, ongoing food from whatever is available."
Serves: continuous   Time: ongoing

History & Context

A heavy pot maintained continuously on the back of the stove, added to daily with whatever vegetable trimmings, leftover grains, and cooking liquids are available, and brought to a full boil once per day to keep it safe. This is not a Depression invention, it is the oldest form of cooking that exists, practiced continuously across human history until refrigeration made it seem unnecessary. It never runs out as long as you keep adding to it. The daily boil is the only rule that cannot be skipped.

Ingredients

- Starting base (Day 1): soup bones or a ham hock, dried beans soaked overnight, diced onion, carrot, celery, salt and pepper, water to fill the pot 3/4 full
- Daily additions, use what you have: vegetable trimmings and peels, leftover cooked grains, cooking liquid from boiled vegetables, small amounts of any leftover cooked meat, a handful of oats or cornmeal to thicken if needed
- Weekly refresh: drain off about 1/3 of the liquid and replace with fresh water and a new base of aromatics

Method

1. Day 1: combine bones, soaked beans, aromatics, salt, and water. Bring to a boil, skim foam, reduce to a low simmer. Cook 2-3 hours until beans are tender.
2. Daily: add whatever vegetable trimmings, grains, or cooking liquids are available. Stir in a handful of oats or cornmeal if the soup needs more body.
3. Once every day without exception: bring the pot to a full rolling boil and hold it there for at least 2 full minutes. This is the food safety step.
4. After boiling: reduce to a simmer or turn off the heat. In a cool kitchen the pot can rest covered at room temperature between boilings. In a warm kitchen, refrigerate it.
5. Taste and adjust daily, add salt, pepper, or a splash of vinegar to brighten.
6. Weekly: when the flavor goes muddy or the color turns very dark, drain off 1/3 of the liquid, add fresh water, and a new base of aromatics.
7. The pot is working correctly when no two bowls taste the same and it never fully runs out.

THE DAILY BOIL IS NOT OPTIONAL. SKIPPING IT ALLOWS DANGEROUS BACTERIA TO MULTIPLY IN THE POT. A SIMMER IS NOT A BOIL. THE ENTIRE POT MUST REACH A FULL ROLLING BOIL AND HOLD IT FOR AT LEAST 2 FULL MINUTES, EVERY SINGLE DAY WITHOUT EXCEPTION.

SIMPLE VEGETABLE SOUP

"Whatever vegetables you have, a pot of water, and salt. The technique is the recipe."

Serves: 6-8   Time: 45 min

History & Context

This is the entry-level soup, the one you make when you are learning, when the pantry is thin, or when you need to feed people from whatever is available. No stock required, no meat required, no special technique. Cheap vegetables simmered in salted water with an onion and whatever seasoning is on hand. The result is genuinely good and genuinely filling. The skill being learned here is how to build flavor from vegetables alone, which is more useful and more transferable than any recipe that depends on meat or stock.

Ingredients

- 2 medium potatoes, diced, the base, provides starch and body
- 2 medium carrots, sliced
- 2 stalks celery, sliced
- 1 medium onion, diced
- 2 cloves garlic, minced
- 1 can (14.5 oz, 410 g) diced or crushed tomatoes
- 1 cup (240 ml) any available vegetables: frozen peas, green beans, corn, cabbage, zucchini
- 6 cups (1.4 L) water
- 1 tsp (5 ml) salt, 1/2 tsp (3 ml) black pepper
- 1/2 tsp (3 ml) dried thyme or Italian seasoning
- 1 tbsp (15 ml) olive oil, lard, or any cooking fat
- Optional: 1/2 cup (120 ml) dried pasta or rice added in the last 15 minutes
- Optional: 1 can drained beans for protein

Method

1. Heat fat in a large pot over medium heat. Add diced onion and cook 5 minutes until softened.
2. Add garlic. Cook 1 minute.
3. Add potatoes, carrots, and celery. Stir to coat in the fat.
4. Add canned tomatoes, water, salt, pepper, and dried herbs. Stir.
5. Bring to a boil. Reduce to a steady simmer.
6. Cook 20 minutes until potatoes and carrots are nearly tender.

7. Add remaining vegetables, optional beans, and optional pasta or rice.
8. Simmer another 10-15 minutes until everything is completely tender.
9. Taste and adjust salt. The soup should taste well-seasoned, not flat.

Field Note: The three things that make this taste like something rather than nothing: fat in the pan at the start, salt added early and tasted at the end, and enough time simmering that the vegetables break down slightly into the broth. A soup that tastes flat is almost always undersalted. Add salt a pinch at a time and taste after each addition. The optional pasta or rice makes this substantially more filling and costs almost nothing extra.

OATMEAL SOUP

"Rolled oats simmered in broth with onion until thick. It sounds wrong. It tastes right."

Serves: 2-3   Time: 20 min

History & Context

Rolled oats stirred into salted broth with a diced onion and simmered until the oats swell and thicken the liquid into something between a soup and a porridge. Scottish and Irish immigrants carried this technique across North America and it survived in working-class kitchens for generations, not because it was fashionable but because it worked. Oats are cheap, shelf-stable for years, and have more protein per dollar than almost any other grain. The broth can be anything: water with a bouillon cube, leftover cooking liquid, or plain salted water. The onion is the only fresh ingredient. The whole pot costs under fifty cents.

Ingredients

- 1/2 cup (120 ml) old-fashioned rolled oats, not instant
- 3 cups (720 ml) chicken broth, vegetable broth, or water with 1 bouillon cube
- 1 small onion, diced
- 1 tbsp (15 ml) butter or lard
- Salt and black pepper
- Optional: pinch of dried thyme, splash of apple cider vinegar at the end

Method

1. Melt butter in a saucepan over medium heat. Add diced onion and cook 5-6 minutes until softened and translucent.
2. Add broth or water with bouillon. Bring to a gentle boil.
3. Stir in rolled oats. Reduce heat to medium-low.
4. Cook 8-10 minutes, stirring occasionally, until oats have swelled and the soup has thickened to the consistency of a thin porridge.
5. Season with salt and pepper. Add optional thyme.
6. A small splash of apple cider vinegar stirred in at the end brightens the flavor considerably.

Field Note: Use old-fashioned rolled oats, not instant, instant oats turn to paste. The finished texture should be thick enough to coat a spoon but still pourable. If it thickens too much on standing, stir in a splash of hot water. A bouillon cube dissolved in water works as well as homemade broth here, keep a jar of bouillon

---

cubes in the pantry, they cost almost nothing and turn plain water into a flavorful base for any soup.

PROTEIN: MEAT, FISH & EGGS

Jerky, pemmican, organ meats, cheap cuts, canned fish, and eggs

Protein is the most expensive macro-nutrient and the one most likely to become scarce first. This chapter addresses that problem from three directions: extending the shelf life of available protein through drying and curing, using the cuts and sources most people overlook, and replacing meat entirely when the shelves are bare. Organ meats cost a fraction of muscle meat and contain more nutrition. Canned sardines provide complete protein and calcium at under two dollars per tin. Eggs are the fastest, cheapest hot protein a kitchen can produce. Marrow bones are frequently free from butchers. The preservation techniques at the start, jerky and pemmican, are the foundation of any serious protein reserve. The final recipes in this chapter are for when meat is simply not available. Lentils and beans, properly seasoned and cooked, satisfy the same protein need. Lentil meat crumbles function as a direct ground beef substitute. Lentil sausage, red lentils cooked to a paste and seasoned with the exact spice profile that signals sausage, replaces breakfast patties, sausage gravy, Italian sausage in pasta, and anywhere else sausage would have gone. These are not vegan novelties. They are contingency plans.

◆ ◆ ◆

BEEF JERKY

"A week of protein in a coat pocket. No refrigeration. No preparation required to eat it."
Serves: makes ~1 lb   Time: 6-8 hours

History & Context

Dried salted meat strips. The technique is simple and the result lasts months at room temperature, longer in a cool location. Fat causes rancidity and must be eliminated entirely, lean cuts only. The jerky from this recipe is drier and harder than commercial jerky, which is deliberate. Dry means shelf-stable. Moist means days, not months.

Ingredients

- 2 lbs (905 g) lean beef, eye of round or flank, all visible fat removed
- 3 tbsp (45 ml) coarse kosher salt
- 1 tsp (5 ml) black pepper
- Optional: 1/2 tsp (3 ml) cayenne, 1 tsp (5 ml) garlic powder

Method

1. Remove every trace of fat from the meat. Fat causes rancidity and will destroy the entire batch within days. Inspect carefully.
2. Slice with the grain into 1/4-inch (0.5 cm) strips.
3. Rub every surface of every strip thoroughly with salt and pepper.
4. Arrange in a single layer on a rack over a baking sheet. No overlapping.
5. Dry in an oven at 170°F (75°C) with the door propped 1 inch (2.5 cm) open for 4-6 hours, flipping once at the midpoint.
6. The jerky is finished when it bends without breaking and shows no moisture when squeezed firmly.
7. Store in a cloth bag or loose container in a cool dry place. Do not seal airtight until completely and thoroughly dry.

Field Note: Any fat remaining on the meat will go rancid within days and ruin the entire batch. This is not an exaggeration, one fatty strip can contaminate everything around it. Lean cuts only. Properly dried jerky keeps 1-2 months at room temperature, 6+ months in a cool cellar.

PEMMICAN

"One pound contains 3,500 calories and keeps for years in a coat pocket. The most calorie-dense portable food ever developed."

Serves: makes ~20 oz   Time: 2 hours

History & Context

Dried meat pounded to powder, combined with rendered fat and dried berries, pressed into bars. The caloric density is extraordinary: 3,500 calories per pound, no refrigeration, years of shelf life when properly made. The fat must be rendered tallow or lard, not butter, which contains water. The meat must be completely dry. These are not details; they are the conditions for the product to function.

Ingredients

- 1 lb (455 g) lean dried beef, completely dry and brittle, not soft jerky
- 1/2 cup (120 ml) rendered beef tallow or lard (not butter, butter contains water and will cause spoilage)
- 1/4 cup (60 ml) dried berries (cranberries, blueberries, or chopped dried cherries)
- Optional: 2 tbsp (30 ml) honey

Method

1. Jerky must be completely dry and brittle, snap it, it should crack. Any residual moisture causes spoilage.
2. Pound or process dried jerky into a coarse powder. Not fine dust, rough crumbs with no large pieces.
3. Render tallow: melt beef suet over very low heat until fat runs completely clear. Strain through cloth. Cool until semi-liquid but not solid.
4. Combine meat powder and dried berries in a bowl. Pour warm (not hot) fat over the mixture and stir thoroughly until everything is coated.
5. Press firmly into a greased pan or roll into logs. Allow to cool completely and harden.
6. Wrap in wax paper or cloth. Store in a cool dry location.

Field Note: The ratio is approximately 50% dried meat and 50% fat by weight. Too little fat and it crumbles. Too much fat and it goes rancid. The berries add carbohydrates and improve palatability, they are not optional if this needs to be eaten regularly.

TURKEY & LEAN MEAT JERKY

"Commercial turkey breast is leaner than beef. That low fat content, usually a cooking disadvantage, becomes a preservation advantage when drying."

Serves: makes ~8 oz   Time: 2-6 hours

History & Context

Commercial turkey breast has dramatically lower fat content than beef. Fat is what goes rancid and shortens shelf life, lean meat dries cleaner and keeps longer. The technique is identical to beef jerky. Any lean cut works: turkey breast, chicken breast, or extra-lean beef round. The lower the fat content, the longer the finished jerky keeps.

Ingredients

- 1-2 lbs (455 to 905 g) boneless skinless turkey breast, chicken breast, or extra-lean beef round, all visible fat removed
- 3 tbsp (45 ml) coarse salt
- 1 tbsp (15 ml) black pepper
- 1 tsp (5 ml) dried sage (for poultry) or dried thyme (for beef)
- Optional: 1 tsp (5 ml) garlic powder, 1/2 tsp (3 ml) cayenne

Method

1. Remove every trace of fat from the meat. Fat is the enemy of long shelf life.
2. Slice with the grain into 1/4-inch (0.5 cm) strips, about 1 inch (2.5 cm) wide and 6-8 inches (15 to 20 cm) long.
3. Rub every surface with salt, pepper, and chosen herbs.
4. Arrange on a rack in a single layer, pieces should not touch.
5. Oven method: arrange on a rack at 170°F (75°C) with door propped 1 inch (2.5 cm) open for 4-6 hours, flipping once.
6. Dehydrator method: 160°F (70°C) for 4-5 hours, flipping once halfway.
7. Finished jerky should crack when bent sharply and transfer no moisture to your fingers when squeezed.

Field Note: Turkey breast is the most practical choice for most people, it is available boneless and skinless at any grocery store, already trimmed of most fat, and inexpensive per pound. If turkey is unavailable, chicken breast works identically. Extra-lean beef round (labeled 'London broil' or 'eye of round') is the best beef option, cheaper cuts have too much fat marbling to dry safely for long storage.

ORGAN MEAT STEW

"Heart, liver, and kidney cost a fraction of muscle meat and contain more nutrients per pound than any other cut."

Serves: 6-8   Time: 3 hours

History & Context

Organ meats are the most nutrient-dense and cheapest cuts available at any butcher. Heart is mild and meaty. Liver is assertive but rich in iron and B vitamins. Kidney requires a soak but has a deep flavor. Together in a stew they produce something genuinely rich at a cost per serving that muscle meat cannot approach. The key is controlling the liver ratio, it is the most assertive flavor and should be used sparingly.

Ingredients

- 1-2 lbs (455 to 905 g) mixed organ meats: beef or pork heart (diced), liver (a small amount only, 2-3 oz, 55 to 85 g), kidneys (pre-soaked 1 hour in salted water and drained)
- 2 onions diced
- 2 dried chili peppers crushed, or 1 tsp (5 ml) chili powder
- Salt and black pepper
- 2 tbsp (30 ml) lard
- Water to cover

Method

1. Soak diced kidneys in heavily salted water 1 hour. Drain and rinse thoroughly.
2. Heat lard in a Dutch oven or heavy pot over high heat until nearly smoking.
3. Brown the diced organ meats in batches, each piece should develop a dark sear before the next batch goes in.
4. Add diced onions. Cook until softened and beginning to brown.
5. Add crushed chilies, salt, pepper, and enough water to just cover.
6. Reduce to a low simmer, cover, and cook 2-3 hours. The broth will become dark and rich.
7. Serve with biscuits or cornbread.

Field Note: Use liver sparingly, 2-3 oz (55 to 85 g) maximum for this quantity. More than that and the assertive flavor of the liver dominates everything else. Heart is the main body of the stew. If organ meats are unavailable, substitute beef chuck with marrow bones.

FRIED CHICKEN, ANY CUT

"The lid-on method ensures the interior cooks through before the crust burns. The technique works for every piece from wing to thigh."

Serves: 4   Time: 45 min

History & Context

Chicken cut into pieces, coated in seasoned flour, and fried in fat. The technique, lid on for the first half to steam and cook the interior through, lid off for the second half to develop and set the crust, is what separates properly cooked fried chicken from chicken that is burnt outside and raw inside. It works for any cut: bone-in thighs, drumsticks, breasts, or a whole bird broken down. Bone-in thighs are the best value, more fat, more flavor, cheaper per pound, and more forgiving of timing than breast meat.

Ingredients

- 3-4 lbs (1.4 to 1.8 kg) bone-in chicken pieces, thighs and drumsticks are the best value; breast pieces work but cook faster
- 1.5 cups (360 ml) flour
- 2 tsp (10 ml) salt
- 1 tsp (5 ml) black pepper
- 1/2 tsp (3 ml) cayenne
- Lard or fat for frying, at least 2 inches (5 cm) deep in the pan

Method

1. Pat chicken pieces completely dry. Moisture prevents the coating from adhering.
2. Combine flour, salt, pepper, and cayenne in a wide bowl. Dredge each piece, pressing firmly so the coating adheres to every surface.
3. Heat lard to 350°F (175°C) in a large cast iron skillet. A pinch of flour dropped in should sizzle immediately.
4. Add larger pieces (thighs, drumsticks) first, skin-side down. Cover with a lid for the first 10 minutes.
5. Remove lid, increase heat slightly, cook 5-8 more minutes until the bottom is deeply golden.
6. Flip and cook uncovered another 10 minutes. Done when juices run clear and internal temp reaches 165°F (75°C).
7. Salt immediately after removing from fat.

LOW & SLOW BRAISED CHICKEN THIGHS

"Cheap tough cuts cooked at low heat for two hours produce more flavor than expensive cuts cooked fast. This is the technique."

Serves: 4-6   Time: 2.5 hours

History & Context

Bone-in chicken thighs are among the cheapest cuts at any grocery store. They are also among the most forgiving, the connective tissue and fat that make them tough when cooked quickly converts to gelatin when given sustained low heat, producing a rich broth and meat that falls from the bone. The same technique applies to any bone-in braising cut: pork neck bones, beef short ribs, turkey legs, or turkey thighs. The principle is the same regardless of the animal, low heat, liquid, time.

Ingredients

- 2-3 lbs (0.9 to 1.4 kg) bone-in chicken thighs, or turkey thighs, pork neck bones, or beef short ribs
- 2 tbsp (30 ml) lard or cooking oil
- 1 large onion diced
- 2 cloves garlic
- Salt, black pepper, cayenne
- 1 tsp (5 ml) dried sage or thyme
- 2 cups (480 ml) water or broth

Method

1. Pat meat dry. Season heavily with salt and pepper on all sides.
2. Heat lard in a Dutch oven or heavy pot over high heat until nearly smoking.
3. Brown meat in batches, each piece should develop a dark sear before the next batch goes in. Do not crowd the pot. This step is not optional.
4. Remove browned meat. Add diced onion to the same pot. Cook until softened and beginning to brown.
5. Return all meat to pot. Add garlic, cayenne, herbs, and water or broth to come halfway up the meat.
6. Cover tightly and cook over the lowest possible heat for 1.5-2 hours until meat pulls from the bone with no resistance.
7. Serve in the broth with cornbread or flat dumplings.

Field Note: Low and slow is the only method for bone-in braising cuts. High heat seizes the proteins and produces meat that stays dry and stringy no matter how long you cook it afterward. If chicken thighs are unavailable at the store, turkey thighs and drumsticks are identical in technique. Pork neck bones take 2.5-3 hours and produce a richer, porkier broth. Beef short ribs take 3+ hours and are the most expensive option but the most luxurious result.

PRAIRIE OYSTER SCRAMBLE

"Organ protein that costs almost nothing. Properly cooked, the flavor is mild."

Serves: 4   Time: 20 min

History & Context

Animal testicles are edible protein available from butchers who process whole animals, ask directly, as they are rarely displayed in the retail case. Specialty butchers, Latin meat markets, and farm-supply butcher counters are the most likely sources. The flavor is genuinely mild when properly cooked. Most negative reactions come from prior knowledge rather than from the actual taste. Dusted in cornmeal and fried in hot fat, they are indistinguishable from other offal. The point is not novelty, it is using every part of an animal that someone paid for.

Ingredients

- 6-8 calf, lamb, or pig testicles from a specialty butcher or Latin meat market
- 1/2 cup (120 ml) cornmeal
- 1/2 cup (120 ml) flour
- 1 tsp (5 ml) salt
- 1/2 tsp (3 ml) black pepper
- 1/4 tsp (1 ml) cayenne
- Lard or fat for frying
- 4 eggs
- Apple cider vinegar for serving

Method

1. Rinse thoroughly. Optionally split lengthwise to allow faster, more even cooking.
2. Combine cornmeal, flour, salt, pepper, and cayenne. Dredge each piece, pressing coating firmly.
3. Heat lard in a cast iron skillet over medium-high until shimmering.
4. Fry 3-4 minutes per side until golden and crisp. Done when firm to the touch.
5. In the same pan with remaining fat, scramble eggs.
6. Serve together with a splash of apple cider vinegar.

Field Note: The cornmeal coating and high-heat frying are essential to the flavor. Undercooking produces an unpleasant texture. Overcooking produces something tough. If these are unavailable from your butcher, this recipe's technique applies equally well to chicken gizzards, widely available, cheap, and similarly overlooked.

CHICKEN & FLAT DUMPLINGS

"One cheap cut of chicken stretched into a complete meal for five by a pot of broth and flat dumplings."

Serves: 4-6   Time: 2.5 hours

History & Context

Bone-in chicken thighs simmered in water for two hours produce a rich broth and tender falling-off-the-bone meat. The flat dumplings are not the fluffy drop dumplings of modern cooking. They are thin, dense, and rolled, becoming slippery and chewy as they cook through, more filling per square inch, and they stretch the meal further. A two-dollar package of chicken thighs becomes six servings with this technique.

Ingredients

- 2 lbs (905 g) bone-in chicken thighs, or turkey thighs, bone-in chicken drumsticks
- 1 large onion diced
- Salt and black pepper
- 1 tsp (5 ml) dried sage or thyme
- 4 cups (960 ml) water
- Flat dumplings: 2 cups (480 ml) flour, 1/2 tsp (3 ml) salt, 1/4 cup (60 ml) lard, 1/2 cup (120 ml) cold water

Method

1. Season chicken pieces with salt and pepper. Place in a Dutch oven with diced onion and herbs.
2. Add water. Bring to a boil, reduce to a low simmer. Cover and cook 1.5-2 hours until meat falls freely from the bone.
3. Remove chicken pieces. Strip all meat from bones and return meat to the broth. Discard bones.
4. Make flat dumplings: combine flour and salt. Cut in lard until crumbly. Add cold water until dough holds, stiffer than biscuit dough.
5. Roll very thin on a floured surface, 1/8-inch (0.5 cm). Cut into rough 1x3-inch (2.5x7.5 cm) strips.
6. Bring broth back to a gentle simmer. Drop in dumplings a few at a time, stirring gently to prevent sticking.
7. Cook 8-10 minutes until dumplings are cooked through and slightly translucent.

Field Note: *Roll the dumplings thin enough to almost see light through, 1/8-inch*

(0.5 cm) or less. Thick dumplings are dense and heavy. Thin dumplings become slippery, silky, and genuinely filling. If chicken thighs are out of stock, turkey thighs and drumsticks are a direct substitute at similar price. Bone-in pork neck bones produce a richer broth and work identically, allow an extra 30-45 minutes of simmering time.

ROASTED MARROW BONES

"Butchers frequently give these away. The marrow inside is one of the richest and most calorie-dense foods available from an animal."

Serves: 4   Time: 20 min

History & Context

Bone marrow is concentrated fat and protein that requires almost no preparation to eat. Roasted in an oven or directly in coals for 15-20 minutes, it becomes soft, spreadable, and intensely beefy. It costs almost nothing because most customers do not know what to do with it, ask your butcher directly.

Ingredients

- 4-6 large beef femur or leg bones, cut crosswise 3 inches (7.5 cm), ask butcher specifically for marrow bones
- Coarse salt and black pepper
- Toasted bread or biscuits for serving

Method

1. Bring bones to room temperature if refrigerated, about 30 minutes.
2. Stand bones cut-side up in a baking pan. Season the exposed marrow with salt and pepper.
3. Oven method: 450°F (230°C) for 15-20 minutes. Done when the marrow is soft throughout and just beginning to melt at the edges.
4. Campfire method: nestle bones upright directly in hot coals. Roast 15-20 minutes until marrow bubbles.
5. Serve immediately upright with a small spoon. Spread on toast or biscuits.
6. Consume within 10 minutes, marrow firms quickly as it cools.

Field Note: The marrow should appear creamy and beige. Gray marrow was cooked too long. Ask butchers for marrow bones specifically, they are often inexpensive or free because demand is low. Femur bones provide the most marrow per bone.

SALMON PATTIES

"Canned salmon is complete protein, omega-3 fats, and significant calcium, all in a shelf-stable can that costs under two dollars."

Serves: 4 patties   Time: 20 min

History & Context

Canned salmon provides complete protein, omega-3 fatty acids, and significant calcium from the soft pressure-cooked bones, which are fully edible and undetectable in texture. Shelf-stable for several years. Formed into patties with cracker crumbs and a beaten egg, fried until golden, it is one of the most nutritionally complete cheap meals available from canned goods.

Ingredients

- 1 can (14.75 oz, 420 g) salmon, drained
- 1/2 cup (120 ml) saltine cracker crumbs
- 1 egg beaten
- 2 tbsp (30 ml) diced onion
- 1 tbsp (15 ml) yellow mustard
- Salt and black pepper
- Oil or lard for frying
- Bread or crackers for serving

Method

1. Drain salmon. Leave the small soft bones in and mash them into the mixture, they provide calcium and are undetectable.
2. Combine salmon, cracker crumbs, beaten egg, onion, and mustard. Mix with a fork.
3. Season with salt and pepper. The mixture should hold together when squeezed.
4. Form into 3/4-inch (2 cm) thick patties about 3 inches (7.5 cm) across.
5. Heat 2 tbsp (30 ml) oil in a skillet over medium-high.
6. Cook 3-4 minutes per side without moving until golden-brown and firm.
7. Serve on bread or crackers with mustard or hot sauce.

Field Note: *The soft bones in canned salmon are pressure-cooked to complete softness during the canning process. Mash them in, they provide substantial calcium and have no detectable texture. A single can of salmon and a sleeve of crackers* *produces four filling patties for about two dollars total.*

DEVILED HAM

"Aggressively seasoned ground ham paste. A small amount feels substantial."
Serves: 6-8 sandwiches worth   Time: 20 min

History & Context

Ground ham seasoned with mustard, vinegar, and spices until intensely flavored, a small amount spread thick on bread delivers enough flavor to constitute a meal. Canned ham has a long shelf life and can be used in place of fresh. The homemade version is substantially better than the commercial equivalent.

Ingredients

- 1 lb (455 g) cooked ham or canned ham
- 2 tbsp (30 ml) yellow mustard
- 1 tbsp (15 ml) apple cider vinegar
- 1/2 tsp (3 ml) black pepper
- 1/4 tsp (1 ml) cayenne
- 1/4 tsp (1 ml) garlic powder
- Pinch of ground cloves
- Salt to taste

Method

1. Cut ham into chunks. Include any caramelized darker exterior if using leftover baked ham.
2. Process or mince ham until very fine, almost paste-like.
3. Add mustard, vinegar, pepper, cayenne, garlic powder, and cloves. Mix until fully incorporated.
4. Taste and adjust, the mixture should be assertive and peppery.
5. Pack into a jar. Refrigerate at least 2 hours before using.
6. Spread thickly on bread.

Field Note: The cloves seem unusual but contribute a warm complexity that distinguishes this from plain ground ham. Keeps refrigerated for a week. Canned ham stores for years at room temperature and is a legitimate shelf-stable protein source.

HEAD CHEESE

"Pork neck bones, hocks, or feet simmered until the meat falls off, set in their own gelatin. Protein from the cheapest cuts."

Serves: 4-6 sandwiches   Time: 4 hours + overnight

History & Context

Head cheese is not cheese. It is shredded meat from pork neck bones, hocks, or feet combined with the naturally gelatinous cooking liquid, seasoned with vinegar and spices, poured into a mold and refrigerated overnight until it sets firm enough to slice. The cheapest cuts of pork, the ones with the most collagen, produce the firmest, best result. This is protein from the parts of the animal that cost almost nothing.

Ingredients

- 2-3 lbs (0.9 to 1.4 kg) pork neck bones, hocks, or pig's feet
- 1 large onion quartered
- 3 cloves garlic
- 2 bay leaves
- 1 tbsp (15 ml) apple cider vinegar
- 1 tsp (5 ml) black pepper
- 1 tsp (5 ml) salt
- Optional: 1/4 tsp (1 ml) allspice, 1/4 tsp (1 ml) nutmeg
- Rye bread, mustard, and pickles for serving

Method

1. Place pork pieces in a large pot. Cover with cold water by 2 inches (5 cm). Bring to a boil and skim all foam during the first 15 minutes.
2. Add onion, garlic, bay leaves, vinegar, salt, and pepper. Reduce to a low simmer. Cover and cook 3-4 hours until all meat falls freely from the bones.
3. Remove all meat pieces. Strain the broth and return to the pot. Boil uncovered until reduced by about one-third.
4. Pick all meat from bones. Discard bones.
5. Combine picked meat with reduced broth. Add optional spices. Taste and adjust salt and vinegar.
6. Pour into a loaf pan or bowl. Refrigerate overnight until firmly set.
7. Unmold and slice 1/4-inch (0.5 cm) thick. Serve on bread with mustard and pickles.

SOUSE, PICKLED PRESSED PORK

"Head cheese's sharper cousin. The vinegar brine both preserves the meat and makes the sandwich."

Serves: 4-6 sandwiches   Time: 3 hours + overnight

History & Context

The same technique as head cheese but brined in vinegar after pressing, which adds a sharp tang and extends shelf life further. Made from pig's feet, ears, or hocks, the cheapest cuts that cost almost nothing. Keeps refrigerated in its brine for up to a week.

Ingredients

- 2 lbs (905 g) pig's feet, ears, or hocks, cleaned thoroughly
- 1 large onion
- 3 cloves garlic
- 2 bay leaves
- Brine: 2 cups (480 ml) apple cider vinegar, 1 cup (240 ml) water, 1 tbsp (15 ml) salt, 1 tsp (5 ml) black pepper, 1/2 tsp (3 ml) red pepper flakes, 1/4 tsp (1 ml) allspice
- White bread, raw onion, and hot sauce for serving

Method

1. Scrub pig's feet or ears under cold water. Place in a large pot with onion, garlic, and bay leaves. Cover with water by 2 inches (5 cm).
2. Bring to a boil, skim foam 15 minutes. Reduce to a low simmer, cover, cook 2.5-3 hours until all meat is very tender.
3. Remove meat. Cool until handleable. Strip all meat and soft cartilage from bones. Discard bones.
4. Combine brine ingredients in a saucepan. Bring to a boil to dissolve salt.
5. Pack shredded meat tightly into a loaf pan. Pour hot brine over until just covered.
6. Weight the meat down with a plate and refrigerate overnight.
7. Slice thin. Serve on bread with raw onion and hot sauce.

> **Field Note:** *Use apple cider vinegar rather than white distilled vinegar for a rounder flavor. The brine both flavors and preserves, souse kept submerged in its brine in the refrigerator holds for a week.*

LIVERWURST SANDWICH

"Spreadable pork liver sausage on rye bread with raw onion and mustard. Liver nutrients at sandwich prices."

Serves: 1-2   Time: 3 min

History & Context

Liverwurst and braunschweiger are spreadable sausages made from pork liver, fat, and seasonings. They cost a fraction of whole muscle meat, provide complete protein, iron, zinc, and B vitamins in concentrations that muscle meat cannot match, and require no cooking. This is one of the most nutritionally dense things you can put on bread for under two dollars.

Ingredients

- 2 slices dark rye bread or any available bread
- 2-3 oz (55 to 85 g) liverwurst or braunschweiger, at room temperature
- 1 thin slice raw onion
- Yellow mustard
- Optional: sliced dill pickle

Method

1. Allow liverwurst to come to room temperature, cold liverwurst tears bread.
2. Spread a generous layer across one slice of bread.
3. Add a thin line of yellow mustard.
4. Lay the onion slice over the mustard.
5. Add pickle if using.
6. Press the second slice on top.

Field Note: Liverwurst keeps refrigerated for 1-2 weeks. The strong flavor mellows significantly when paired with rye bread's sourness and raw onion's sharpness. This sandwich provides more nutritional value per dollar than almost anything else in this book.

SCRAPPLE

"Ground pork and cornmeal cooked together into a firm loaf, sliced thin and fried until shattering. Every part of the animal used."

Serves: 6-8   Time: 45 min + chilling

History & Context

Scrapple uses ground pork, cornmeal, and seasoning to produce a firm sliceable loaf that keeps for days and fries up with a crackling crust. It uses the scraps and trimmings that would otherwise be discarded. The cornmeal stretches the protein and adds carbohydrates. Combined, they produce something more complete than either ingredient alone.

Ingredients

- 1 lb (455 g) ground pork (or a mix of pork and up to 1/4 lb (115 g) pork liver for more nutrition)
- 4 cups (960 ml) water or pork broth
- 1 cup (240 ml) yellow cornmeal
- 1 tsp (5 ml) salt
- 1/2 tsp (3 ml) black pepper
- 1/4 tsp (1 ml) dried sage
- 1/4 tsp (1 ml) dried thyme
- 1/8 tsp (1 ml) cayenne
- Lard or bacon drippings for frying

Method

1. Cook ground pork in a saucepan over medium heat, breaking into very fine crumbles. Drain excess fat, leaving about a tablespoon in the pan.
2. Add water or broth and bring to a boil. Add all seasonings.
3. Pour cornmeal in a thin stream while stirring constantly. Stir vigorously to prevent lumps.
4. Reduce heat to low. Cook, stirring frequently, for 20-25 minutes until very thick and pulling from the sides of the pan.
5. Pour into a greased loaf pan, smooth top, cover, and refrigerate at least 4 hours or overnight.
6. Unmold. Slice 3/8 to 1/2-inch (1 to 1.5 cm) thick.
7. Heat lard in a cast iron skillet over medium-high until nearly smoking. Fry slices 3-4 minutes per side without moving until a shattering crust forms.

FRIED EGG SANDWICH

"One egg, two slices of bread, a hot pan. The fastest protein meal a kitchen can produce."

Serves: 1   Time: 5 min

History & Context

One egg cracked into hot fat in a skillet, cooked until the edges are lacy and brown, placed on bread with salt and pepper. A dozen eggs at current prices means twelve hot protein meals. The technique, hot pan, enough fat, not moving the egg until the edges are set, produces something better than a pale rubbery egg in an insufficient pan.

Ingredients

- 2 slices white sandwich bread
- 1 large egg
- 1 tsp (5 ml) bacon drippings or lard
- Salt and black pepper

Method

1. Heat a skillet over medium heat until a drop of water dances and evaporates. Add bacon drippings and swirl to coat.
2. Crack the egg into the hot fat. It will set immediately around the edges.
3. Season with salt and pepper directly on the yolk.
4. Cook until the white is fully set and edges are golden and lacy, 2-3 minutes. For travel, press the yolk gently until it just breaks and sets.
5. Place egg on one slice of bread. Press the second slice on top firmly. Eat immediately.

Field Note: Golden lacy edges come from a hot enough pan with enough fat. A pale rubbery egg means the pan was not hot enough. The browned fat on the white edges is where the flavor is.

EGG IN A HOLE

"An egg cooked inside a slice of bread. Nothing wasted, not even the bread scrap."

Serves: 1   Time: 8 min

History & Context

A hole cut in a slice of bread, an egg cracked into it. The bread scrap is fried alongside and used for dipping. Nothing is discarded. The lid-on technique, covering the pan briefly after flipping, sets the white with trapped steam without requiring you to flip the egg and risk breaking the yolk.

Ingredients

- 1 slice white sandwich bread, at least 3/4-inch (2 cm) thick
- 1 large egg
- 1 tbsp (15 ml) butter or bacon drippings
- Salt and black pepper
- A round glass or cutter about 2.5-3 inches (6.5 to 7.5 cm) across

Method

1. Press a glass or round cutter firmly into the center of the bread and remove the circle. Set the circle aside.
2. Melt butter in a skillet over medium heat until foaming.
3. Place the bread frame and the bread circle in the skillet. Toast the first side about 90 seconds until golden.
4. Flip both pieces. Immediately crack the egg into the hole.
5. Season with salt and pepper. Cover the pan with a lid for 1-2 minutes, trapped steam sets the white without flipping.
6. The white should be fully set with no translucent spots; the yolk should still jiggle slightly.
7. Slide onto a plate with the bread circle alongside for dipping.

Field Note: The lid technique works for any fried egg where you want a fully set white and a runny yolk. Once you know it, you will use it every time.

TUNA NOODLE CASSEROLE

"Two cans of tuna, a can of soup, egg noodles, and crackers. Feeds four for under four dollars."

Serves: 4-6   Time: 35 min

History & Context

Tuna noodle casserole became a weekly standard in American households during the postwar years because it checked every box that mattered: cheap, filling, made entirely from shelf-stable canned and dry goods, and something children would actually eat without complaint. A can of condensed cream of mushroom soup thinned with milk becomes the sauce. Egg noodles provide the bulk. Crackers on top provide the crust. The whole thing takes 35 minutes and costs about $3.50 at current grocery prices. It is one of the most practical recipes in this book for the target audience, someone who has never cooked much and needs to feed a family from pantry staples.

Ingredients

- 2 cans (5 oz, 140 g each) tuna in water or oil, drained
- 1 can condensed cream of mushroom soup, do not add water
- 1/2 cup (120 ml) whole milk, or reconstituted powdered milk
- 2 cups (480 ml) egg noodles, cooked and drained
- 1/2 cup (120 ml) frozen or canned peas, drained
- 1/2 tsp (3 ml) black pepper
- 1/4 tsp (1 ml) garlic powder
- 1/2 cup (120 ml) crushed crackers or breadcrumbs for topping
- 1 tbsp (15 ml) butter or lard, melted

Method

1. Preheat oven to 375°F (190°C). Grease a 2-quart (1.9 L) baking dish.
2. Cook egg noodles in salted boiling water until just barely tender, slightly underdone. Drain.
3. In a large bowl, combine condensed soup and milk. Stir until smooth.
4. Add drained tuna, breaking it into small flakes. Add peas, pepper, and garlic powder.
5. Add cooked noodles. Stir until everything is evenly coated.
6. Pour into the greased baking dish. Spread evenly.
7. Combine crushed crackers with melted butter. Scatter evenly over the top.
8. Bake 20-25 minutes until bubbling at the edges and the topping is golden brown.

9. Rest 5 minutes before serving.

PICKLED EGGS

"Hard boiled eggs in vinegar brine keep for weeks without refrigeration. Complete protein you can carry in a pocket."

Serves: 12 eggs   Time: 20 min active + 1 week

History & Context

Pickled eggs were a standard item in every American tavern, general store, and lunch counter from the 1800s through the mid-20th century, kept in large glass jars on the counter at room temperature for weeks. The vinegar brine preserves them completely. A jar of pickled eggs in a cool location keeps for a month or more without any refrigeration at all. They require no preparation to eat, provide complete protein, and cost almost nothing. A dozen eggs and a cup of vinegar is the entire investment. These are legitimate emergency protein that can be made now and stored for later.

Ingredients

- 12 large eggs
- 2 cups (480 ml) apple cider vinegar or white distilled vinegar
- 1 cup (240 ml) water
- 1 tbsp (15 ml) pickling salt or kosher salt (non-iodized)
- 1 tsp (5 ml) black peppercorns
- 1 tsp (5 ml) sugar
- 2 cloves garlic
- Optional: 1/2 tsp (3 ml) red pepper flakes for heat, 1 tsp (5 ml) dried dill

Method

1. Place eggs in a single layer in a saucepan. Cover with cold water by 1 inch (2.5 cm).
2. Bring to a boil over medium-high heat. Once boiling, cover and remove from heat. Let stand 12 minutes.
3. Transfer eggs to a bowl of ice water immediately. Cool 10 minutes. Peel under cold running water.
4. Combine vinegar, water, salt, sugar, peppercorns, and garlic in a saucepan. Bring to a boil until salt and sugar dissolve. Remove from heat.
5. Pack peeled eggs into a clean quart jar or any clean container with a lid.
6. Pour hot brine over eggs until completely submerged. Add optional spices.
7. Cool to room temperature. Seal and refrigerate, or store in a cool location below 60°F (15°C).

8. Ready to eat in 3-5 days. Best after a full week when the brine has fully
penetrated.

ONION & POTATO FRITTATA

"Potatoes and onions fried soft, eggs poured over and set. A complete skillet meal from three ingredients."

Serves: 4   Time: 25 min

History & Context

A frittata is a skillet egg dish that starts on the stovetop and finishes under a lid, no oven required. The potato provides the bulk and carbohydrates, the onion provides sweetness and depth, and the eggs bind everything into a single cohesive dish that feeds four people from ingredients that cost under two dollars total. It works equally well as breakfast, lunch, or dinner, which is part of why it appeared on Depression-era tables at every meal. One skillet, one cooking session, nothing wasted.

Ingredients

- 3 medium potatoes, peeled and sliced thin, 1/8-inch (0.5 cm)
- 1 large onion, sliced thin
- 4 eggs
- 2 tbsp (30 ml) lard or bacon drippings
- Salt and black pepper
- Optional: 2 tbsp (30 ml) any available cheese, crumbled or shredded
- Optional: pinch of dried thyme or parsley

Method

1. Heat lard in a 10-inch (25 cm) cast iron skillet over medium heat until shimmering.
2. Add potato slices in a single layer if possible. Season with salt and pepper.
3. Cook 5 minutes, turning occasionally, until potatoes begin to soften and color slightly.
4. Add sliced onion over the potatoes. Stir to combine. Cook another 8-10 minutes, stirring occasionally, until both potatoes and onions are completely soft and golden.
5. Spread the potato and onion mixture evenly across the pan bottom.
6. Beat eggs with a pinch of salt and pepper until combined. Pour evenly over the potato mixture.
7. Reduce heat to medium-low. Cover the skillet with a lid or foil.
8. Cook 5-7 minutes until the eggs are fully set with no wet spots on top.
9. If using cheese, scatter over the top in the last 2 minutes of cooking.
10. Slide or cut into wedges directly from the pan.

RICE AND EGG POT

"Rice cooked, egg cracked on top, lid on, heat off. Five minutes later it is dinner."

Serves: 1-2   Time: 25 min

History & Context

A cup of rice cooked in salted water until done, an egg cracked directly onto the surface, the lid replaced and the heat turned off. The residual steam in the pot sets the egg in five minutes, white fully cooked, yolk still soft. You break the yolk over the rice and it runs into every gap. A drizzle of soy sauce or a shake of hot sauce if available. That is the entire meal. One cup of rice and one egg costs under twenty-five cents and provides enough protein and carbohydrate for a complete meal. When the pantry is nearly empty and the energy to cook is gone, this is the answer.

Ingredients

- 1 cup (240 ml) long-grain white rice
- 2 cups (480 ml) water
- 1/2 tsp (3 ml) salt
- 1-2 eggs
- Soy sauce, hot sauce, or a drizzle of any available fat for serving

Method

1. Combine rice, water, and salt in a small saucepan with a tight-fitting lid. Bring to a full boil.
2. Reduce heat to the lowest possible setting. Cover tightly. Cook 18 minutes without lifting the lid.
3. At 18 minutes, the water should be fully absorbed. Do not drain.
4. Crack one or two eggs directly onto the surface of the rice. Replace the lid immediately.
5. Turn the heat completely off. Let stand 5 minutes, the residual steam sets the egg.
6. Check at 5 minutes: white should be fully opaque, yolk should still jiggle slightly.
7. Break the yolk with a fork and stir it gently through the top layer of rice.
8. Add a drizzle of soy sauce, hot sauce, or fat directly in the pot and eat from it.

***Field Note:** The tight lid and residual steam are the entire technique, do not lift the lid during the 5-minute rest or the steam escapes and the egg white stays raw. If the egg white is still translucent at 5 minutes, replace the lid and wait another 2 minutes with the burner on the absolute lowest setting. One egg feeds one person*

---

well. Two eggs make it more substantial. This works with any long-grain white rice, do not use instant rice, which turns mushy from the extended steam. When meat is unavailable entirely, see recipes 3-23 through 3-26, lentil loaf, bean sausage patties, chickpea patties, and lentil meat crumbles that function as direct substitutes in any meal that would normally include meat.

LENTIL LOAF

"Brown lentils, oats, and egg baked in a loaf pan. Slices like meatloaf. Works hot for dinner and cold for sandwiches."

Serves: 6-8 slices   Time: 75 min

History & Context

When the meat case is bare, this is the closest thing to meatloaf that a pantry can produce. Brown lentils cooked until just tender and partially mashed, combined with rolled oats, an egg, onion, garlic, and a spice blend that reads as savory and substantial. Pressed into a loaf pan and baked until firm, then glazed with ketchup or tomato paste and vinegar. It slices cleanly, it holds together, and cold leftover slices make excellent sandwiches. Brown lentils are available at any grocery store for under two dollars a pound and store indefinitely sealed. This is not a compromise version of meatloaf, it is a different thing that satisfies the same need.

Ingredients

- 1 cup (240 ml) dried brown lentils (or 2.5 cups (600 ml) cooked)
- 2.5 cups (600 ml) water for cooking lentils
- 1 cup (240 ml) old-fashioned rolled oats
- 1 egg, beaten
- 1 small onion, finely diced
- 3 cloves garlic, minced, or 1 tsp (5 ml) garlic powder
- 2 tbsp (30 ml) soy sauce or Worcestershire sauce
- 1 tbsp (15 ml) tomato paste or ketchup
- 1 tsp (5 ml) smoked paprika
- 1 tsp (5 ml) dried thyme
- 1/2 tsp (3 ml) black pepper
- 1/2 tsp (3 ml) salt
- Glaze: 3 tbsp (45 ml) ketchup or tomato paste + 1 tbsp (15 ml) apple cider vinegar + 1 tsp (5 ml) sugar

Method

1. Rinse lentils. Combine with 2.5 cups (600 ml) water in a saucepan. Bring to a boil, reduce to a simmer. Cook 20-25 minutes until tender but not mushy. Drain any excess liquid.
2. Preheat oven to 350°F (175°C). Grease a 9x5 inch (23x13 cm) loaf pan.

3. While lentils are warm, mash roughly two-thirds of them with a fork or potato masher, leave the remaining third whole for texture. You want a thick paste with some visible lentils.
4. Heat a small amount of fat in a skillet. Cook diced onion until soft and golden, about 6 minutes. Add garlic and cook 1 minute more.
5. Combine mashed lentils, cooked onion and garlic, oats, beaten egg, soy sauce, tomato paste, smoked paprika, thyme, salt, and pepper. Mix until fully combined.
6. The mixture should hold together when squeezed. If too wet, add another 2 tablespoons (30 ml) of oats. If too dry, add a tablespoon of water.
7. Press firmly and evenly into the greased loaf pan. Smooth the top with the back of a spoon.
8. Mix glaze ingredients and spread evenly over the top.
9. Bake 45-50 minutes until the top is darkened and the loaf feels firm when pressed.
10. Cool in the pan for 15 minutes before slicing, it firms up as it cools. Do not slice while hot.

> *Field Note: The 15-minute rest before slicing is not optional, hot lentil loaf falls apart. Cold lentil loaf slices cleanly. Leftover slices fried in a little fat the next morning develop a crackling crust that is genuinely excellent. If you have no egg, substitute 1 tablespoon (15 ml) ground flaxseed mixed with 3 tablespoons (45 ml) water, rested 5 minutes, it binds identically.*

BEAN & OAT SAUSAGE PATTIES

"White beans, oats, and sausage spices formed into patties and pan-fried. The fennel is what makes them taste like sausage."

Serves: 8 patties   Time: 30 min

History & Context

Fennel seed, smoked paprika, garlic, and sage are the flavor profile that signals sausage to the brain, the specific combination that has defined breakfast and Italian sausage for generations. Mashed white beans provide the protein base, oats provide structure, and an egg binds everything. Pan-fried in a little fat until both sides are dark and crispy, these patties read as sausage in a way that surprises people who expect them to taste like beans. White beans, navy beans, great northern, or cannellini, are shelf-stable, cheap, and available everywhere.

Ingredients

- 1.5 cups (360 ml) cooked white beans, navy, great northern, or cannellini, or one 15oz (425 g) can, drained and rinsed
- 1 cup (240 ml) old-fashioned rolled oats
- 1 egg, beaten
- 1/2 small onion, very finely minced
- 2 cloves garlic, minced, or 1/2 tsp (3 ml) garlic powder
- 1 tbsp (15 ml) soy sauce
- 1 tbsp (15 ml) tomato paste
- 1 tsp (5 ml) fennel seeds, lightly crushed, or 1/2 tsp (3 ml) ground fennel. This is the key ingredient.
- 1 tsp (5 ml) smoked paprika
- 1/2 tsp (3 ml) dried sage
- 1/2 tsp (3 ml) garlic powder
- 1/2 tsp (3 ml) onion powder
- 1/4 tsp (1 ml) cumin
- 1/4 tsp (1 ml) black pepper
- 1/4 tsp (1 ml) salt
- Pinch of cayenne
- Fat for frying

Method

1. Drain and rinse beans thoroughly. Place in a bowl and mash with a fork or potato masher until mostly smooth, some whole beans remaining is fine and adds texture.
2. Add oats, beaten egg, minced onion, garlic, soy sauce, tomato paste, and all spices. Mix until fully combined.
3. The mixture should hold its shape when pressed into a ball. If too wet, add a tablespoon more oats. If too dry, add a teaspoon of water.
4. Divide into 8 equal portions. Shape each into a round patty about 3/4-inch (2 cm) thick.
5. Refrigerate patties for 20 minutes if time allows, they hold together better when cold.
6. Heat fat in a cast iron skillet over medium heat until shimmering.
7. Fry patties 4-5 minutes per side without moving until a deeply dark crust forms on each side.
8. Drain briefly and serve immediately.

> *Field Note: Fennel seed is the single ingredient that makes these taste like sausage rather than spiced beans. Do not skip it. Whole fennel seeds lightly crushed in your palm release more flavor than pre-ground. These patties freeze well, form them, freeze on a flat surface until solid, then store in a bag. Cook from frozen in a covered skillet over medium-low for 6-7 minutes per side.*

CHICKPEA PATTIES

"Chickpeas mashed with flour, egg, and spices. Pan-fried until crispy. On a plate, in a sandwich, or alongside anything."

Serves: 6 patties   Time: 25 min

History & Context

Chickpeas, garbanzo beans, are one of the most complete plant proteins available, with more protein per cup than most other legumes. Mashed by hand with flour as a binder, a beaten egg, and a spice blend built around cumin and smoked paprika, they form patties that hold together in the pan and develop a genuinely crispy exterior. No food processor, no specialty ingredients, no technique beyond mashing with a fork. A can of chickpeas costs under a dollar and makes six patties. Dried chickpeas soaked overnight cost even less. These work as a burger replacement, a protein alongside rice and beans, or sliced cold in a sandwich.

Ingredients

- 1.5 cups (360 ml) cooked chickpeas, one 15oz (425 g) can, drained and rinsed, or cooked from dried
- 3 tbsp (45 ml) all-purpose flour or cornmeal, cornmeal gives a crispier result
- 1 egg, beaten
- 2 tbsp (30 ml) finely minced onion, or 1/2 tsp (3 ml) onion powder
- 1 tsp (5 ml) cumin
- 1 tsp (5 ml) smoked paprika
- 1/2 tsp (3 ml) garlic powder
- 1/2 tsp (3 ml) salt
- 1/4 tsp (1 ml) black pepper
- Pinch of cayenne
- Fat for frying

Method

1. Drain and rinse chickpeas. Place in a bowl.
2. Mash with a fork until mostly broken down, aim for a rough paste with some whole chickpeas still visible. Do not puree completely, texture holds the patty together.
3. Add flour, beaten egg, onion, and all spices. Mix until combined.
4. The mixture should hold together when squeezed into a ball. If it falls apart, add another tablespoon of flour. If too dry, add a teaspoon of water.

5. Divide into 6 portions. Form each into a round patty about 3/4-inch (2 cm) thick.
6. Heat fat in a skillet over medium-high until shimmering.
7. Fry 3-4 minutes per side without moving until each side is deeply golden and crisp.
8. Season with a pinch of salt immediately after removing from fat.

Field Note: Partial mashing is the key, a completely smooth chickpea puree produces a patty that steams rather than crisps. Rough texture with visible whole chickpeas creates the structure that develops a proper crust. Cornmeal as the binder instead of flour produces a slightly crunchier exterior. These hold together better after 20 minutes of refrigeration before frying, if time allows, chill the formed patties before cooking.

LENTIL MEAT CRUMBLES, GROUND BEEF SUBSTITUTE

"Seasoned cooked lentils that look, cook, and eat like ground beef. Use anywhere ground meat would go."

Serves: 4   Time: 30 min

History & Context

This is the most practical meat substitute in the book because it requires no forming, no special technique, and no pretending it is something it is not. Cooked brown or green lentils seasoned with soy sauce, smoked paprika, garlic, cumin, and a small amount of fat produce a loose, savory crumble that functions as a direct replacement for ground beef in any application: tacos, pasta sauce, rice bowls, chili, stuffed peppers, sloppy joes. The texture is not identical to ground beef, it is slightly softer, but the flavor profile is close enough that most people eating it in a taco with toppings do not notice the difference. At a time when ground beef costs five dollars a pound and brown lentils cost two dollars for an entire bag, this is not a compromise. It is arithmetic.

Ingredients

- 1 cup (240 ml) dried brown or green lentils, not red lentils, which dissolve instead of holding shape
- 2.5 cups (600 ml) water or broth for cooking
- 2 tbsp (30 ml) soy sauce
- 1 tsp (5 ml) smoked paprika
- 1 tsp (5 ml) garlic powder
- 1 tsp (5 ml) onion powder
- 1 tsp (5 ml) cumin
- 1/2 tsp (3 ml) black pepper
- 1/2 tsp (3 ml) chili powder
- 1 tbsp (15 ml) cooking fat
- Optional: 1 tbsp (15 ml) tomato paste, splash of apple cider vinegar for brightness

Method

1. Rinse lentils. Cook in water or broth over medium heat, bring to a boil, reduce to a simmer, cook 20-25 minutes until tender but still holding their shape. They should be firm, not mushy. Drain completely.
2. Heat fat in a skillet over medium-high heat.

3. Add drained lentils to the hot skillet in a single layer as much as possible. Do not stir immediately, let them sit 2-3 minutes until the bottom layer begins to crisp and darken slightly.

4. Stir and repeat, let sit, then stir. This develops a slightly caramelized exterior that adds texture.

5. Add all spices, soy sauce, and optional tomato paste. Stir to coat every lentil.

6. Cook 3-4 more minutes until the mixture is dark, fragrant, and slightly dried out. It should look like cooked ground meat.

7. Taste and adjust salt, spice, and heat.

8. Use immediately or refrigerate for up to 5 days.

Field Note: Brown or green lentils only, red lentils dissolve during cooking and produce a paste rather than a crumble. The two-step cooking process matters: boil the lentils first, then fry them in the skillet. Frying dried-out boiled lentils develops the caramelized exterior that makes them read as meat crumbles rather than plain cooked lentils. Use these anywhere ground beef would go: tacos with any available toppings, stirred into canned tomatoes over pasta, mixed into rice, added to soup for protein. A batch made on Sunday feeds a household all week.

LENTIL SAUSAGE

"Red lentils cooked down to a paste, seasoned like sausage, shaped into patties or a sliceable log. No meat, no casing, no specialty ingredients."

Serves: 6-8 patties or 1 log   Time: 40 min + chilling

History & Context

Red lentils cooked in water and blended or mashed to a smooth paste become, with the right spice profile, something that satisfies the same role as sausage in a meal. The technique comes from necessity: smoked paprika, garlic, fennel, Italian herbs, and cayenne are the flavor signals that the brain reads as sausage. The lentil paste picks them up completely. The result works as breakfast patties alongside eggs, crumbled into gravy over biscuits in place of sausage gravy, sliced from a chilled log and fried until crispy, or crumbled into pasta sauce, bean soup, or rice dishes anywhere sausage would have gone. Red lentils cook in 12 minutes from dry with no soaking, faster than any other protein in this book. A one-pound bag costs under two dollars and contains enough for multiple batches. This recipe follows the four meat substitutes before it: it is not a vegan identity choice. It is what you make when the meat case is empty and people need to eat.

Ingredients

- 1 cup (240 ml) dried red lentils
- 3 cups (720 ml) hot water
- 1/2 tsp (3 ml) salt for cooking
- 1 tbsp (15 ml) olive oil, lard, or any cooking fat
- 1 tsp (5 ml) smoked paprika
- 1 tsp (5 ml) garlic powder
- 1 tsp (5 ml) Italian seasoning or dried oregano
- 1 tsp (5 ml) onion powder
- 1/2 tsp (3 ml) fennel seeds, lightly crushed, or 1/4 tsp (1 ml) ground fennel. This is what signals sausage.
- 1/2 tsp (3 ml) black pepper
- 1/4 tsp (1 ml) cayenne pepper, adjust to taste
- 2 tbsp (30 ml) soy sauce
- 2 tbsp (30 ml) Worcestershire sauce
- 3 tbsp (45 ml) all-purpose flour or fine cornmeal, for binding
- Fat for frying

Method

1. Rinse lentils thoroughly under cold water.
2. Combine rinsed lentils, hot water, and salt in a saucepan. Bring to a boil, reduce to a low simmer.
3. Cook over low heat, stirring frequently, until all water is absorbed and the mixture reaches a very thick, mashed-potato-like consistency, about 15-20 minutes. It should pull away from the sides of the pan. Do not rush this step; undercooked paste falls apart when formed.
4. Remove from heat. Stir in cooking fat, all spices, soy sauce, and Worcestershire sauce while the paste is still hot. Mix until fully incorporated.
5. Add flour or cornmeal and stir in. The mixture should be thick enough to hold a shape when scooped. If too wet, add another tablespoon of flour.
6. Taste the mixture and adjust seasoning, it should taste assertively spiced, not mild.
7. FOR PATTIES: let the mixture cool until handleable. Divide into 6-8 portions. Shape each into a round patty about 3/4-inch (2 cm) thick. Refrigerate at least 30 minutes before frying, cold patties hold together far better than warm ones.
8. FOR A SLICEABLE LOG: scoop the warm mixture onto a sheet of plastic wrap, foil, or a clean damp cloth. Roll into a tight log shape, twist the ends closed, and refrigerate at least 2 hours or overnight. Unwrap and slice into rounds 1/2-inch (1.5 cm) thick.
9. To cook: heat fat in a cast iron skillet over medium heat. Fry patties or slices 4-5 minutes per side without moving until a dark, crispy crust forms on each side.
10. FOR CRUMBLES: skip the shaping entirely. Spoon the cooked paste directly into a hot oiled skillet and break it apart with a spatula as it fries. Cook until browned and slightly dried out. Use anywhere crumbled sausage would go.

Field Note: The chilling step before frying is the difference between patties that hold together and paste that spreads in the pan. The log method, chilled overnight in foil or cloth, produces rounds that slice cleanly and fry beautifully. Beyond patties: crumble the cooked paste into sausage gravy (Recipe 1-12 method, replacing sausage with lentil crumbles); stir into canned tomatoes over pasta exactly as you would with Italian sausage; add to bean soup for a smoky, meaty depth; fry sliced rounds and serve alongside eggs and biscuits as a complete breakfast. A batch made ahead and refrigerated keeps 5 days. Form and freeze uncooked patties for up to 3 months, fry from frozen over lower heat.

WORCESTERSHIRE SAUCE CONTAINS ANCHOVIES. IT IS NOT VEGETARIAN. SUBSTITUTE SOY SAUCE DOUBLED IF SERVING TO ANYONE AVOIDING FISH OR MEAT PRODUCTS.

BEANS, GRAINS & VEGETABLES

Dried beans, cornmeal, grits, vegetables, and the staples that store for years

Dried beans are the most cost-effective protein and calorie source available to anyone with a pot and a heat source. A five-gallon bucket of mixed dried beans costs around sixty dollars, stores indefinitely when sealed, and represents approximately six months of protein for one person. There is no more practical food reserve. Free food exists in plain sight. Dandelion greens grow in most yards, they cost nothing and provide genuine nutrition. Know what you are picking before you pick it. The final recipe in this chapter is Recipe 4-19: Beans & Rice. It is last because it is the most important. Every civilization on earth with agriculture arrived at this combination independently. Beans and rice together form a complete protein. They cost under one dollar to feed four people. They are already in your pantry. If you read nothing else in this book, read that recipe.

◆ ◆ ◆

JUST BEANS

"A pound of dried beans costs under two dollars, yields eight servings of protein, and stores for years. This is the foundation."

Serves: 6-8   Time: 2-3 hours

History & Context

Dried beans soaked overnight and simmered in water. The bean varies, navy, pinto, black-eyed peas, great northern, but the principle is consistent: the cheapest complete protein available, indefinite shelf life, and enough calories per serving to constitute a full meal when served with cornbread. A 5-gallon (18.9 L) bucket of mixed dried beans is the foundation of any serious food reserve.

Ingredients

- 1 lb (455 g) dried beans of any variety
- 8 cups (1.9 L) water
- 1 tsp (5 ml) salt, added at the end only, salt added early toughens the skins
- Optional: 1 onion, garlic cloves, bay leaf, piece of salt pork or bacon

Method

1. Sort beans and remove any debris. Rinse under cold water.
2. Soak overnight in 3x their volume of cold water, OR quick-soak: cover with water, boil 2 minutes, remove from heat, soak 1 hour.
3. Drain soaking water. Place beans in a pot with 8 cups (1.9 L) fresh water.
4. Add optional aromatics: halved onion, garlic, bay leaf, salt pork.
5. Bring to a boil. Reduce to a low simmer and skim any foam during the first 10 minutes.
6. Simmer partially covered 1.5-3 hours depending on bean type until completely tender.
7. Season with salt only after cooking is complete.
8. Serve with cornbread or any available bread.

Field Note: A pound of dried beans costs under $2, yields 6-8 full servings, and stores indefinitely when sealed. 50 lbs (22.7 kg) of mixed dried beans is approximately six months of protein for one person, takes up less than two cubic feet of space, and costs around $60. There is no more cost-effective food reserve available.

BURGOO, EVERYTHING POT

"No recipe. Only principles. Whatever is available goes in. Whatever goes in becomes a meal."

Serves: variable   Time: 2-4 hours

History & Context

Burgoo is the answer to the question of what to cook when the only ingredients available are small amounts of several different things that will otherwise go to waste. Everything into one pot, cooked long enough that the result becomes coherent. It has no recipe because it cannot have one, the ingredient list changes every time. The principle does not change.

Ingredients

- Whatever remains, this is the honest ingredient list
- Typically: pre-cooked or canned beans, any available meat (small amounts), any available vegetables or canned goods
- A handful of cornmeal or flour for thickening
- Salt, pepper, dried chilies or hot sauce if available
- Water to cover

Method

1. Brown any available meat in fat at the bottom of a heavy pot first. This is the flavor foundation.
2. Add onions or any available alliums. Cook until softened.
3. Add all remaining vegetables, beans, and any cooked meat.
4. Stir in a handful of cornmeal to begin thickening the broth.
5. Add water to cover everything by at least an inch. Season with salt, pepper, and any available spices.
6. Bring to a boil, reduce to the lowest possible simmer. Cover and cook 2-4 hours.
7. Serve with any available bread.

Field Note: The cornmeal thickening technique transforms thin broth into something with body and substance. A tablespoon of vinegar or hot sauce added at the end brightens a pot that has been cooking for hours. Burgoo tastes better the second day.

CHILI, NO BEANS, NO TOMATOES

"Beef and dried chilies. Nothing else. This is what chili was before anyone added beans or tomatoes."

Serves: 6-8   Time: 3 hours

History & Context

Whole dried chili peppers toasted, soaked, and blended into a paste, combined with beef browned in fat and simmered for hours until the sauce reduces to something thick and dark. No tomatoes, no beans, no fillers. The complexity of the dried chili paste is what makes this worth eating, it cannot be replicated with chili powder from a jar.

Ingredients

- 2 lbs (905 g) beef chuck or brisket, cut into 1/2-inch (1.5 cm) cubes
- 3 dried ancho or pasilla chili peppers, stemmed and seeded
- 2 dried guajillo peppers, stemmed and seeded
- 3 cloves garlic minced
- 2 tsp (10 ml) ground cumin
- 1 tsp (5 ml) dried oregano
- 1 tsp (5 ml) salt
- 2 tbsp (30 ml) lard or beef fat
- 2 cups (480 ml) water or broth

Method

1. Toast whole dried chilies in a dry skillet 30 seconds per side until they blister and smell fragrant. Do not burn them.
2. Soak toasted chilies in 1 cup (240 ml) hot water 20 minutes until soft.
3. Blend softened chilies with soaking water, garlic, cumin, oregano, and salt into a thick paste.
4. Heat lard in a Dutch oven until nearly smoking. Brown beef in batches, dark sear on all sides.
5. Pour chili paste over browned beef. Stir to coat every piece.
6. Add remaining water. Bring to a boil then reduce to the lowest possible simmer.
7. Cover and cook 2-3 hours until beef is completely tender and sauce has thickened.
8. Serve with cornbread.

POTATO AND ONION PIE

"Thin-sliced potatoes and onions sealed under a lard crust and baked until the onions caramelize inside. A complete meal from root vegetables."

Serves: 6-8   Time: 70 min

History & Context

Potatoes and onions are the two cheapest, longest-keeping vegetables available. Sealed inside a pastry and baked for an hour, the onions caramelize into something sweet and complex and the potatoes become soft and yielding. The long bake inside sealed pastry produces a result dramatically different from simply roasting the vegetables open.

Ingredients

- 4 medium potatoes, sliced very thin, use a mandoline or sharp knife
- 2 large onions, thinly sliced
- Salt, black pepper, dried thyme or sage
- 2 tbsp (30 ml) lard for dotting over the layers
- Crust: 1.5 cups (360 ml) flour, 1/2 tsp (3 ml) salt, 1/2 cup (120 ml) cold lard, 4 tbsp (60 ml) cold water

Method

1. Make crust: combine flour and salt, cut in cold lard until crumbly, add cold water until dough holds. Divide in half.
2. Preheat oven to 375°F (190°C). Grease a deep 9-inch (23 cm) pie pan or cast iron skillet.
3. Roll one half of crust thin and press into the bottom and sides.
4. Layer potato slices slightly overlapping. Season with salt, pepper, and herbs.
5. Add a layer of sliced onions. Season again. Dot with small pieces of lard.
6. Repeat layers, finishing with potato.
7. Roll out second crust half, place over the top, crimp edges. Cut steam vents.
8. Bake 50-60 minutes until crust is golden and a knife meets no resistance in the potatoes.
9. Rest 10 minutes before cutting.

Field Note: Thin slices are critical, a mandoline or very sharp knife. Thick slices cook unevenly. The lard dotted between layers melts during baking and bastes the interior.

OATMEAL WITH FAT AND SALT

"Oats, water, fat, and salt. Works as breakfast, supper, or anything in between. The most shelf-stable grain you own."

Serves: 2-3   Time: 10 min

History & Context

Rolled oats cooked in salted water and finished with fat. When oats were what was available and nothing else was, this appeared on the table morning and evening. The distinction between breakfast oatmeal and supper oatmeal is entirely the seasoning and the base liquid, sugar and milk for morning, salt and lard for evening. Both versions are the same technique. A tablespoon of fat adds roughly 120 calories and converts a bowl of porridge into something that sustains hard physical work all morning or carries a person through the night. The fat also slows digestion, extending the window before hunger returns. Rolled oats sealed in Mylar bags with oxygen absorbers keep for 25-30 years. At current prices, a 25-lb (11.3 kg) bag costs around $15 and represents approximately 50 meals.

Ingredients

- 1 cup (240 ml) old-fashioned rolled oats
- 2 cups (480 ml) water, or thin broth for the supper version
- 1/2 tsp (3 ml) salt
- 1-2 tbsp (15 to 30 ml) lard, butter, or bacon drippings
- Black pepper
- Optional: fried egg on top for supper, a drizzle of sorghum or honey for breakfast

Method

1. Bring water or broth to a boil with salt.
2. Stir in oats and reduce heat to medium. Cook 5 minutes, stirring occasionally.
3. Remove from heat. Add fat and stir vigorously until completely melted and incorporated.
4. Taste and add more salt if needed.
5. For supper: season with black pepper and top with a fried egg if available.
6. For breakfast: a small drizzle of sorghum or honey makes it worth eating willingly.

Field Note: This is one of the cheapest complete meals available. The fat is not optional, plain oats in water provide calories but the fat is what keeps you from being hungry again in two hours. Use broth instead of water for the evening version

CORNMEAL MUSH

"A pot of cornmeal cooked in water. One preparation produces two completely different meals, hot porridge now, fried cakes tomorrow."

Serves: 4-6   Time: 30 min

History & Context

Cornmeal cooked in salted water produces a hot porridge. Poured into a loaf pan, chilled overnight, sliced, and fried the next morning in hot fat, it produces something with a crackling golden crust and a creamy interior. One cooking session produces breakfast for two days. Stone-ground cornmeal stored sealed keeps for a decade or more.

Ingredients

- 1 cup (240 ml) stone-ground yellow or white cornmeal (not instant)
- 4 cups (960 ml) cold water, divided
- 1 tsp (5 ml) salt
- 1 tbsp (15 ml) lard or bacon drippings (optional)
- Sorghum, buttermilk, or a fried egg for serving

Method

1. Whisk the cornmeal into 1 cup (240 ml) of cold water until smooth with no lumps.
2. Bring the remaining 3 cups (720 ml) of water and salt to a full rolling boil.
3. Pour the slurry slowly into the boiling water while stirring constantly. Keep stirring for two full minutes.
4. Reduce heat to lowest setting. Cook uncovered 20-25 minutes, stirring every few minutes and scraping the bottom. Done when it pulls from the sides of the pot.
5. Serve hot immediately with your topping, OR pour into a greased loaf pan, smooth the top, and refrigerate overnight.
6. For fried mush: unmold, slice 3/4-inch (2 cm) thick, fry in hot lard 3-4 minutes per side until a dark golden crust forms.

Field Note: The slurry method, mixing cornmeal with cold water before adding to boiling water, prevents the lumps that form when dry meal hits hot liquid. Always start with a cold slurry.

FRIED CORNMEAL WITH BLACKSTRAP MOLASSES

"Chilled mush fried hard in lard, covered with blackstrap molasses. Cheap, calorie-dense, and worth eating."

Serves: 4   Time: 10 min + overnight chilling

History & Context

Blackstrap molasses, the darkest, least-refined product of sugarcane processing, is cheap, calorie-dense, and contains meaningful amounts of iron, calcium, potassium, and magnesium. Poured over hot fried cornmeal it creates a meal that provides genuine nutritional value beyond just calories. It costs less than a dollar per serving.

Ingredients

- Cold leftover cornmeal mush, sliced 3/4-inch (2 cm) thick
- 2 tbsp (30 ml) lard or bacon drippings
- Blackstrap molasses for serving, not regular or light molasses, which are less nutritious

Method

1. The fried cornmeal only works from cold firm mush, it must have been refrigerated overnight. Remove the loaf and slice 3/4-inch (2 cm) thick.
2. Heat lard in a cast iron skillet over medium-high until very hot.
3. Lay slices flat in a single layer. Press gently with a spatula to ensure full contact with the pan.
4. Cook without disturbing 4-5 minutes until a dark crispy crust forms on the bottom.
5. Flip once. Cook another 3-4 minutes.
6. Transfer to a plate and drizzle blackstrap molasses immediately over the top.

Field Note: Blackstrap molasses specifically, not regular or light molasses. Blackstrap is the third pressing of sugarcane and contains the concentrated minerals that the first two pressings extract. Regular molasses has most of these removed. The label should say 'blackstrap.' A tablespoon provides a meaningful daily amount of iron.

GRITS WITH REDEYE GRAVY

"Slow-cooked stone-ground grits take 30 minutes and cannot be rushed. The result is worth the patience."

Serves: 4   Time: 40 min

History & Context

Stone-ground grits, not instant, not quick-cook, cooked slowly in salted water for 30 minutes with constant stirring produce something with a depth of corn flavor that the quick-cook version cannot replicate. The difference is not subtle. Topped with redeye gravy from fried country ham and black coffee, this is a complete meal from shelf-stable ingredients.

Ingredients

- 1 cup (240 ml) stone-ground white or yellow grits (not instant)
- 4 cups (960 ml) water
- 1 tsp (5 ml) salt
- 1 tbsp (15 ml) butter or lard (optional)
- Redeye gravy: 4-6 slices country ham or heavily cured bacon, 1/2 cup (120 ml) strong black coffee

Method

1. Bring 4 cups (960 ml) of water and salt to a boil.
2. Pour grits slowly into boiling water while stirring. Stir continuously for 2 minutes.
3. Reduce to lowest possible heat, partially cover. Cook 25-35 minutes, stirring every 5 minutes and scraping the bottom. Done when no grittiness remains.
4. Stir in butter or lard if using. Cover and keep warm.
5. Fry country ham in a dry cast iron skillet over medium-high, 2-3 minutes per side.
6. Remove ham. Pour black coffee into the hot skillet. Stir and scrape hard to dissolve the fond. Let bubble one minute.
7. Spoon grits into a wide bowl. Ladle thin dark gravy over the top.

Field Note: Low heat, long cook, frequent stirring. These are the three requirements for proper stone-ground grits. Quick-cook grits skip these requirements and produce a different product. Stone-ground grits store well in a cool dry location for years.

FRIED MUSH AND EGGS

"Cold cornmeal mush fried until crackling. Fried eggs in the same pan. The yolk becomes the sauce."

Serves: 2   Time: 15 min + overnight chilling

History & Context

The simplest combination of the two cheapest calorie sources in the pantry: cornmeal and eggs. The fried mush provides carbohydrates and a crackling crust. The egg provides protein and fat. The yolk, broken and run over the hot mush, enriches every bite. Cook them in sequence in the same pan, the residual cornmeal fond adds flavor to the eggs.

Ingredients

- Cold leftover cornmeal mush, sliced 3/4-inch (2 cm) thick
- 2 eggs per person
- Lard or bacon drippings for frying
- Salt and black pepper

Method

1. Slice cold firm mush 3/4-inch (2 cm) thick.
2. Heat 2 tbsp (30 ml) lard in a large cast iron skillet over medium-high until nearly smoking.
3. Add mush slices in a single layer. Do not move them. Cook 4-5 minutes until a dark golden crust forms.
4. Flip once. Cook another 3-4 minutes. Remove to a warm plate.
5. In the same pan with the same fat, fry the eggs until edges are lacy and whites are set.
6. Plate the mush slices and slide the eggs directly on top.
7. Break the yolk with the edge of a fork and let it run across the mush.

Field Note: *Do not clean the pan between the mush and the eggs. The residual cornmeal fond in the pan adds flavor to the eggs. The yolk that runs over the hot mush is the sauce for the entire plate.*

LEFTOVER POTATO CAKES

"Cold mashed potatoes from last night become this morning's best breakfast. Two meals from one cooking."

Serves: 4   Time: 20 min

History & Context

Cold mashed potatoes mixed with a beaten egg and a little flour form patties that hold together in the pan and develop a crackling golden crust. The cold is essential, warm freshly mashed potatoes do not have the retrograded starch structure that makes the cakes hold together and develop a proper crust. Always make extra mashed potatoes at dinner.

Ingredients

- 2 cups (480 ml) cold mashed or boiled potatoes, cold from the refrigerator, not warm
- 1 egg, beaten
- 2-3 tbsp (30 to 45 ml) all-purpose flour
- 1/2 tsp (3 ml) salt
- 1/4 tsp (1 ml) black pepper
- Optional: 2 tbsp (30 ml) finely minced onion
- 2-3 tbsp (30 to 45 ml) bacon drippings or lard for frying

Method

1. Use potatoes directly from the cold refrigerator. If using boiled whole potatoes, mash coarsely, leave some texture.
2. Combine cold potatoes, beaten egg, flour, salt, and pepper. Mix until incorporated. Should hold together when pressed but not be wet.
3. Form into round patties about 3/4-inch (2 cm) thick and 3 inches (7.5 cm) across.
4. Heat bacon drippings in a cast iron skillet over medium-high until shimmering and nearly smoking.
5. Add patties in a single layer without crowding. Do not move them.
6. Cook 4-5 minutes until a deeply golden-brown crust has formed. Flip once carefully.
7. Cook 3-4 more minutes until the second side matches.

Field Note: *Cold potatoes are not a detail. The partially retrograded starch in cold potatoes creates a structure that holds during frying and produces a crispier crust.*

DANDELION GREEN SALAD

"Dandelions grow for free in almost any lawn or open area. Young spring leaves wilted with hot bacon fat and vinegar are genuinely good."

Serves: 4   Time: 15 min

History & Context

Dandelion greens harvested from pesticide-free areas in early spring, before the plant flowers, when the leaves are youngest and least bitter, wilted with hot bacon drippings and a splash of apple cider vinegar. The bitterness that the fat and acid counteracts indicates flavonoids and vitamins that are genuinely useful. This costs nothing if you have access to a pesticide-free lawn, park, or open area. Do not harvest from roadsides, treated lawns, or anywhere that may have been sprayed.

Ingredients

- 4 cups (960 ml) young dandelion leaves (harvested before flowering, from pesticide-free areas, wash thoroughly)
- 3 strips bacon
- 2 tbsp (30 ml) apple cider vinegar
- 1 tsp (5 ml) sugar
- Salt and black pepper
- Optional: thin-sliced raw onion, hard-boiled egg

Method

1. Harvest young dandelion leaves before the plant flowers. Wash thoroughly.
2. Fry bacon until crisp. Remove and crumble. Leave rendered fat in the pan.
3. With skillet still hot on medium heat, add apple cider vinegar, sugar, and a pinch of salt to the fat. Stir briefly.
4. Pour hot dressing immediately over the dandelion greens in a large bowl. The greens will wilt slightly.
5. Toss to coat. Top with crumbled bacon, sliced onion, and sliced hard-boiled egg if available.
6. Eat while still warm.

Field Note: Early spring leaves are mild. Summer leaves are more bitter. Hot fat dressing reduces bitterness considerably. Identify dandelions correctly before harvesting, they are a distinctive plant and difficult to confuse if you look at the whole plant rather than just a leaf.

NEVER HARVEST ANY WILD PLANT YOU CANNOT POSITIVELY IDENTIFY. NEVER HARVEST FROM ROADSIDES, TREATED LAWNS, GOLF COURSES, OR ANYWHERE THAT MAY HAVE BEEN SPRAYED WITH PESTICIDES OR HERBICIDES. WHEN IN DOUBT, DO NOT EAT IT.

FRIED GREEN TOMATOES

"Any unripe tomato that won't ripen before frost is worth frying rather than wasting."

Serves: 4   Time: 20 min

History & Context

Unripe tomatoes harvested at the end of the growing season before frost, cornmeal-coated and fried until the crust is dark and crackling. The green tomato's firm starchy texture holds up to frying in a way that ripe tomatoes cannot. The starch gelatinizes during frying, producing a creamy interior against a crunchy exterior.

Ingredients

- 3-4 large green (unripe) tomatoes
- 1 cup (240 ml) cornmeal
- 1/4 cup (60 ml) flour
- 1 tsp (5 ml) salt
- 1/2 tsp (3 ml) black pepper
- 1/4 tsp (1 ml) cayenne
- 1 egg beaten with 2 tbsp (30 ml) buttermilk or water
- Lard or bacon drippings for frying

Method

1. Slice tomatoes 1/3 to 1/2-inch (1 to 1.5 cm) thick. This thickness matters, thinner falls apart, thicker stays raw in the center.
2. Combine cornmeal, flour, salt, pepper, and cayenne in a wide bowl.
3. Dip each tomato slice in the egg wash, then press firmly into the cornmeal mixture on both sides.
4. Heat 1/4-inch (0.5 cm) of lard in a cast iron skillet over medium-high until shimmering.
5. Fry in a single layer 3-4 minutes per side without moving.
6. The crust should be deeply golden-brown.
7. Drain and season immediately with a pinch of salt.

Field Note: The tomatoes must be genuinely unripe, firm and green throughout, not starting to blush. A tomato beginning to ripen lacks the starch structure that makes the fried version work.

HOMINY, NIXTAMALIZED CORN

"An alkaline soak unlocks nutrients in dried corn that the body cannot access any other way. This is why populations that ate nixtamalized corn did not develop pellagra."

Serves: 4-6 cups   Time: overnight + 3 hours

History & Context

Nixtamalization, soaking dried corn in an alkaline solution of pickling lime and water, converts the niacin locked in untreated corn into a bioavailable form. Populations that ate untreated corn as a staple developed pellagra, a devastating niacin deficiency disease. Populations that nixtamalized their corn did not. Food-grade pickling lime is available at Latin grocery stores as 'cal' for a few dollars. This is one of the most important food processing techniques that exists.

Ingredients

- 2 cups (480 ml) dried field corn kernels (hard, dried dent or flint corn, not sweet corn)
- 2 tbsp (30 ml) food-grade pickling lime (calcium hydroxide, sold as 'cal' at Latin grocery stores)
- 8 cups (1.9 L) water plus additional for rinsing

Method

1. Combine corn, water, and pickling lime in a large non-reactive pot (not aluminum). Stir to dissolve.
2. Bring to a simmer. Simmer 30 minutes, stirring occasionally. Hulls will begin separating.
3. Remove from heat. Soak overnight (8-12 hours).
4. Drain and rinse under cold running water. Rub kernels together to remove loose hulls. Requires 3-4 thorough rinses.
5. Cover with fresh water and simmer 2-4 hours until kernels are tender throughout.
6. Season with salt.

Field Note: Use only food-grade calcium hydroxide, not builder's lime or garden lime, which are not food-safe. It is sold in small bags at Latin grocery stores as 'cal' and is inexpensive. Nixtamalization is what makes corn a complete food rather than a nutritional trap.

SPOTTED PUP, QUICK RICE PUDDING

"White rice with raisins, a spoonful of sugar, and a splash of milk. Sweet, hot, and done in 30 minutes."

Serves: 4-6   Time: 30 min

History & Context

White rice with raisins scattered through it, the raisins look like spots on a dog, which is where the name comes from. This is not the slow-simmered creamy rice pudding in Chapter VII. That version cooks rice in milk for nearly an hour and produces something rich and custardy. This version cooks rice in water first, then adds a small amount of milk and sugar at the end. It is faster, uses less milk, and produces a lighter result, something between a sweet rice dish and a proper pudding. Both are valid. This one is the quick weeknight version made when you want something sweet and warm from ingredients already on the shelf.

Ingredients

- 1 cup (240 ml) long-grain white rice
- 2.5 cups (600 ml) water
- 1/2 tsp (3 ml) salt
- 1/2 cup (120 ml) raisins or dried currants
- 3 tbsp (45 ml) brown sugar
- 1/4 cup (60 ml) canned, powdered, or fresh milk
- 1/4 tsp (1 ml) cinnamon

Method

1. Bring rice, water, and salt to a boil. Reduce to lowest heat, cover, cook 18 minutes without lifting the lid.
2. Remove from heat. Scatter raisins over top without stirring. Replace lid. Steam 5 more minutes.
3. Add brown sugar, milk, and cinnamon. Stir gently from the bottom up.
4. Return to very low heat uncovered for 3-5 minutes, stirring, until slightly thickened.
5. Serve warm. Spotted pup thickens considerably as it cools, it will be looser than you expect straight off the heat.

Field Note: *This works with any dried fruit, chopped dried apricots, dried cherries, or cranberries all substitute for raisins. For the slow-cooked creamy version that*

RICE AND MILK

"Cold leftover rice from dinner, cold milk, a spoon of sugar. Two minutes of preparation, no cooking, a complete breakfast."

Serves: 1-2   Time: 2 min

History & Context

Cold leftover rice from the previous evening's supper, covered with cold milk and sprinkled with sugar. The rice was already cooked, the only cost is not throwing it away. Always make extra rice at dinner. The cold leftover from supper is breakfast tomorrow at zero additional cost or effort.

Ingredients

- 1 cup (240 ml) cold cooked white rice (leftover from the previous meal)
- 3/4 to 1 cup (180 to 240 ml) cold whole milk or reconstituted powdered milk
- 1-2 tsp (5 to 10 ml) white sugar
- Optional: pinch of salt, sprinkle of cinnamon

Method

1. Place cold rice directly into a bowl. Do not heat it.
2. Pour cold milk over the rice until just covered.
3. Sprinkle sugar over the top.
4. Eat immediately or wait five minutes for a thicker, more porridge-like consistency.

Field Note: Always make extra rice at dinner. Every pot of rice made for supper automatically provides breakfast the next morning. This two-meal-from-one-cook principle is fundamental to efficient food management under any conditions.

RED LENTIL DAL WITH FLATBREAD

"Red lentils cook in 12 minutes with no soaking. Complete protein from the cheapest dried legume available."

Serves: 4-6   Time: 35 min

History & Context

Red lentils dissolve into a silky thick curry without soaking, without hours of cooking, and without meat. A one-cup bag costs under a dollar and feeds four people a high-protein meal. Combined with canned tomatoes, an onion, and a small amount of spice, they produce something that tastes far more substantial than the ingredient list suggests. The two-ingredient flatbread cooks in a dry pan in under three minutes per side with no yeast, no rising time, and no oven. Together this is a complete meal for a family of four for approximately two dollars.

Ingredients

- 1 cup (240 ml) red lentils, rinsed, no soaking required
- 1 can (14 oz, 395 g) crushed or diced tomatoes
- 2 tbsp (30 ml) tomato paste
- 2.5 cups (600 ml) water or any available broth
- 1 medium onion, diced
- 2 cloves garlic, minced
- 1 tsp (5 ml) fresh or dried ginger
- 1 tbsp (15 ml) cooking oil or lard
- 2 tsp (10 ml) curry powder
- 1 tsp (5 ml) ground cumin
- 1/2 tsp (3 ml) turmeric
- 1 tsp (5 ml) paprika (optional)
- 1/4 tsp (1 ml) chili flakes or cayenne (omit for mild)
- 1 tsp (5 ml) salt, 1/2 tsp (3 ml) black pepper
- Flatbread: 1.5 cups (360 ml) self-raising flour, or all-purpose + 1.5 tsp (8 ml) baking powder
- Flatbread: 3/4 cup (180 ml) plain yogurt
- Flatbread: 1/2 tsp (3 ml) salt, 1 tbsp (15 ml) oil or butter (optional)
- Optional: butter, 1 garlic clove minced, dried coriander for finishing

Method

1. Rinse red lentils. Place in a pot with water or broth. Bring to a boil then reduce to a simmer. Cook 12 minutes, stirring occasionally. The lentils will swell and begin to dissolve. Remaining liquid goes into the curry. Set aside.
2. Make flatbread dough: combine flour, yogurt, salt, and optional oil. Mix until a soft slightly tacky dough forms. Cover and rest 10 minutes.
3. Heat oil in a heavy pan over medium. Add diced onion and cook 6-8 minutes until golden and browning at the edges.
4. Add garlic and ginger. Stir and cook 2-3 minutes until the raw smell fades.
5. Reduce heat to low. Add curry powder, cumin, turmeric, paprika, and chili. Stir constantly 60-90 seconds, toasting not burning. Low heat is essential.
6. Add canned tomatoes and tomato paste. Stir hard to lift everything from the pan bottom. Cook 3 minutes over medium.
7. Add cooked lentils and all their liquid. Stir to combine. Simmer 15 minutes until thick and silky. Taste and adjust salt.
8. Cook flatbreads: heat a dry skillet over medium-high until very hot. Divide dough into 4-6 balls. Roll or press each to about 1/4-inch (0.5 cm) thick.
9. Place in the dry pan with no oil. Bubbles appear within 60-90 seconds. Press gently with a cloth to push air around evenly.
10. Cook 2-3 minutes until dark spots appear and surface looks dry. Flip. Cook 2 more minutes.
11. Optional: while still hot, rub flatbread with butter mixed with minced garlic and a pinch of dried coriander.
12. Serve curry over rice if available, with flatbreads for scooping.

Field Note: Red lentils are the only dried legume that needs no soaking and cooks in 12 minutes, they dissolve into the sauce naturally, thickening it without any added starch. A 1-lb (455 g) bag costs under and makes at least two full batches. Without yogurt for the flatbread, substitute 3/4 cup (180 ml) water mixed with 1 tbsp (15 ml) apple cider vinegar rested 5 minutes, the acid activates the leavening the same way yogurt does.

OVEN-ROASTED SWEET POTATOES

"Cut side down first. That is the technique. Everything else is seasoning."

Serves: 4   Time: 50 min

History & Context

Sweet potatoes are among the most nutritionally complete cheap foods available, more vitamin A per dollar than almost anything else in the grocery store, substantial potassium and fiber, and they store for months in a cool dry location without refrigeration. Roasting them cut-side down in an oiled pan caramelizes the flesh surface, producing a deeply sweet, slightly crisp interior face that boiling or steaming cannot replicate. The herb side and the cinnamon side cook separately because they go on different surfaces, savory on the cut face that meets the pan, warm spice on the skin side that faces up. Melted butter at the end is not optional.

Ingredients

- 4 medium-to-large orange-flesh sweet potatoes
- Any neutral cooking oil, enough to coat the pan generously
- Dried rosemary, a good pinch per potato
- Dried thyme, a good pinch per potato
- Pink salt or coarse salt
- Ground cinnamon
- Optional: a shake of adobo seasoning
- 2 tbsp (30 ml) melted butter for finishing

Method

1. Preheat oven to 350-400°F (175 to 205°C). Higher if you want more caramelization and a slightly shorter cook time.
2. Cut each sweet potato in half lengthwise.
3. Oil a baking pan generously, coat the entire surface. Any oil works.
4. Season the cut faces of the potatoes: rosemary, thyme, and salt directly on the flesh.
5. Place cut-side down in the oiled pan. Press flat so the entire cut surface contacts the pan.
6. Season the skin side now facing up: cinnamon instead of salt. Add adobo if using.
7. Roast 20-25 minutes until the cut side is deeply caramelized and pulling slightly from the pan.
8. Flip each half cut-side up. The flesh should be golden to dark brown.

9. Continue roasting another 15-20 minutes until completely tender throughout, a fork should meet no resistance.

10. Brush melted butter over the cut faces while still hot. Let it soak in for 2 minutes before serving.

POTATO PUFF BAKE

"Cold leftover mashed potatoes from last night become something completely new. One egg and fifteen minutes of oven time."

Serves: 4-6   Time: 25 min + leftover mashed potatoes

History & Context

Cold mashed potatoes mixed with a beaten egg, shaped into mounds, and baked until puffed and golden. The outside develops a light crust. The inside stays soft and creamy. This is not the same dish as the original mashed potatoes, the egg changes the texture entirely, and the oven produces a surface that the original never had. The rule is the same as potato cakes: always make extra mashed potatoes at dinner. The leftovers are tomorrow's second meal at zero additional cost.

Ingredients

- 2 cups (480 ml) cold mashed potatoes, from the refrigerator, not freshly made
- 1 egg, beaten
- 1 tbsp (15 ml) butter or lard, melted
- Salt and black pepper to taste
- Optional: 2 tbsp (30 ml) shredded cheese, 1 tbsp (15 ml) finely minced onion, pinch of dried herbs

Method

1. Preheat oven to 375°F (190°C). Grease a baking sheet with lard or line with foil.
2. Combine cold mashed potatoes, beaten egg, and melted butter. Mix until fully incorporated.
3. Taste and adjust salt and pepper. Add optional cheese, onion, or herbs if using.
4. Scoop mixture into mounds on the baking sheet, about 1/3 cup (80 ml) each, roughly the size of a large dinner roll. Space them 2 inches (5 cm) apart.
5. Use the back of a spoon to smooth the tops slightly.
6. Bake 18-22 minutes until the tops and sides are golden and the mounds have puffed slightly.
7. Rest 3 minutes before serving, they firm up as they cool slightly.

> *Field Note: Cold mashed potatoes are essential, warm freshly made mash is too soft to hold its shape and will spread flat on the pan. The egg is what causes the puff and creates the slight crust. If you have no oven, this mixture can be formed into patties and fried in a skillet exactly like the potato cakes in recipe 4-11, same ingredients,*

BEANS & RICE

"Kidney, pinto, black, navy, chickpeas, lentils, or peanuts, with rice, grits, cornbread, or any grain"

This is the meal that feeds the world.

Serves: 4-6   Time: 25 min with lentils / 90 min with dried beans

---

History & Context

Every civilization on earth with agriculture arrived at this combination independently. The Romans ate it. Medieval Europe ate it. Every culture across Asia, Africa, Central America, and South America ate it. They did not learn it from each other. They discovered it separately because it works, and it works because of a specific nutritional fact that took modern science centuries to confirm: legumes and grains are nutritionally incomplete on their own, but together they supply every essential amino acid the human body requires. Beans provide lysine and isoleucine. Grains provide methionine and cysteine. Each has what the other lacks. Combined in a single bowl, they form a complete protein equivalent to meat, egg, or dairy, at a cost of under one dollar for a meal that feeds four people. This is not a recipe invented by any one culture. It is the solution that hunger and agriculture produce wherever they meet. The specific bean does not matter. The specific grain does not matter. Red beans and white rice is the Louisiana version. Black beans and rice is the Cuban version. Lentils and rice is dal and chawal, eaten across the Indian subcontinent by more people every day than any other meal on earth. Chickpeas over rice or flatbread is eaten from Morocco to Pakistan. Pinto beans and cornbread is the American South. Peanuts and rice is eaten across West Africa and Southeast Asia. Peanuts are a legume, not a nut. They grow underground, fix nitrogen like beans, and carry the same complete protein mechanism when combined with any grain. If peanuts or peanut butter are what your pantry holds, they belong in this recipe. The combination is the recipe. Make it from whatever you have.

Ingredients

- LEGUME, use any one:
- 1 cup (240 ml) dried lentils (red, green, or brown), no soaking required, ready in 20-25 minutes, highest-protein option
- 1 cup (240 ml) dried beans (kidney, pinto, black, navy, or great northern), soak overnight in cold water, then drain before cooking
- 1 can (15 oz, 425 g) any beans, drained and rinsed, fastest option, ready in 10 minutes
- 1 cup (240 ml) dried chickpeas, soak overnight, then drain; or use 1 can (15 oz, 425 g) chickpeas, drained

- 1 cup (240 ml) roasted peanuts, shelled, or 3 tbsp (45 ml) natural peanut butter stirred into the finished dish off the heat; peanuts are a legume and provide the same complete protein effect with any grain
- GRAIN, use any one:
- 1 cup (240 ml) long-grain white rice cooked in 2 cups (480 ml) salted water
- 1 cup (240 ml) stone-ground grits cooked in 4 cups (960 ml) salted water
- A batch of skillet cornbread from Recipe 1-3, serve the beans over or alongside
- AROMATICS AND FAT:
- 1 medium onion, diced
- 3 cloves garlic, minced (or 1/2 tsp (3 ml) garlic powder)
- 2 tbsp (30 ml) lard, bacon drippings, or vegetable oil
- 1 tsp (5 ml) salt, plus more to taste
- 1/2 tsp (3 ml) black pepper
- OPTIONAL SEASONING, any combination:
- 1 tsp (5 ml) cumin, 1/2 tsp (3 ml) smoked paprika, 1 bay leaf, splash of vinegar or hot sauce at the table

Method

1. If using dried beans or chickpeas: soak overnight in cold water covering by 3 inches (7.5 cm). Drain and rinse before cooking. Do not soak lentils, they need no preparation.
2. Cook your grain according to its method and set aside covered to stay warm.
3. In a heavy pot, heat fat over medium heat. Add diced onion and cook 5-7 minutes, stirring occasionally, until soft and translucent.
4. Add garlic and any dry spices. Stir and cook 1 minute until fragrant.
5. FOR LENTILS: add lentils and 3 cups (720 ml) of water or any available broth. Bring to a boil, reduce to a simmer, cook 20-25 minutes until completely tender. Add salt in the last 5 minutes, salting too early toughens lentils.
6. FOR SOAKED DRIED BEANS: add drained beans and water to cover by 2 inches (5 cm). Bring to a boil, reduce to a low simmer. Cook 60-90 minutes until completely tender throughout, no chalky center. Salt in the last 15 minutes.
7. FOR CANNED BEANS OR CHICKPEAS: add drained beans directly to the cooked onion and garlic. Add 1/2 cup (120 ml) water or broth. Simmer 10 minutes until heated through and flavors have combined. Salt to taste.
8. FOR PEANUTS: add shelled roasted peanuts to the cooked onion and garlic. Add 1.5 cups (360 ml) water, bring to a simmer, cook 15 minutes until peanuts have softened slightly and the liquid has reduced to a thick sauce. Alternatively, stir 3 tablespoons (45 ml) of natural peanut butter into any finished grain dish off the heat, thin with a splash of water if needed. Season with salt, a squeeze of vinegar, and cayenne if available.
9. Taste before serving. Well-seasoned and fully soft throughout. Under-salted tastes flat, add salt a pinch at a time until the flavor opens up.

10. Serve over or alongside the grain. Add vinegar or hot sauce at the table if available.

11. The bean cooking liquid is not waste. It is thick, flavorful, and nutritious. Spoon it generously over the grain.

Field Note: The complete protein mechanism works across every legume and grain combination in this recipe including peanuts. A bowl of peanuts and rice, peanut butter stirred into oatmeal, or roasted peanuts alongside cornbread all deliver complete protein. This matters most when other beans are unavailable, if your pantry holds peanut butter and any grain, you have everything you need. The complete protein argument requires no precise ratio, a bowl that is roughly half legume and half grain by volume covers the nutritional need. Leftovers improve overnight as the flavors continue to develop. Cold leftover beans mashed onto bread the next morning is a complete breakfast. The cooking liquid thickens as it cools and makes an excellent base for the next day's soup. Nothing from this pot should be discarded. A household that keeps dried lentils and white rice in its pantry always has a complete, nutritionally adequate meal available regardless of what else is missing. That is the point of this recipe and the point of this book.

SANDWICHES & QUICK MEALS

Sixteen sandwiches, two skillet quick meals, cowboy coffee, and the honest record of the wish sandwich

A sandwich is what you make when there is not enough of anything to constitute a full meal but there is bread and something to put between two slices. This chapter documents that logic from both ends: the satisfying quick meals and the honest record of what people ate when those were not available. The wish sandwich is included not as a recipe but as a record. It happened. It should not be forgotten. Everything else in this chapter exists so that it does not have to happen again.

◆ ◆ ◆

SUGAR SANDWICH

"Butter, white bread, granulated sugar. Feeding children on almost nothing."

Serves: 1   Time: 2 min

History & Context

Sugar on buttered white bread. Cheap, immediate, and functional, provides fat and rapid energy at almost no cost. Children ate these at school and said nothing about what was inside.

Ingredients

- 2 slices soft white bread
- 1.5 tbsp (23 ml) softened butter or lard
- 1.5 tbsp (23 ml) granulated white sugar
- Optional: pinch of coarse salt

Method

1. Spread fat evenly across one slice to the edges, room temperature is essential.
2. Sprinkle sugar in a visible layer over the fat. Press gently so it adheres.
3. Optional pinch of coarse salt amplifies the flavor.
4. Press the second slice on top. Eat immediately while the sugar still has crunch.

Field Note: The fat-sugar combination provides rapid energy. The salt bridges the flavors. Room temperature fat spreads cleanly; cold fat tears the bread.

MUSTARD SANDWICH

"Two slices of bread and yellow mustard. The sandwich of genuine necessity."

Serves: 1   Time: 1 min

History & Context

Yellow mustard spread thick on bread with nothing else. A jar of yellow mustard costs almost nothing, lasts weeks, and provides enough acid and salt to create the sensation of eating something with substance even when the sandwich delivers very little nutrition. Add raw onion if available, onion provides actual nutritional value.

Ingredients

- 2 slices bread
- Yellow mustard, generous application, this is the filling not a condiment
- Optional: thin-sliced raw onion

Method

1. Spread yellow mustard generously on both slices, thick enough to be the filling.
2. Add raw onion if available.
3. Press together and eat.

Field Note: *Yellow mustard contains turmeric, vinegar, and salt. Adding a thin smear of lard or butter to the bread before the mustard adds fat, which slows digestion and makes the meal more sustaining.*

KETCHUP SANDWICH

"When the only thing left in the pantry is condiments."

Serves: 1   Time: 1 min

History & Context

Ketchup on white bread. The sandwich of last resort. Provides tomato-derived vitamin C, vinegar, and some sugar. Toast the bread first, it holds up better against the moisture and makes the result more worth eating.

Ingredients

- 2 slices white bread
- 3-4 tbsp (45 to 60 ml) ketchup
- Optional: thin-sliced raw onion, black pepper, hot sauce

Method

1. Toast the bread first if possible, it holds up better and creates a better texture.
2. Spread ketchup generously across one or both slices.
3. Add raw onion and black pepper if available.
4. Press together and eat immediately.

Field Note: Toasting the bread extends the window before it goes soggy and improves the texture significantly. Homemade ketchup from canned tomatoes, vinegar, sugar, and spices is shelf-stable and worth knowing how to make.

POTATO SANDWICH

"Cold mashed potatoes on bread. Dense, filling, and nearly free."

Serves: 1   Time: 3 min

History & Context

Cold leftover mashed potatoes spread thick on bread. Potatoes are among the cheapest calories available. The cold mash from last night becomes today's lunch at no additional cost.

Ingredients

- 2 slices bread
- 1/2 to 3/4 cup (120 to 180 ml) cold mashed potatoes, must be stiff and cold from the refrigerator
- Salt and pepper
- Optional: thin-sliced onion, smear of butter, ketchup

Method

1. Spread cold mash thickly across one slice to the edges.
2. Season aggressively with salt and pepper directly on the potato.
3. Add optional onion or condiment.
4. Press firmly together. Eat within 30 minutes.

***Field Note:** Cold potatoes have firmer structure than warm ones, the starch partially retrogrades during refrigeration, which is why cold potato sandwiches hold together. Always use cold leftovers.*

ONION SANDWICH

"Raw onion sliced paper-thin on buttered bread. Onions cost almost nothing and keep for weeks without refrigeration."

Serves: 1   Time: 5 min

History & Context

Raw onion, fat, salt. Onions cost almost nothing, keep for weeks without refrigeration, and provide genuine nutritional value, vitamins that prevented deficiency diseases in families who rarely saw fresh produce. The social cost of eating raw onion at lunch is real. The nutritional benefit is also real.

Ingredients

- 2 slices bread
- 1 tbsp (15 ml) softened butter, lard, or bacon drippings
- 1/2 medium yellow onion, sliced paper-thin
- Salt and black pepper
- Optional: yellow mustard

Method

1. Slice the onion as thin as possible, thin enough to be translucent.
2. Spread fat generously on both slices.
3. For milder flavor: salt the onion slices, wait 10 minutes, rinse and pat dry.
4. Layer onion across one slice. Season with salt and pepper.
5. Press together and eat.

Field Note: *Thin slices are the entire technique. Thick onion overwhelms everything. Fresh parsley chewed after eating neutralizes onion breath effectively.*

PEANUT BUTTER AND PICKLE SANDWICH

"The acidity of pickle brine cuts through peanut butter fat the same way lemon juice cuts through cream."

Serves: 1   Time: 3 min

History & Context

Peanut butter and dill pickle. The flavor chemistry is not accidental, acid cuts fat, making both ingredients taste more complete than they do separately. The salt in the brine amplifies the sweetness of the peanut butter.

Ingredients

- 2 slices bread
- 3 tbsp (45 ml) peanut butter
- 6-8 dill pickle slices
- Optional: thin layer of yellow mustard

Method

1. Spread peanut butter generously on one slice, thick.
2. Lay pickle slices in a single layer over the peanut butter.
3. Optional mustard on the second slice.
4. Press together firmly so pickle slices embed slightly into the peanut butter.
5. Eat immediately, the pickle crunch is the point.

Field Note: *The acidity of pickle brine cuts peanut butter fat through the same mechanism as lemon juice cutting cream. These flavors are not complementary by accident.*

PIMENTO CHEESE SANDWICH

"Grated sharp cheddar, jarred pimentos, mayonnaise. One of the cheapest high-protein sandwich fillings available."

Serves: 4-6 sandwiches   Time: 15 min + chilling

History & Context

Finely grated sharp cheddar, chopped pimento peppers from a jar, and enough mayonnaise to bind them. Spreadable, keeps for a week refrigerated, and stretches across more sandwiches per dollar than most alternatives. Grate your own cheese, pre-shredded contains anti-caking agents that prevent proper binding.

Ingredients

- 1.5 cups (360 ml) sharp cheddar, finely grated, grate yourself
- 1/4 cup (60 ml) pimento peppers from a jar, drained and roughly chopped
- 3-4 tbsp (45 to 60 ml) mayonnaise
- 1/4 tsp (1 ml) black pepper
- Pinch of cayenne
- Salt to taste

Method

1. Grate cheese on the fine side of a box grater.
2. Drain and pat-dry the pimentos. Chop into 1/4-inch (0.5 cm) pieces.
3. Combine cheese, pimentos, 3 tbsp (45 ml) mayonnaise, pepper, and cayenne. Mix vigorously.
4. Taste before adding salt, cheese is already salty.
5. Refrigerate at least 30 minutes before serving.
6. Spread generously on bread.

Field Note: *Pimento cheese improves over the first two days as the flavors meld. Also works on crackers and melted on toast.*

HOT WATER CORNBREAD SANDWICH

"Cornmeal patties fried until the exterior cracks open and filled with whatever is available."

Serves: 4-5 patties   Time: 20 min

History & Context

Cornmeal mixed with boiling water and salt, shaped with wet hands into a patty, fried in lard until the exterior cracks and the inside stays creamy, then split and filled. The boiling water activates the starch immediately, creating a cohesive dough without eggs or fat. Cold water produces a patty that falls apart in the pan.

Ingredients

- 1 cup (240 ml) white cornmeal
- 1/2 tsp (3 ml) salt
- Boiling water, approximately 3/4 cup (180 ml), added gradually
- Lard for frying
- Filling: sorghum syrup, bacon grease, butter, or beans

Method

1. Measure cornmeal and salt into a bowl.
2. Pour boiling water slowly over the cornmeal while stirring. Add just enough to create a thick moldable dough.
3. Rest 2 minutes. The cornmeal continues absorbing water.
4. Wet hands thoroughly. Press dough between wet palms into patties about 3 inches (7.5 cm) across and 1/2-inch (1.5 cm) thick.
5. Heat generous lard in a cast iron skillet over medium-high until very hot.
6. Fry 4-5 minutes per side until deeply golden and the exterior is firm and crackly.
7. Split open while hot and add filling.

Field Note: *Boiling water gelatinizes the cornmeal starch immediately, creating the cohesive structure that holds during frying. Cold water simply wets the flour and produces a crumbly patty.*

BREAD AND BUTTER PICKLE SANDWICH

"Thirty jars put up in summer from a kitchen garden feeds a family through winter."

Serves: 1 sandwich / several jars   Time: 30 min + resting

History & Context

Bread and butter pickles layered thick between buttered bread. A small garden produces enough cucumbers in summer to fill 30 jars at almost no cost, providing this sandwich through the cold months. Home pickling is among the most practically valuable food preservation skills.

Ingredients

- Pickles: 4 lbs (1.8 kg) cucumbers sliced 1/4-inch (0.5 cm), 2 medium onions sliced, 1/4 cup (60 ml) pickling salt
- Brine: 2 cups (480 ml) white vinegar, 2 cups (480 ml) sugar, 1 tbsp (15 ml) mustard seed, 1 tsp (5 ml) celery seed, 1/2 tsp (3 ml) turmeric
- Sandwich: bread, butter, pickle slices

Method

1. Combine cucumber and onion slices with pickling salt, cover with ice, refrigerate 2-3 hours.
2. Drain, rinse twice under cold water, drain very well.
3. Combine brine ingredients in a pot, bring to a boil until sugar dissolves.
4. Add drained cucumbers. Heat to just simmering. Remove from heat immediately.
5. Pack into sterilized jars and seal. Ready after 24 hours; improves over a week.
6. Sandwich: butter both slices. Layer pickles generously. Press firmly.

Field Note: The bread-and-butter formula works with cucumbers, green tomatoes, onions, and many other vegetables. Properly processed sealed jars are shelf-stable for a year or more.

THE WISH SANDWICH

"Two slices of bread. Nothing between them. This happened. It should be remembered."

Serves: 1   Time: 0 min

History & Context

Two slices of bread with nothing between them. This is a record, not a recipe. Millions of families during the worst years of the Depression sat children down to lunch with two slices of bread and nothing else because there was nothing else. It is included here not for culinary value but because it is true, and because every other recipe in this book exists so that this one does not have to be made. Stock your pantry accordingly.

Ingredients

- 2 slices bread
- Nothing

Method

1. Place two slices of bread on the table.
2. Eat them.
3. Understand that this happened, that it was real, and that the people who ate it did not consider themselves defeated by it.
4. Every other recipe in this book exists so that this one does not have to be made.
5. If you are reading this because you genuinely have nothing: reach out to someone in your community.

Field Note: *This recipe is included because it is true. Stock your pantry before you need it.*

LARD SANDWICH

"Lard spread thick on bread with coarse salt. Nine hundred calories. For people doing hard physical labor, that was the point."

Serves: 1   Time: 2 min

History & Context

Lard spread on day-old bread with coarse salt. Made by miners' wives and handed to husbands heading underground for twelve-hour shifts. The fat content was not incidental, it was the meal's entire purpose. Men burning thousands of calories in cold dark tunnels needed concentrated fuel. Lard delivers it at a fraction of the cost of any alternative. Room temperature lard spreads cleanly; cold lard tears bread.

Ingredients

- 2 slices day-old white bread
- 2 tbsp (30 ml) lard or rendered pork fat, at room temperature
- Coarse salt
- Optional: black pepper, thin-sliced raw onion

Method

1. Allow lard to come fully to room temperature, spreadable, not solid.
2. Spread lard generously across both slices, all the way to the edges.
3. Shake coarse salt evenly over the lard on one slice. Add pepper and onion if using.
4. Press the second slice firmly on top.
5. Wrap tightly in wax paper if traveling.

Field Note: The salt is not optional, it is the entire seasoning. Without it the result is flat and greasy rather than rich and savory.

BREAD AND GRAVY SANDWICH

"The roast is gone. The pan drippings are not. Three more meals live in that pan."

Serves: 2-3   Time: 15 min

History & Context

Pan drippings from any roasted or fried meat, made into gravy with flour and water, poured between two slices of bread. A single roast fed a Depression family in sequence: the hot meal, cold slices the next day, gravy sandwiches the day after, then bones for soup. Nothing moved to waste until it was completely exhausted.

Ingredients

- Pan drippings from any roasted or fried meat, do not clean the pan
- 2 tbsp (30 ml) all-purpose flour
- 1 to 1.5 cups (240 to 360 ml) water or any available thin broth
- Salt and black pepper
- White or whole wheat bread for serving

Method

1. Leave the pan with all drippings and browned bits over medium heat.
2. Add flour directly to the hot fat and stir constantly 2-3 minutes until the roux turns golden-brown.
3. Pour in water or broth slowly while whisking hard. Add in three additions, whisking smooth after each.
4. Bring to a simmer and cook 4-5 minutes until the gravy is pourable.
5. Season with salt and pepper.
6. Ladle generously between two slices of bread. Eat immediately.

Field Note: The browned fond on the pan bottom is concentrated flavor. Never rinse the pan before making gravy, that fond is the entire point of the dish.

TOAST SANDWICH

"A slice of hot buttered toast tucked between two slices of soft bread. Texture was the entire recipe."

Serves: 1   Time: 5 min

History & Context

A piece of freshly buttered toast placed between two slices of soft untoasted bread. The warm crisp buttery interior against soft outer slices produces a genuinely different eating experience from plain bread, enough different to constitute a meal rather than simply bread. It requires only bread, butter, and a heat source.

Ingredients

- 3 slices white sandwich bread
- 1 tbsp (15 ml) real butter
- Salt and pepper

Method

1. Toast one slice until golden and firm on both sides.
2. While still hot, butter it generously on both sides.
3. Place the hot buttered toast between the two untoasted slices.
4. Press together gently. The warmth will slightly soften the inner surfaces of the outer slices.
5. Eat immediately while the interior toast is still warm and crisp.

Field Note: The toast must go between the soft slices while still hot. A cold toast sandwich loses its entire purpose, the warmth and texture contrast are the recipe.

FRIED HOT DOG SANDWICH

"Split lengthwise and fried flat. More surface area, more crust, more meal from the same amount of meat."

Serves: 1   Time: 8 min

History & Context

Split the hot dog lengthwise, fry flat, place on regular bread not a bun. Buns are a bakery indulgence. Bread is already in the house. The split-and-fried preparation increases the surface area in the pan, creating caramelized edges across the full cut surface. A whole hot dog in bread is a round object on a flat surface, most of it touches nothing. A split flat hot dog covers the full surface of the bread.

Ingredients

- 2 slices white bread
- 1 hot dog or frankfurter
- 1 tsp (5 ml) butter or bacon drippings
- Yellow mustard, ketchup, or both
- Optional: thin-sliced raw onion

Method

1. Split the hot dog lengthwise from end to end with a single clean cut. Open it flat.
2. Heat fat in a skillet over medium-high until shimmering.
3. Place the hot dog cut-side down in the hot fat. Press flat with a spatula.
4. Cook without moving 2-3 minutes until the cut surface is deeply browned and slightly crispy.
5. Flip and cook the skin side 1-2 minutes.
6. Place on one slice of bread, cut-side up. Add condiments and onion.
7. Press the second slice on top.

Field Note: *The lengthwise split is the entire technique. A whole hot dog in bread provides minimal surface contact with condiments or bread. A split-flat hot dog covers the full bread surface.*

BANANA SANDWICH

"Sliced bananas on buttered bread. Cheap, sweet, and requires no cooking."

Serves: 1   Time: 3 min

History & Context

Bananas are among the cheapest fresh fruit available. Sliced on buttered white bread they require no cooking, no preparation, and produce something genuinely sweet and satisfying at minimal cost. Use the ripest bananas available, spotted skin means fully converted starch, which means sweeter flavor and softer texture.

Ingredients

- 2 slices soft white bread
- 1 ripe banana, spotted skin means maximum sweetness
- 1 tbsp (15 ml) softened butter
- Optional: pinch of sugar, light dusting of cinnamon

Method

1. Spread butter evenly across both slices.
2. Peel the banana. Slice into coins about 1/4-inch (0.5 cm) thick.
3. Layer banana slices across one buttered slice in a single overlapping layer.
4. Optional: dust lightly with cinnamon.
5. Press the second slice on top firmly.
6. Eat immediately, banana discolors and softens quickly.

Field Note: *A very ripe, well-spotted banana makes a dramatically better sandwich than an underripe one. Never use a firm yellow banana for this.*

CREAMED CHIPPED BEEF ON TOAST

"Dried salt beef in a flour gravy over toast. Fast, filling, and entirely from shelf-stable ingredients."

Serves: 4   Time: 15 min

History & Context

Dried salt beef shredded into a white sauce and spooned over toast. Became a weekly standard in postwar American households because it is fast, uses shelf-stable ingredients, and produces something filling from almost nothing. For field use: reconstitute dried beef in hot water, make the roux with powdered milk reconstituted thick, and you have a hot high-calorie meal from entirely shelf-stable ingredients.

Ingredients

- 1 jar (2.5 oz, 70 g) dried chipped beef, or very thinly sliced salt beef
- 2 tbsp (30 ml) unsalted butter
- 3 tbsp (45 ml) all-purpose flour
- 2 cups (480 ml) whole milk or reconstituted powdered milk, warmed
- Generous black pepper
- Salt only after tasting, the beef is very salty

Method

1. Separate beef slices. Taste, if extremely salty, rinse briefly under cold water. Tear into rough 1-inch (2.5 cm) pieces.
2. Melt butter in a saucepan over medium heat. Add flour and stir continuously 2 minutes.
3. Add warm milk slowly while whisking constantly until all milk is incorporated and gravy thickens, about 5 minutes.
4. Add generous black pepper. Taste before adding salt.
5. Fold in torn beef pieces. Simmer on low 2 minutes.
6. Ladle over firmly toasted bread.

Field Note: Dried chipped beef and canned salt beef are both excellent long-shelf-life proteins. Powdered whole milk reconstituted thick makes this entirely shelf-stable, no refrigeration needed for any ingredient.

VEGETABLE FRIED RICE

"Cold leftover rice, one egg, whatever vegetables are available. Fifteen minutes in a hot pan."

Serves: 2-4   Time: 15 min

History & Context

Fried rice exists because leftover cold rice is already everywhere. Cold rice fries better than fresh, the overnight refrigeration dries the grains slightly so they separate in the pan instead of clumping. A hot skillet, a little fat, an egg, whatever vegetables are on hand, and soy sauce if you have it. The method is the same whether you have three ingredients or eight. This version is built from what a depleted pantry reliably holds: rice, egg, onion, and fat. Every ingredient beyond that improves it further.

Ingredients

- 2 cups (480 ml) cold cooked rice, leftover from the day before, not freshly made
- 1-2 eggs
- 1 medium onion, diced small
- 2 tbsp (30 ml) lard, bacon drippings, or vegetable oil
- 2 tbsp (30 ml) soy sauce, or 1/2 tsp (3 ml) salt if no soy sauce
- Black pepper to taste
- OPTIONAL VEGETABLES, use any available: frozen peas, diced carrots, shredded cabbage, canned corn, sliced green onion, diced bell pepper
- OPTIONAL PROTEIN, use any available: diced leftover meat or poultry, crumbled sausage, diced Spam, flaked canned tuna or salmon

Method

1. Heat a large cast iron skillet or any wide pan over high heat until very hot, a drop of water should evaporate on contact.
2. Add fat. When it shimmers, add diced onion and any vegetables that need cooking (carrots, cabbage, bell pepper). Cook stirring frequently 3-4 minutes until softened and edges begin to brown.
3. Push everything to one side of the pan. Crack eggs into the empty side and scramble them quickly in the pan, break them up as they set, about 30 seconds. Mix the egg into the vegetables.
4. Add cold rice all at once. Press it flat against the pan with a spatula and let it sit undisturbed 1-2 minutes to develop some color on the bottom.

5. Stir and press flat again. Repeat once more, the goal is some grains with toasted spots, not uniform grey mush.

6. Add soy sauce around the edge of the pan so it hits the hot surface and sizzles before mixing in. Stir everything together.

7. Add any tender vegetables or protein that just needs heating through (peas, canned corn, cooked meat). Toss and serve immediately.

Field Note: The single most important rule: the pan must be very hot before anything goes in. A lukewarm pan steams the rice instead of frying it and produces a wet mass. High heat is the technique. Cold rice is the second rule, warm or freshly cooked rice is too moist and will clump. If you have no soy sauce, a splash of Worcestershire sauce or just salt and pepper work fine.

EGG AND POTATO HASH

"Diced potatoes, an egg, and a hot skillet. Works as breakfast, lunch, or supper."

Serves: 2-3   Time: 25 min

History & Context

Potatoes and eggs in a cast iron pan. This combination feeds people at any hour because both ingredients keep well and cook fast. The technique is simple: dice the potatoes small so they cook through before the outside burns, get them properly browned on at least two sides, then add the egg. Onion and fat make it better. Nothing else is required.

Ingredients

- 3 medium potatoes, diced into 1/2-inch (1.5 cm) cubes, no need to peel
- 2-3 eggs
- 1 medium onion, diced
- 3 tbsp (45 ml) lard, bacon drippings, or any cooking fat
- 1/2 tsp (3 ml) salt
- 1/2 tsp (3 ml) black pepper
- Optional: 1/4 tsp (1 ml) garlic powder, pinch of paprika
- Optional protein: diced leftover meat, crumbled sausage, diced Spam or canned ham

Method

1. Heat lard in a cast iron skillet over medium-high heat until shimmering.
2. Add diced potatoes in a single layer as much as possible. Season with salt and pepper. Do not stir, let them sit undisturbed 4-5 minutes until the bottom is golden-brown.
3. Add diced onion. Stir everything and press flat again. Let sit another 3-4 minutes undisturbed.
4. Stir and test a potato, it should be completely tender inside and browned on at least one side. If still firm, continue cooking 3-4 minutes more, stirring occasionally.
5. If using optional protein, add it now and stir through until heated.
6. Make 2-3 wells in the hash with a spoon. Crack one egg into each well.
7. Reduce heat to medium. Cover the pan with a lid or a piece of foil. Cook 3-4 minutes until the egg whites are fully set but yolks are still slightly soft, or cook fully through if preferred.
8. Serve directly from the skillet.

> **Field Note:** *Small dice is the key, 1/2-inch (1.5 cm) cubes cook through reliably before the outside burns. Larger chunks mean the outside chars while the inside stays raw. If the potatoes are browning too fast before they are tender, add 2 tablespoons (30 ml) of water to the pan and cover for 2-3 minutes. The steam cooks them through and then the water evaporates, letting the browning resume.*

COWBOY COFFEE

"Grounds directly in the pot, brought to a boil, cold water splash to settle them. The correct method when there is no filter."

Serves: 4 cups   Time: 10 min

History & Context

Coffee grounds placed directly in cold water in a pot, brought to a boil, then settled with a splash of cold water dropped in from height. No filter, no equipment beyond a pot. The cold water splash creates a thermal shock that drops the grounds to the bottom. Boiled coffee extracts more fully than drip coffee due to longer contact time.

Ingredients

- 4 cups (960 ml) cold water
- 1/4 cup (60 ml) coarsely ground dark roast coffee
- Cold water, a small splash for settling

Method

1. Place cold water and ground coffee directly into a pot, no filter.
2. Bring to a full boil over high heat, stirring once.
3. As soon as it boils, reduce to a simmer briefly, then pull from heat.
4. Drop a small splash of cold water into the pot from height, this thermal shock drops the grounds.
5. Let sit undisturbed 2 full minutes without touching.
6. Pour very slowly into cups, leaving the last 1/4 cup (60 ml) of sludge in the pot.

Field Note: *The cold water splash genuinely settles the grounds through thermal shock. This method works with any heat source, any pot, and any coarsely ground coffee. An eggshell added to the grounds before brewing also helps settle them.*

SNACKS & STAPLES

Small cheap things that sustain people between meals

This chapter is the between-meals chapter. Not full recipes, not complete meals, but the small preparations that keep people functional through a long day when full meals are not available at regular intervals. Several of these require no cooking at all. Sardines on crackers is protein, fat, and a tin. Cornbread in cold milk is two ingredients in a bowl. The skill required is approaching these without embarrassment, recognizing that food does not need to be elaborate to be real food. Bacon drippings get their own recipe because they are the most useful free ingredient that most kitchens produce and then pour down the drain. Save them. The final recipe in this chapter is Recipe 6-15: Garlic Aioli and Homemade Mayonnaise. Oil, eggs, and an acid blended together produce mayonnaise. Add garlic confit from Recipe 8-14 and it becomes something better. Both the garlic preparation and the emulsification technique are worth knowing.

✦ ✦ ✦

BREAD AND BACON GREASE

"Toast spread with saved bacon drippings. The most useful cooking fat in any kitchen costs nothing to collect."

Serves: 4-6   Time: 5 min

History & Context

Rendered bacon fat collected in a jar kept beside the stove. Spread on toast it costs nothing, it is a byproduct of cooking bacon, which you are already doing. It keeps at room temperature for two weeks or refrigerated for months. It is more useful as a cooking fat than any purchased alternative and produces a deeply savory spread from what most people pour down the drain.

Ingredients

- 2 thick slices day-old white bread
- 1-2 tbsp (15 to 30 ml) rendered bacon drippings, at room temperature
- Coarse salt

Method

1. Save bacon drippings every time you cook bacon. Pour warm fat through a fine strainer into a clean glass jar. Store at room temperature away from sunlight up to two weeks, or refrigerate for months.
2. Allow drippings to soften to room temperature, spreadable consistency, not liquid.
3. Toast bread until both sides are firm and golden.
4. While still warm, spread drippings generously across the surface to the edges.
5. Season with coarse salt. Eat immediately.

Field Note: Never pour bacon drippings down the drain. A jar of bacon fat beside the stove is the most versatile, cheapest cooking fat available. It goes in everything, beans, cornbread, gravies, fried eggs, vegetables.

MILK TOAST

"Warm milk poured over toast. The simplest comforting meal a kitchen can produce."

Serves: 1-2   Time: 10 min

History & Context

Toast in warm salted milk. The preparation requires no skill, no special equipment, and nothing beyond bread and milk. It is easy on the stomach, gentle in flavor, and provides protein and carbohydrates in a form that is easy to eat when nothing else sounds appealing. Powdered whole milk reconstituted to full strength works perfectly.

Ingredients

- 2 slices white sandwich bread
- 1 to 1.5 cups (240 to 360 ml) whole milk or reconstituted powdered milk
- 1 tsp (5 ml) butter
- Pinch of salt
- 1/2 tsp (3 ml) sugar (optional)

Method

1. Toast bread until uniformly golden and firm throughout.
2. Warm milk in a small saucepan over medium-low with butter, salt, and optional sugar. Do not boil, heat until steaming and just below a simmer.
3. Place toast flat in a wide shallow bowl or break into large pieces.
4. Pour hot milk directly over toast.
5. Let rest 60-90 seconds. The ideal texture is toast that still has some resistance in the center with softened edges.

Field Note: *Powdered whole milk reconstituted to full strength works perfectly and is shelf-stable for years. This is the substitution to know when fresh milk is unavailable.*

BACON GREASE TOAST AND JELLY

"Warm grease and cold jelly on the same piece of toast. The contrast is the point."

Serves: 1-2   Time: 5 min

History & Context

Toast spread with bacon drippings, topped with cold jelly. The warm fat soaks slightly into the toast, the cold jelly sits distinct on top, and the contrast between the two, temperature, sweet versus savory, salt, creates something greater than either alone. It costs nothing extra beyond what every kitchen already has.

Ingredients

- 2 slices white bread, toasted golden and firm
- 1.5 tbsp (23 ml) bacon drippings at room temperature
- 1.5 tbsp (23 ml) any fruit jelly, jam, or preserves
- Pinch of coarse salt

Method

1. Toast bread until both sides are golden and firm.
2. While still hot, spread bacon drippings across the full surface.
3. Add the jelly on top, it should sit distinct on the drippings rather than melting in.
4. Shake a tiny pinch of coarse salt over the jelly.
5. Eat while the toast is still warm.

Field Note: The pinch of salt on the jelly bridges the sweet and savory and completes the combination. It sounds wrong and tastes right.

CLABBER AND CORNBREAD

"Naturally fermented milk crumbled with cold cornbread. A probiotic food that costs almost nothing."

Serves: 2   Time: 10 min + overnight fermenting

History & Context

Plain yogurt mixed with whole milk and left at room temperature for 18-24 hours produces a tangy fermented dairy product similar to clabber. Cold cornbread crumbled into it provides carbohydrates, fiber, and texture. The fermentation produces beneficial bacteria. This is a functionally complete meal from pantry staples that requires almost no preparation.

Ingredients

- Clabber substitute: 2 cups (480 ml) whole milk + 2 tbsp (30 ml) plain yogurt with live cultures, rested 18-24 hours at room temperature
- OR: 1 cup (240 ml) commercial full-fat plain yogurt thinned slightly with whole milk
- 2-3 pieces cold cornbread, crumbled
- Optional: drizzle of sorghum or honey

Method

1. Make clabber substitute: combine whole milk and plain yogurt. Stir, cover loosely, leave at room temperature 18-24 hours until thickened and tangy.
2. Make cornbread (see 1-3) the day before. Cool and refrigerate overnight.
3. Crumble cold cornbread into a large glass or wide bowl.
4. Pour the clabber or thickened yogurt over the crumbled cornbread.
5. Add sorghum or honey if desired.

Field Note: *Ultra-pasteurized milk will not ferment correctly, it has been sterilized too thoroughly. Standard pasteurized milk works. The label should say 'pasteurized' not 'ultra-pasteurized' or 'UHT.'*

BISCUITS AND POT LIQUOR

"The dark cooking liquid from boiled greens is loaded with nutrients leached from the vegetables. Never discard it."

Serves: 4-6   Time: 75 min

History & Context

Pot liquor, the cooking liquid left after boiling collard greens, turnip greens, or cabbage with a ham hock for an hour, is dark, minerally, and loaded with nutrients that leached from the vegetables during the long cook. Split biscuits soaked in it is a complete meal. Reheated pot liquor over biscuits was a standard breakfast when nothing else was available. Never discard it.

Ingredients

- 1 large bunch collard greens, turnip greens, or cabbage
- 6 cups (1.4 L) water
- 1 ham hock, salt pork, or 3-4 strips bacon
- 1 tsp (5 ml) salt, 1/2 tsp (3 ml) black pepper
- Biscuits for serving (see 1-7)

Method

1. Place ham hock or salt pork in the pot with water. Bring to a boil and cook 15 minutes.
2. Wash greens. Remove tough center stems. Tear roughly.
3. Add greens, salt, pepper. Press down as they wilt.
4. Reduce to a low simmer, partially cover, cook 45-60 minutes until greens are completely tender.
5. Ladle the pot liquor, the cooking broth, into a separate container. Refrigerate.
6. In the morning, reheat pot liquor until steaming. Adjust seasoning.
7. Split hot biscuits into a wide bowl. Ladle steaming pot liquor over them.

Field Note: Never discard pot liquor. Any time you boil vegetables, the cooking liquid contains leached minerals and vitamins. Save it in a jar, refrigerate for up to five days, and use it as the base for soup, gravy, or this preparation.

COFFEE SOUP

"Hot black coffee poured over stale bread with cream and sugar. A Scandinavian farm breakfast that requires no cooking."

Serves: 1   Time: 5 min

History & Context

Stale bread covered with hot black coffee, topped with cream and sugar. Swedish and Norwegian farming families brought this tradition because it required no cooking beyond already-made coffee and used bread that had gone too hard to eat plain. Provides caffeine, calories, and warmth from what is already in the kitchen.

Ingredients

- 1-2 slices day-old bread, slightly stale
- 1 cup (240 ml) hot strong-brewed black coffee
- 2 tbsp (30 ml) heavy cream or whole milk
- 1-2 tsp (5 to 10 ml) sugar to taste

Method

1. Tear stale bread into rough 1-2 inch (2.5 to 5 cm) pieces and place in a wide bowl.
2. Pour hot black coffee over the bread pieces until just submerged.
3. Add cream or milk. Add sugar to taste and stir gently.
4. Let sit 1-2 minutes before eating. Bread should be softened but still identifiable.

Field Note: This requires no cooking, no fire, and no equipment beyond a bowl and spoon. Hard biscuits, hardtack, and stale cornbread all work as the bread base. Hot coffee is already being made.

FRIED BOLOGNA CUPS

"A thick slice of bologna in a hot dry skillet buckles into a cup in 90 seconds. Fill it."

Serves: 1-2   Time: 5 min

History & Context

Bologna's curious behavior in a hot dry skillet, the way a thick slice curls upward and buckles into a cup as the center fat renders, makes it both food and vessel. The charred crispy edges taste better than plain bologna. The cup holds condiments, eggs, or whatever is available.

Ingredients

- 4 thick slices bologna, ask specifically for thick-cut
- Yellow mustard, ketchup, or relish for filling
- Optional: a cracked egg

Method

1. Heat a dry cast iron skillet over medium-high. No oil needed.
2. Place a thick slice of bologna flat in the hot pan.
3. Within 60-90 seconds the edges curl upward and the slice buckles into a cup.
4. Once fully formed with charred crispy edges, remove from pan.
5. Fill immediately with condiment.
6. Bonus: crack an egg into the cup while still in the skillet. Cover with a lid for 2 minutes.

Field Note: Thick-sliced bologna is essential, thin slices fry flat and do not form cups. Ask the deli counter for thick-cut specifically.

CINNAMON SUGAR TOAST

"91 seconds under a broiler. The sugar caramelizes into something genuinely worth eating."

Serves: 1   Time: 3 min

History & Context

Butter spread on bread, covered with cinnamon sugar, placed under a broiler for 90 seconds. The sugar caramelizes into a crunchy golden layer at the edges and a gooey center. It costs four cents in ingredients and produces something that requires no explanation to children.

Ingredients

- 1-2 slices white bread
- 1 tbsp (15 ml) softened butter
- 2 tsp (10 ml) white granulated sugar
- 1/2 tsp (3 ml) ground cinnamon

Method

1. Mix sugar and cinnamon, 4:1 ratio. More cinnamon becomes bitter.
2. Spread butter evenly across the bread to the edges.
3. Sprinkle cinnamon-sugar evenly over the butter.
4. Place bread on the highest rack under the broiler.
5. Broil 90 seconds exactly. Watch continuously. Remove the moment the sugar turns golden and bubbles.
6. Let cool 60 seconds before eating, the caramelized sugar is molten when it first comes out.

Field Note: *Watch it continuously. The difference between perfect and burned is about 30 seconds under a broiler. Pull it the moment you see golden bubbling across the surface.*

CORNBREAD IN COLD MILK

"Leftover cornbread crumbled into cold milk and eaten with a spoon. No cooking. No preparation."

Serves: 1   Time: 2 min

History & Context

Leftover cornbread crumbled into cold milk eaten with a spoon from a tall glass. No cooking, no preparation, thirty seconds of assembly. Day-old or older cornbread holds its texture longer in the milk, producing a range of textures, firm at the center, softened at the edges, within a single bowl.

Ingredients

- 1-2 thick slices leftover cornbread
- 1 cup (240 ml) cold whole milk or buttermilk
- Optional: pinch of salt, spoonful of sorghum

Method

1. Crumble the cornbread into rough chunks directly into a tall glass or wide bowl.
2. Pour cold milk over the cornbread until nearly covered.
3. Wait 30 seconds as the cornbread begins absorbing milk.
4. Eat with a spoon.

Field Note: Use day-old or older cornbread. Fresh cornbread goes mushy immediately. Day-old cornbread holds texture long enough to eat.

SALTINES AND BUTTER

"Work the softened butter into the holes with a table knife. Room temperature butter only."
Serves: as desired   Time: 2 min

History & Context

Saltine crackers spread with real butter worked carefully into the perforated holes with a table knife. Room temperature butter spreads cleanly and fills the holes. Cold butter tears the cracker. Melted butter soaks through and makes it soggy. There is exactly one correct temperature.

Ingredients

- 1 sleeve saltine crackers
- Real butter at room temperature, not cold, not melted

Method

1. The butter must be at room temperature, not cold, not melted.
2. Hold a cracker flat. Press softened butter onto the surface and work it into the holes with a table knife.
3. The surface should be glossy and evenly coated.
4. Eat while the cracker still has its snap.

Field Note: *Room temperature only. This is the entire technique.*

SARDINES ON CRACKERS

"Complete protein, omega-3 fats, significant calcium. Under two dollars a tin. One of the most nutritionally complete shelf-stable foods available."

Serves: as desired   Time: 2 min

History & Context

Canned sardines on crackers with mustard. The bones in canned sardines are pressure-cooked to complete softness during canning and are fully edible, they provide significant calcium. The oil they are packed in is nutritious and should not be drained. A tin and a sleeve of crackers is a complete high-protein meal for about two dollars.

Ingredients

- 1 tin (3.75 oz, 105 g) sardines in olive oil or water
- Crackers
- Yellow mustard
- Optional: hot sauce, thin-sliced raw onion

Method

1. Open the tin. Do not drain the olive oil if packed in oil.
2. Lift each sardine onto a cracker, whole, not mashed.
3. Add a small squeeze of yellow mustard to each.
4. Optional: a small slice of raw onion or a drop of hot sauce.
5. Eat in one or two bites while the cracker is still crisp.

Field Note: The soft bones are completely edible and undetectable in texture. Eat them, they provide calcium. Keep a minimum of 24 cans in your pantry at all times. Shelf life is typically 3-5 years.

FRIED SPAM

"Spam sliced thick and fried in a dry skillet until both cut surfaces are mahogany brown. A different product from the cold version."

Serves: 2-3   Time: 8 min

History & Context

Spam fried until both cut surfaces develop a deep brown crust is a genuinely different product from cold Spam eaten from the can. The Maillard reaction creates flavor compounds during frying that the cold version structurally lacks. Shelf-stable for years, 7g protein per serving, functional when other protein sources are unavailable.

Ingredients

- 1 can Spam, sliced 3/8-inch (1 cm) thick
- No oil needed, Spam provides its own fat
- Optional: honey, soy sauce, or hot sauce glaze

Method

1. Slice Spam 3/8 to 1/2-inch (1 to 1.5 cm) thick.
2. Heat a dry cast iron skillet over medium-high until hot.
3. Place slices in the dry pan. No oil.
4. Do not move the slices. Cook 2-3 minutes until the bottom is very deeply browned, nearly mahogany.
5. Flip once. Cook 2-3 more minutes.
6. For glazed version: drizzle honey or soy sauce over slices in the last 30 seconds.
7. Eat on rice, bread, or directly from the pan.

Field Note: *Do not move the slices during frying. The crust must form undisturbed before they are flipped. Keep multiple cans in rotation, they are shelf-stable for years and are one of the most reliable shelf-stable protein sources available.*

VELVEETA ON CRACKERS UNDER THE BROILER

"Sixty seconds under a broiler turns a cracker and a thin slice of Velveeta into something worth eating."

Serves: as desired   Time: 5 min

History & Context

Ritz crackers with thin slices of Velveeta, run under a broiler for exactly 60 seconds. Velveeta's lower melting temperature means it fuses into the cracker surface rather than simply melting on top. The result is a crunch followed by a smooth molten interior. Velveeta stores well at room temperature before opening.

Ingredients

- 1 sleeve Ritz crackers or any cracker
- 4 oz (115 g) Velveeta, sliced very thin
- Optional: a drop of hot sauce on each

Method

1. Set broiler to high. Place rack on highest position.
2. Arrange crackers on a baking sheet.
3. Slice Velveeta as thin as possible, about 1/8-inch (0.5 cm). Place one slice on each cracker.
4. Set a timer for 60 seconds. Place under broiler.
5. Watch through the oven door. Remove at 60 seconds.
6. Let cool 30 seconds before eating.

Field Note: 60 seconds is precise. Velveeta goes from perfect to overcooked in under a minute under a hot broiler.

STOVETOP POPCORN

"Half a cup of kernels, two tablespoons of fat, a lid, and a pot. The original before microwave bags."

Serves: 4   Time: 10 min

History & Context

Popcorn kernels cooked in hot fat in a covered heavy pot, tipped into a bowl, covered with melted butter. Stovetop popcorn has a crispier hull and more developed corn flavor than microwave popcorn because the direct dry heat creates different caramelization. Popcorn kernels store indefinitely.

Ingredients

- 1/2 cup (120 ml) popcorn kernels
- 2 tbsp (30 ml) lard, coconut oil, or any cooking fat
- 3 tbsp (45 ml) butter melted
- Coarse salt

Method

1. Heat a heavy pot with a lid over medium-high. Add fat.
2. Add 3 test kernels. When they pop, the fat is at the right temperature.
3. Add remaining kernels and cover the lid, tilted slightly to allow steam to escape.
4. Keep at medium-high. Corn will begin popping vigorously within 1-2 minutes.
5. Shake the pot every 30 seconds while holding the lid down.
6. When popping slows to 2-3 seconds between pops, remove from heat immediately.
7. Pour melted butter over the top and toss. Season with coarse salt.

Field Note: The tilted lid allows steam to escape, which is what makes stovetop popcorn crisp rather than chewy. Sealed lid produces soft popcorn. Tilted lid produces crisp popcorn.

GARLIC AIOLI, HOMEMADE MAYONNAISE

"Oil, eggs, and an acid blended together. The result is mayonnaise. Add garlic or onion and it becomes something better."

Serves: about 1 cup   Time: 10 min

History & Context

Mayonnaise is an emulsion, oil droplets suspended in water by the lecithin in egg yolk. When you blend oil and eggs together with an acid, the lecithin molecules arrange themselves between the oil and water and hold them together in a stable creamy suspension. That is the entire science. The technique is an immersion blender and 60 seconds. Commercial mayonnaise is shelf-stable because it is pasteurized and sealed in a sterile jar. Homemade mayonnaise is not shelf-stable, it must be refrigerated and used within a week. What it provides in return is something richer, cleaner, and more flavorful than commercial equivalents, made from ingredients already in your pantry. Adding garlic confit from Recipe 8-14, soft golden garlic cooked in the same oil used here, transforms plain mayonnaise into a garlic aioli. Adding caramelized onion cooked the same way produces an onion aioli. Both are more useful than plain mayonnaise and more interesting on anything you put them on: bread, potatoes, eggs, cold meat, or eaten directly from the jar, which is the honest outcome.

Ingredients

- 2 large eggs, at room temperature, cold eggs resist emulsification
- 1 cup (240 ml) neutral oil, vegetable oil or light olive oil. Do not use extra-virgin olive oil, it can turn bitter when blended
- 1 tbsp (15 ml) apple cider vinegar or white vinegar
- 1 tsp (5 ml) yellow mustard, this helps stabilize the emulsion as well as adding flavor
- 1/2 tsp (3 ml) salt
- FOR GARLIC AIOLI: add 4-6 cloves of garlic confit from Recipe 8-14, or 2 cloves raw garlic for a sharper version
- FOR ONION AIOLI: cook 1 medium onion, roughly chopped, in 1 cup (240 ml) of oil over medium heat until deep golden and caramelized, about 20-25 minutes. Cool completely before using. Use this onion-infused oil in place of plain oil below.
- FOR PLAIN MAYONNAISE: use the base recipe with no additions

Method

1. Make sure eggs are at room temperature. Cold eggs are the most common reason emulsification fails. If eggs are cold, submerge them in warm water for 5 minutes before using.
2. If making garlic or onion aioli: prepare your flavored oil first. For garlic confit aioli, use the oil from Recipe 8-14 as your 1 cup (240 ml) of oil and add the soft garlic cloves directly to the jar. For onion aioli, cook the onion in the oil until deeply caramelized, then cool completely.
3. Place eggs, vinegar, mustard, and salt in a tall narrow jar or container. If using garlic confit cloves, add them now.
4. Pour all the oil on top. Do not stir.
5. Place an immersion blender at the very bottom of the jar, pressing it against the base. Turn it on.
6. Hold it still at the bottom for 10-15 seconds without moving it. You will see mayonnaise forming around the blender head.
7. Once you see the bottom half of the jar has turned white and creamy, begin slowly pulling the blender upward while keeping it running. Take 20-30 seconds to move from bottom to top.
8. By the time the blender reaches the top, the entire jar should be thick, creamy, and fully emulsified.
9. If using whole garlic confit cloves or caramelized onion pieces: the blender will break these down into the mayonnaise, producing pieces throughout. For a completely smooth result, blend longer. For texture with flavor bursts, stop sooner.
10. Taste and adjust salt and vinegar. Transfer to a sealed jar. Refrigerate immediately. Use within one week.

> *Field Note: If the emulsion breaks and you end up with oily liquid rather than cream: pour the broken mixture into a new jar, add one fresh egg yolk, and re-blend from the bottom as described above. The fresh yolk almost always rescues a broken batch. The immersion blender method works because holding it stationary at the bottom forces the blender to process oil and egg together before either can separate. The key variables are room temperature eggs, the right jar size (narrow and tall, not wide and flat), and patience on the upward pull. Once you have this technique it takes under two minutes and produces something better than anything in a commercial jar.*

DESSERTS & SWEET TABLE

Twenty-four cheap sweet things. Morale matters.

Morale is a legitimate survival resource. People who maintain some normalcy and pleasure during extended hardship make better decisions and sustain effort longer. A dessert once a week is not a luxury. It is a functional investment in the people eating it. Every recipe in this chapter costs under three dollars to make and serves at least six people. Several use entirely shelf-stable ingredients with no fresh eggs or dairy required. Wacky Cake was developed during the Depression specifically because eggs and butter were unavailable, and it produces genuine chocolate cake from pantry staples. If the oven is unavailable (power outage, generator failure, cooking over fire), three recipes in this chapter require no oven at all: Recipe 7-1 (No-Bake Chocolate Oatmeal Cookies, done on the stovetop in 20 minutes), Recipe 7-3 (Icebox Cake, set in the refrigerator overnight with no heat at all), and Recipe 7-23 (Potato Candy, no cooking required). When there is no electricity, these three are your dessert options.

❖ ❖ ❖

NO-BAKE CHOCOLATE OATMEAL COOKIES

"60 seconds at a full rolling boil. Use a timer. The entire recipe is in that one minute."

Serves: 30 cookies   Time: 20 min

History & Context

Sugar, butter, cocoa, and milk brought to a full rolling boil for exactly one minute, then poured over oats and peanut butter and dropped to set. No oven. Under 15 minutes. The critical variable is timing: 60 seconds at a true rolling boil sets firm. Less produces chocolate puddles. More produces dry crumbling sand. That 60-second window is the entire skill.

Ingredients

- 2 cups (480 ml) granulated sugar
- 1/2 cup (120 ml) whole milk
- 1 stick (1/2 cup, 120 ml) unsalted butter
- 3 tbsp (45 ml) unsweetened cocoa powder
- 1/2 tsp (3 ml) salt
- 3 cups (720 ml) old-fashioned rolled oats
- 1/2 cup (120 ml) natural peanut butter
- 2 tsp (10 ml) vanilla extract
- Wax paper for dropping

Method

1. Line a baking sheet or counter with wax paper. Measure all remaining ingredients and have them ready before starting, once the boil begins there is no time.
2. Combine sugar, milk, butter, cocoa, and salt in a heavy saucepan over medium heat. Stir until butter melts.
3. Increase to medium-high. Bring to a full rolling boil, bubbles breaking rapidly across the entire surface that cannot be stirred down.
4. Time exactly 60 seconds from the full rolling boil. Stir constantly.
5. Remove from heat immediately. Stir in peanut butter until melted and combined.
6. Stir in oats and vanilla. The mixture will thicken rapidly.
7. Drop by rounded tablespoons onto wax paper immediately.
8. Cool 20-30 minutes at room temperature. Do not refrigerate to speed setting.

> **Field Note:** *A full rolling boil cannot be stirred down, the bubbles break rapidly*

PINEAPPLE UPSIDE-DOWN CAKE

"One flip. The caramelized pineapple cascades down. Confidence is the only skill required."

Serves: 8-10   Time: 55 min

History & Context

Brown sugar and butter caramelized in the pan, pineapple rings arranged on top, batter poured over, baked, then flipped. The 5-minute rest before flipping is the critical window, too soon and the caramel runs, too late and it sticks. A can of pineapple rings costs about $1.50. The whole cake costs under $3 and feeds ten.

Ingredients

- Topping: 4 tbsp (60 ml) butter, 1/2 cup (120 ml) packed brown sugar, 1 can (20 oz, 565 g) pineapple rings drained (reserve juice), maraschino cherries
- Batter: 1.5 cups (360 ml) flour, 1.5 tsp (8 ml) baking powder, 1/4 tsp (1 ml) salt, 1/2 cup (120 ml) softened butter, 3/4 cup (180 ml) sugar, 2 eggs, 1 tsp (5 ml) vanilla, 1/2 cup (120 ml) reserved pineapple juice

Method

1. Preheat oven to 350°F (175°C).
2. Melt 4 tbsp (60 ml) butter in a 10-inch (25 cm) cast iron skillet over medium heat. Add brown sugar and stir until dissolved and bubbling. Remove from heat.
3. Arrange pineapple rings over the brown sugar. Place a cherry in the center of each ring.
4. Make batter: whisk flour, baking powder, and salt. Cream butter and sugar until fluffy, 3 minutes. Beat in eggs one at a time, then vanilla. Add flour alternating with pineapple juice, beginning and ending with flour.
5. Pour batter evenly over the pineapple.
6. Bake 35-40 minutes until a toothpick comes out clean.
7. Cool exactly 5 minutes. Run a knife around the edge. Place a plate face-down over the skillet. Flip in one decisive motion. Lift the skillet.

Field Note: The flip requires decisiveness. One clean confident rotation is better than a slow uncertain one. Hesitation allows the caramel to shift during inversion.

ICEBOX CAKE

"The refrigerator does the baking. Eight hours of cold turns plain crackers into something indistinguishable from cake."

Serves: 8   Time: 15 min + overnight

History & Context

Graham crackers layered with whipped cream and refrigerated overnight. Moisture from the cream permeates the crackers, transforming them into something with the texture of soft cake layers. No oven. No cooking. A dessert that assembles in 15 minutes and is finished by morning.

Ingredients

- 2 cups (480 ml) heavy whipping cream, very cold
- 3 tbsp (45 ml) powdered sugar
- 1 tsp (5 ml) vanilla extract
- 1 box graham crackers
- Optional: sliced strawberries, banana slices, or chocolate syrup between layers

Method

1. Chill a metal bowl and beaters in the freezer 10 minutes.
2. Beat cold cream to soft peaks. Add powdered sugar and vanilla. Beat to stiff peaks.
3. Spread a thin layer of whipped cream on a rectangular platter or in a 9x13 pan.
4. Lay graham crackers in a single layer over the cream, breaking pieces to fill gaps.
5. Spread a generous layer of whipped cream. Add optional fruit.
6. Repeat, crackers, cream, optional fruit, until all crackers and cream are used. End with a cream layer.
7. Cover tightly and refrigerate at least 8 hours, preferably overnight.
8. Slice and serve cold.

Field Note: 8 hours minimum. 6 hours is not enough, the crackers will still have slight crunch. 10 hours is ideal. The cake should cut cleanly with no cracker resistance.

BROWN BETTY

"Stale bread, apples, butter, brown sugar. One of the oldest American desserts, recorded since the 1860s."

Serves: 6-8   Time: 55 min

History & Context

Alternating layers of buttered breadcrumbs and sliced apples, sweetened with brown sugar and spiced with cinnamon, baked until the crumbs caramelize and the apple juices soak upward through every layer. An answer to the simultaneous problem of stale bread and abundance of apples. Served warm with cold cream.

Ingredients

- 3 cups (720 ml) coarse fresh breadcrumbs from day-old white bread, tear, do not use fine dry crumbs
- 4 tbsp (60 ml) unsalted butter, melted
- 4-5 medium tart apples (Granny Smith or similar), peeled, cored, sliced thin
- 3/4 cup (180 ml) packed brown sugar
- 1 tsp (5 ml) cinnamon, 1/4 tsp (1 ml) nutmeg, pinch of salt
- 2 tbsp (30 ml) lemon juice or apple cider vinegar
- 1/4 cup (60 ml) water or apple juice

Method

1. Preheat oven to 375°F (190°C). Butter a 2-quart (1.9 L) baking dish.
2. Toss breadcrumbs with melted butter until evenly coated.
3. Toss sliced apples with brown sugar, cinnamon, nutmeg, salt, and lemon juice.
4. Layer: spread 1/3 of crumbs in the bottom. Cover with half the apples. Another third of crumbs. Remaining apples. Final third of crumbs.
5. Pour water or apple juice evenly over the top.
6. Cover tightly with foil. Bake 30 minutes covered.
7. Remove foil. Bake another 15-20 minutes until top crumbs are deeply golden.
8. Serve warm with cream poured around the edges.

Field Note: Fresh coarse breadcrumbs are essential, fine dry crumbs turn to paste. Tear the bread into rough pea-sized pieces. The covered baking phase creates steam that keeps the interior moist.

TAPIOCA PUDDING, FROM SCRATCH

"Small pearl tapioca, not instant. An hour of patient stirring produces something the instant version cannot replicate."

Serves: 4-6   Time: 75 min

History & Context

Small pearl tapioca soaked in milk, then cooked slowly with egg yolks, sugar, and vanilla until the pearls turn translucent and the mixture thickens into something silky. Chilled overnight it sets into a cool, creamy dessert with each pearl offering gentle resistance. The instant version is a different product.

Ingredients

- 1/3 cup (80 ml) small pearl tapioca, not instant
- 3 cups (720 ml) whole milk, divided
- 1/4 tsp (1 ml) salt
- 2 eggs, separated
- 1/2 cup (120 ml) granulated sugar, divided
- 1 tsp (5 ml) vanilla extract

Method

1. Soak pearl tapioca in 1 cup (240 ml) of milk for 30 minutes. The pearls will swell slightly.
2. Combine soaked tapioca and milk with remaining 2 cups (480 ml) milk and salt. Cook over medium-low, stirring frequently, until just simmering, about 15 minutes.
3. Beat egg yolks with 1/4 cup (60 ml) sugar until pale.
4. Reduce heat to low. Cook, stirring constantly, 15-20 more minutes until pearls become translucent.
5. Temper the yolks: slowly ladle 1/2 cup (120 ml) hot pudding into the yolk mixture while whisking constantly. Pour tempered yolks back into the pot, stirring continuously.
6. Cook 5 more minutes, stirring constantly, until thick and glossy.
7. Remove from heat. Stir in vanilla.
8. Pour into dishes. Press plastic wrap directly onto the surface. Refrigerate at least 4 hours.

Field Note: Adding hot pudding to the yolks slowly while whisking is called tempering, it prevents the eggs from scrambling by raising their temperature

BANANA PUDDING, FROM SCRATCH

"The custard is the skill. Egg yolks, whole milk, sugar, flour cooked on the stovetop. Layered with wafers and bananas."

Serves: 8-10   Time: 50 min + chilling

History & Context

A genuine vanilla custard made from egg yolks, whole milk, sugar, and flour on the stovetop, layered with vanilla wafers and sliced bananas, topped with meringue made from the reserved whites and baked until the peaks are golden. This is a dessert that requires real technique and rewards it.

Ingredients

- Custard: 3/4 cup (180 ml) sugar, 1/3 cup (80 ml) flour, 1/4 tsp (1 ml) salt, 3 cups (720 ml) whole milk, 3 egg yolks beaten, 2 tbsp (30 ml) butter, 2 tsp (10 ml) vanilla
- Assembly: 1 box vanilla wafers, 4-5 ripe bananas sliced
- Meringue: 3 egg whites, 1/4 tsp (1 ml) cream of tartar, 6 tbsp (90 ml) sugar

Method

1. Whisk sugar, flour, and salt in a heavy saucepan. Gradually whisk in milk until smooth.
2. Cook over medium heat, stirring constantly, until thick and bubbling, 10-12 minutes. Once bubbling, cook 2 more minutes.
3. Temper yolks: ladle 1/2 cup (120 ml) hot custard into beaten yolks while whisking. Return to pot.
4. Cook 2 more minutes, stirring. Remove from heat. Stir in butter and vanilla.
5. Layer wafers across a 2-quart (1.9 L) baking dish. Add sliced bananas. Pour half the hot custard over. Repeat layers.
6. Make meringue: beat egg whites with cream of tartar to soft peaks. Gradually add sugar, beat to stiff glossy peaks.
7. Spread meringue over hot pudding, sealing completely to the edges.
8. Bake at 325°F (165°C) for 15-20 minutes until meringue peaks are golden.
9. Cool to room temperature, then refrigerate at least 2 hours before serving.

Field Note: Spread meringue onto hot pudding, not cooled, the heat from below helps cook the bottom of the meringue and prevents weeping. Sealing to the edges prevents shrinkage.

RICE PUDDING

"Rice and milk simmered together for 50 minutes until they become a single creamy thing."

Serves: 6   Time: 60 min

History & Context

Rice and whole milk, simmered together over low heat for the better part of an hour until the liquid thickens into a dense creamy pudding. Sugar and vanilla go in at the end. This is one of the oldest desserts in recorded cooking and requires almost no skill, just patience and occasional stirring. White rice stores for 25+ years. This dessert is available as long as the rice is.

Ingredients

- 1 cup (240 ml) long-grain white rice
- 4 cups (960 ml) whole milk or reconstituted powdered milk
- 1/2 cup (120 ml) granulated sugar
- 1/4 tsp (1 ml) salt
- 2 tsp (10 ml) vanilla extract
- 1/2 tsp (3 ml) cinnamon for serving
- Optional: 1/2 cup (120 ml) raisins added during last 10 minutes

Method

1. Combine rice, milk, and salt in a heavy-bottomed saucepan over medium heat.
2. Bring to a gentle simmer, stirring frequently to prevent scorching.
3. Reduce heat to low. Cook uncovered 45-50 minutes, stirring every 3-4 minutes and scraping the bottom.
4. Done when rice is very soft and the mixture has thickened to a pourable but creamy consistency.
5. Remove from heat. Stir in sugar and vanilla. Add raisins if using.
6. For warm serving: ladle into bowls and dust with cinnamon.
7. For cold serving: press plastic wrap directly onto the surface and refrigerate at least 3 hours.

Field Note: The pudding thickens substantially as it cools, slightly thin when hot is correct. Refrigerated pudding that seems too thick the next day can be loosened with a splash of cold milk.

OATMEAL CAKE WITH BROILED COCONUT TOPPING

"Oats soaked in boiling water, baked into a spice cake, topped with brown sugar coconut and run under a broiler."

Serves: 12-15   Time: 60 min

History & Context

Oats soaked in boiling water produce an unusually moist crumb that stays soft for days longer than a flour-only cake. The broiled topping, butter, brown sugar, evaporated milk, coconut, pecans, spread over the warm cake and run under a broiler until it caramelizes in dark patches. The contrast between the chewy oat cake and the intensely sweet caramelized topping is the entire composition.

Ingredients

- Cake: 1.5 cups (360 ml) boiling water, 1 cup (240 ml) quick oats, 1/2 cup (120 ml) butter softened, 1 cup (240 ml) granulated sugar, 1 cup (240 ml) brown sugar, 2 eggs, 1.5 cups (360 ml) flour, 1 tsp (5 ml) baking soda, 1 tsp (5 ml) cinnamon, 1/2 tsp (3 ml) nutmeg, 1/4 tsp (1 ml) salt
- Frosting: 1/4 cup (60 ml) butter, 1/2 cup (120 ml) brown sugar, 1/4 cup (60 ml) evaporated milk or cream, 1 cup (240 ml) shredded coconut, 1/2 cup (120 ml) chopped nuts, 1 tsp (5 ml) vanilla

Method

1. Pour boiling water over oats in a bowl. Let stand 20 minutes until cooled to room temperature.
2. Preheat oven to 350°F (175°C). Grease a 9x13 inch (23x33 cm) pan.
3. Cream butter with both sugars until fluffy, 3 minutes. Beat in eggs one at a time.
4. Whisk flour, baking soda, cinnamon, nutmeg, and salt together. Add to butter mixture alternating with soaked oats. Stir just until combined.
5. Pour into pan. Bake 35-40 minutes until a toothpick comes out clean.
6. Make frosting while cake is still warm: melt butter, add brown sugar and evaporated milk. Bring to a boil, stirring. Remove from heat. Stir in coconut, nuts, and vanilla.
7. Spread warm frosting over warm cake.
8. Place under broiler 4-6 inches (10 to 15 cm) from heat for 2-4 minutes until frosting caramelizes in dark patches.
9. Watch continuously. Pull immediately when dark-patched and caramelized.

CHOCOLATE COBBLER

"You pour boiling water over dry cocoa and raw batter without stirring. Then you walk away. What comes out of the oven is in two layers."

Serves: 8   Time: 55 min

History & Context

A thin chocolate batter in a buttered dish, dry cocoa and brown sugar scattered over it without stirring, boiling water poured over the entire assembly without stirring, then baked for 45 minutes. What emerges has separated into two layers: risen cake above, thick fudge sauce below. The chemistry is legitimate. It looks like magic every time.

Ingredients

- Batter: 1 cup (240 ml) flour, 3/4 cup (180 ml) granulated sugar, 2 tbsp (30 ml) cocoa, 2 tsp (10 ml) baking powder, 1/4 tsp (1 ml) salt, 1/2 cup (120 ml) whole milk, 1/3 cup (80 ml) butter melted, 1 tsp (5 ml) vanilla
- Topping: 1 cup (240 ml) packed brown sugar, 1/4 cup (60 ml) cocoa, 1.75 cups (420 ml) boiling water

Method

1. Preheat oven to 350°F (175°C). Melt butter directly in a 9-inch (23 cm) square baking dish in the oven.
2. Whisk flour, granulated sugar, 2 tbsp (30 ml) cocoa, baking powder, and salt.
3. Add milk and vanilla. Stir into a thick batter.
4. Spread batter evenly over the melted butter. Do not stir butter into batter.
5. Mix brown sugar and 1/4 cup (60 ml) cocoa. Scatter evenly over raw batter. Do not stir.
6. Pour boiling water slowly over the entire surface. Do not stir.
7. Bake immediately 40-45 minutes until the top looks set.
8. Serve warm, scooping through both layers.

Field Note: The boiling water must be genuinely boiling, not hot tap water. The temperature differential between boiling water and batter is part of the mechanism. Pouring warm water produces a muddy result without the clean layer separation.

APPLESAUCE CAKE

"A full cup of applesauce replaces most of the fat and eggs. Stays moist for five days."

Serves: 12   Time: 55 min

History & Context

Unsweetened applesauce provides moisture, structure, and pectin that extends shelf life, an applesauce cake stays moist for five days versus two or three for a conventional butter cake. During wartime and Depression-era baking, fruit purees stretched expensive fat and egg rations. A jar of applesauce is cheap. The whole cake costs under a dollar.

Ingredients

- 1.5 cups (360 ml) flour, 1 tsp (5 ml) baking soda, 1/2 tsp (3 ml) cinnamon, 1/4 tsp (1 ml) cloves, 1/4 tsp (1 ml) nutmeg, 1/4 tsp (1 ml) salt
- 1/2 cup (120 ml) butter softened, 1 cup (240 ml) sugar, 1 egg, 1 cup (240 ml) unsweetened applesauce
- Optional: 1/2 cup (120 ml) raisins, 1/2 cup (120 ml) walnuts

Method

1. Preheat oven to 350°F (175°C). Grease and flour a 9x13 pan.
2. Whisk together flour, baking soda, cinnamon, cloves, nutmeg, and salt.
3. Cream butter and sugar until pale and fluffy, 3 minutes. Beat in egg.
4. Add flour mixture in three additions alternating with applesauce in two. Stir only until just combined after each.
5. Fold in raisins and walnuts if using.
6. Pour into pan. Bake 35-40 minutes until toothpick comes out clean.
7. Cool completely before frosting or cutting.

Field Note: *Unsweetened applesauce only, sweetened makes the cake cloying. Flavor and moistness improve after 24 hours as the spices meld.*

PRUNE CAKE WITH BUTTERMILK GLAZE

"Nobody admits it contains prunes until after the second piece. The standard practice is to call it spice cake."

Serves: 12   Time: 60 min

History & Context

Prunes simmered and mashed into a spiced cake batter. The natural sugars in the prune caramelize during baking, giving the crumb a dark toffee-like depth. A hot buttermilk glaze poured over the cake the moment it comes from the oven soaks in completely and makes the surface slightly glossy. The finished cake keeps for nearly a week without drying. The protocol when serving is to answer the question 'what kind of cake is this?' with 'spice cake,' which is accurate.

Ingredients

- 1 cup (240 ml) pitted prunes, simmered in 1 cup (240 ml) water 10 min, drained and mashed
- 1.5 cups (360 ml) flour, 1 tsp (5 ml) baking soda, 1 tsp (5 ml) cinnamon, 1/2 tsp (3 ml) nutmeg, 1/2 tsp (3 ml) allspice, 1/4 tsp (1 ml) salt
- 1/2 cup (120 ml) oil, 1 cup (240 ml) sugar, 2 eggs, 1 tsp (5 ml) vanilla, 1/2 cup (120 ml) buttermilk
- Glaze: 1/2 cup (120 ml) buttermilk, 1/2 cup (120 ml) sugar, 1/4 cup (60 ml) butter, 1/2 tsp (3 ml) baking soda, 1 tsp (5 ml) vanilla

Method

1. Preheat oven to 350°F (175°C). Grease a 9x13 pan.
2. Simmer prunes in water 10 minutes. Drain and mash. Cool.
3. Whisk flour, baking soda, cinnamon, nutmeg, allspice, and salt.
4. Beat oil and sugar. Beat in eggs one at a time, then vanilla.
5. Add flour in three additions alternating with buttermilk. Fold in mashed prunes.
6. Pour into pan. Bake 35-40 minutes until toothpick comes out clean.
7. Make glaze: combine buttermilk, sugar, butter, and baking soda in a saucepan. It will foam. Cook over medium heat, stirring, until foam subsides and glaze turns light golden, about 5 minutes. Stir in vanilla.
8. The moment the cake comes out of the oven: poke holes all over the surface with a skewer. Pour hot glaze slowly over hot cake. It absorbs completely.
9. Cool in the pan before cutting.

DREAM BARS

"Brown sugar shortbread below, coconut caramel above. Community cookbooks from every state between 1965 and 1985 contain some version of this."

Serves: 24 bars   Time: 50 min

History & Context

A crisp brown sugar shortbread base, barely set in the oven, then covered with eggs, brown sugar, coconut, vanilla, and nuts that bake on top into a deeply caramelized yielding layer. Two components that contrast absolutely. The contrast between the firm buttery base and the sweet caramelized topping is the entire dessert.

Ingredients

- Base: 1 cup (240 ml) flour, 1/3 cup (80 ml) packed brown sugar, 1/2 cup (120 ml) cold butter cut in pieces
- Topping: 2 eggs beaten, 1 cup (240 ml) brown sugar, 1 tsp (5 ml) vanilla, 2 tbsp (30 ml) flour, 1 tsp (5 ml) baking powder, 1/4 tsp (1 ml) salt, 1.5 cups (360 ml) shredded coconut, 1 cup (240 ml) chopped nuts

Method

1. Preheat oven to 350°F (175°C). Grease a 9x13 pan.
2. Make base: combine 1 cup (240 ml) flour and 1/3 cup (80 ml) brown sugar. Cut in cold butter until mixture resembles coarse crumbs.
3. Press firmly and evenly into the pan bottom.
4. Bake base alone 12-15 minutes until just barely set, pale and slightly underdone.
5. Make topping: beat eggs with brown sugar. Add vanilla, flour, baking powder, and salt. Stir in coconut and nuts.
6. Pour evenly over warm base.
7. Return to oven 20-25 minutes until topping is golden-brown and a toothpick comes out with moist crumbs.
8. Cool completely, at least 1 hour. Cut into small bars.

Field Note: Cutting before completely cooled produces ragged edges and a filling that has not set. The hour of cooling is not optional. Use a sharp knife and clean it between cuts.

LARD AND VINEGAR PIE CRUST

"Lard for flake, vinegar to prevent toughness, one egg to bind. The pie crust that works."

Serves: 2 crusts   Time: 15 min + 30 min chilling

History & Context

Lard produces a flakier crust than butter because of its fat crystal structure, and it costs less. The vinegar inhibits gluten development, which is what makes crust tough when overworked. The egg binds the dough and adds richness. These three things together produce a crust that is more forgiving to make and better to eat than one made with butter or shortening alone.

Ingredients

- 3 cups (720 ml) all-purpose flour
- 1 tsp (5 ml) salt
- 1 1/4 cups (300 ml) cold lard or vegetable shortening
- 1 egg, beaten
- 1 tbsp (15 ml) distilled white vinegar
- 4 tbsp (60 ml) cold water

Method

1. Combine flour and salt in a large bowl.
2. Cut cold lard into the flour using a pastry cutter, two knives, or fingertips until the mixture resembles coarse crumbs with pea-sized pieces of fat. Work quickly, warm fat makes a mealy crust.
3. In a small bowl, whisk together beaten egg, vinegar, and cold water.
4. Pour liquid over flour mixture a little at a time, stirring with a fork. Add only enough that the dough just holds together when pressed, rough and shaggy, not smooth.
5. Divide in two. Press each half into a flat disc. Wrap and refrigerate at least 30 minutes.
6. Roll each disc on a lightly floured surface to about 12 inches (30 cm) across for a 9-inch (23 cm) pie pan.
7. For a pre-baked shell: prick bottom all over with a fork, line with foil, fill with dried beans, bake at 425°F (220°C) for 12 minutes. Remove weights and bake 3-5 minutes more until pale gold.

Field Note: The single most common mistake is adding too much water. Add it

WATER PIE

"No eggs. No milk. No fruit. Water is the main ingredient. It sets into something that tastes like mild custard."

Serves: 6-8   Time: 70 min + chilling

History & Context

Flour, sugar, butter, vanilla, and water in an unbaked pie shell. That is the complete ingredient list. The chemistry works: flour and sugar dissolve into the water during baking, butter melts through the filling, and the whole thing sets into a soft translucent custard as it cools. It does not taste like water. It tastes like a mild sugar cookie filling, sweet, buttery, faintly vanilla. The pie looks completely liquid when it comes out of the oven. This is correct. It sets in the refrigerator, not in the oven.

Ingredients

- 1 unbaked deep-dish pie crust (see 8-13, or store-bought)
- 1 1/2 cups (360 ml) water, room temperature
- 3 tbsp (45 ml) all-purpose flour
- 1 cup (240 ml) granulated sugar
- 1/4 tsp (1 ml) salt
- 2 tsp (10 ml) vanilla extract
- 5 tbsp (75 ml) unsalted butter, cut into 5 equal pats

Method

1. Preheat oven to 400°F (205°C). Place the unbaked pie shell in its pan on a baking sheet, the filling will slosh when moved.
2. Pour the water directly into the unbaked crust.
3. Stir together flour, sugar, and salt in a small bowl. Sprinkle evenly over the water. Do not stir.
4. Drizzle vanilla evenly over the surface. Do not stir.
5. Place the 5 pats of butter evenly spaced across the top.
6. Bake at 400°F (205°C) for 30 minutes.
7. Reduce to 375°F (190°C). Cover crust edges with foil if browning too fast. Bake another 30 minutes.
8. Remove from oven. The pie will look completely liquid in the center. This is correct.
9. Cool completely at room temperature, at least 1 hour. Cover and refrigerate at least 3 hours before cutting.

VINEGAR PIE

"Apple cider vinegar replaces the lemon that wasn't available. The palate registers it as tart custard."

Serves: 6-8   Time: 55 min

History & Context

A custard pie made with apple cider vinegar instead of lemon juice. The acid provides the sharp tart note that lemon would normally supply, and cider vinegar's mellower profile produces a convincing substitute. This technique, substituting a cheap available acid for an expensive unavailable one, is fundamental to Depression-era and survival cooking.

Ingredients

- 1 unbaked 9-inch (23 cm) pie crust (see 8-13)
- 3 eggs
- 1 cup (240 ml) sugar
- 1/4 cup (60 ml) apple cider vinegar, not white distilled vinegar
- 2 tbsp (30 ml) melted butter
- 1/4 tsp (1 ml) nutmeg
- 1/4 tsp (1 ml) cinnamon

Method

1. Blind-bake crust: press into a 9-inch (23 cm) pie pan. Bake 10 minutes at 375°F (190°C).
2. Whisk eggs and sugar until pale and smooth, at least 2 minutes. Sugar must be fully dissolved.
3. Add melted butter, vinegar, nutmeg, and cinnamon. Whisk until combined.
4. Pour into the par-baked crust.
5. Bake at 325°F (165°C) for 35-40 minutes until the center is set but barely jiggles.
6. Cool completely before cutting, texture improves significantly after an hour.

Field Note: Apple cider vinegar specifically, not white distilled vinegar. Cider vinegar's fruitier acidity creates a convincing lemon-adjacent flavor. White vinegar at the same concentration reads as harsh.

DUTCH OVEN PEACH COBBLER

"Dried peaches rehydrated and baked under a rough biscuit crust in a Dutch oven. No oven required."

Serves: 8-10   Time: 50 min

History & Context

Dried peaches rehydrated in water until pliable, sweetened with brown sugar and warm spices, baked under a rough lard-and-flour crust in a Dutch oven over coals. This works with any dried fruit and requires no oven, just a Dutch oven and a fire. Dried fruit stores for years and costs very little per serving.

Ingredients

- 2 cups (480 ml) dried peaches or dried apples
- 1 cup (240 ml) water for soaking
- 1/2 cup (120 ml) brown sugar
- 2 tbsp (30 ml) whiskey or apple cider vinegar
- 1/2 tsp (3 ml) cinnamon, 1/4 tsp (1 ml) nutmeg
- Crust: 2 cups (480 ml) flour, 1 tbsp (15 ml) baking powder, 1/2 tsp (3 ml) salt, 1/3 cup (80 ml) lard, 3/4 cup (180 ml) water

Method

1. Soak dried fruit in 1 cup (240 ml) water at least 2 hours until pliable.
2. Drain fruit, reserve soaking liquid. Combine fruit with brown sugar, whiskey or vinegar, cinnamon, nutmeg, and 1/4 cup (60 ml) soaking liquid.
3. Make crust: combine flour, baking powder, and salt. Cut in lard until crumbly. Add water until dough just comes together.
4. Grease Dutch oven. Press 2/3 of dough into bottom and up the sides.
5. Pour fruit filling over dough. Flatten remaining dough into rough pieces over the top.
6. Dutch oven method: lid on. Set on 8 coals, place 12-14 coals on lid. Bake 35-45 minutes, rotating every 10 minutes.
7. Oven method: 375°F (190°C) for 35-40 minutes.

Field Note: Dried fruit is one of the most practical long-term storage foods, light, years of shelf life, and it rehydrates into something far better than it appears dry. A 1-lb (455 g) bag of dried peaches represents multiple cobblers and costs very little.

WACKY CAKE, NO EGGS, NO BUTTER, NO MILK

"Mix it in the pan. No eggs, no butter, no milk. It works because the vinegar and baking soda replace all three."

Serves: 8-10   Time: 40 min

History & Context

Developed during the Depression when government food programs provided flour, sugar, cocoa, and oil but not eggs or dairy. The chemical reaction between vinegar and baking soda provides the leavening that eggs would normally supply. The oil provides fat and moisture that butter would supply. This recipe has been made for ninety years because it reliably produces something worth eating from shelf-stable ingredients.

Ingredients

- 1.5 cups (360 ml) flour
- 1 cup (240 ml) sugar
- 1/4 cup (60 ml) cocoa powder
- 1 tsp (5 ml) baking soda
- 1/2 tsp (3 ml) salt
- 1 tsp (5 ml) vanilla
- 1 tbsp (15 ml) apple cider vinegar
- 5 tbsp (75 ml) vegetable oil or melted lard
- 1 cup (240 ml) cold water

Method

1. Preheat oven to 350°F (175°C). Do not grease the pan, you mix the batter directly in it.
2. Combine flour, sugar, cocoa, baking soda, and salt directly in an 8x8 inch (20x20 cm) baking pan.
3. Make three wells in the dry ingredients.
4. Pour vanilla in the first well, vinegar in the second, oil in the third.
5. Pour cold water over everything at once.
6. Stir quickly with a fork until just combined and no dry flour remains.
7. Bake 30-35 minutes until a toothpick comes out clean.
8. Cool in the pan. Better the next day.

MOCK APPLE PIE, RITZ CRACKER PIE

"Ritz crackers in a lemon-acid syrup, baked in pastry. The tartaric acid mimics malic acid at a level the palate registers as fruit."

Serves: 6-8   Time: 50 min

History & Context

Ritz crackers soaked in a syrup of water, sugar, and cream of tartar, baked in pastry. The tartaric acid in cream of tartar mimics the malic acid in apples at a chemical level that the palate genuinely registers as fruit. This is documented food chemistry. Nabisco printed the recipe on cracker boxes during the Depression specifically to help sell crackers to families who could not afford apples.

Ingredients

- 1 unbaked 9-inch (23 cm) pie crust (see 8-13)
- Filling: 1.5 cups (360 ml) water, 1.5 cups (360 ml) sugar, 2 tsp (10 ml) cream of tartar, 2 tbsp (30 ml) lemon juice or apple cider vinegar
- 1 sleeve Ritz crackers, broken into rough halves
- 2 tbsp (30 ml) butter, 1 tsp (5 ml) cinnamon, pinch of nutmeg

Method

1. Preheat oven to 425°F (220°C).
2. Make syrup: combine water, sugar, and cream of tartar. Bring to a boil until sugar dissolves. Boil 1 minute. Remove from heat. Add lemon juice.
3. Line a 9-inch (23 cm) pie pan with crust. Break crackers into rough halves and layer in the shell.
4. Pour hot syrup over crackers. Dot with butter pieces. Sprinkle cinnamon and nutmeg.
5. Roll out remaining dough for the top crust, cover and crimp edges. Cut steam vents.
6. Bake at 425°F (220°C) for 30-35 minutes until crust is golden.
7. Cool completely before cutting.

Field Note: *The cream of tartar is the functional ingredient, its tartaric acid mimics apple's malic acid. Without it this is sweet crackers in pastry. With it, it is convincing.*

BREAD PUDDING WITH WHISKEY SAUCE

"Stale bread soaked in custard and baked until puffed and golden. The sauce is made from butter, sugar, and one egg yolk."

Serves: 8-10   Time: 55 min

History & Context

Stale bread converted to dessert. Soaked in a custard of milk, eggs, and sugar, baked until puffed and golden, served with a sauce made from butter, powdered sugar, a single egg yolk, and whiskey or vanilla. The egg yolk sauce technique, the residual heat of the just-made sauce cooks the yolk safely without scrambling it, produces something glossy and rich.

Ingredients

- Pudding: 6-8 slices stale bread torn into pieces, 2 cups (480 ml) whole milk, 3 eggs beaten, 3/4 cup (180 ml) sugar, 1 tsp (5 ml) vanilla, 1/2 tsp (3 ml) cinnamon, 2 tbsp (30 ml) melted butter
- Sauce: 4 tbsp (60 ml) butter, 1 cup (240 ml) powdered sugar, 1 egg yolk, 3 tbsp (45 ml) whiskey (or 2 tbsp (30 ml) vanilla + 1 tbsp (15 ml) apple juice)

Method

1. Preheat oven to 350°F (175°C). Butter a baking pan.
2. Combine milk, beaten eggs, sugar, vanilla, and cinnamon. Pour over torn bread. Soak 15-20 minutes, pressing bread down.
3. Pour into prepared pan. Drizzle melted butter over top.
4. Bake 35-45 minutes until puffed, golden, and a knife comes out clean.
5. Make sauce: melt butter in a small saucepan. Add powdered sugar, stir until combined. Remove from heat, cool slightly. Whisk in egg yolk, then add whiskey.
6. Serve pudding warm with sauce poured over.

Field Note: Bread pudding works with any stale bread: white, wheat, cornbread, biscuits, or stale cake. The ratio is approximately 1 cup (240 ml) of custard liquid per 4 slices of bread.

APPALACHIAN STACK CAKE

"Thin layers of spiced gingerbread dough with dried apple filling between each. Assembled tall and rested overnight. Cuts cleanly after 24 hours."

Serves: 10-12   Time: 2 hours + overnight rest

History & Context

Thin rounds of spiced gingerbread-like dough with reconstituted dried apple filling between each layer, assembled and left to rest overnight. The moisture from the apple filling migrates into the cake layers as they rest, binding the entire structure. This cake cannot be cut immediately after assembly, it requires the overnight rest to become cohesive. After 24 hours it slices cleanly and tastes completely different from what it is when first assembled.

Ingredients

- Layers (6-8): 3 cups (720 ml) flour, 1 cup (240 ml) sugar, 1/2 cup (120 ml) lard, 2 eggs, 1/2 cup (120 ml) buttermilk, 1 tsp (5 ml) baking soda, 1 tsp (5 ml) ginger, 1/2 tsp (3 ml) cinnamon
- Filling: 1.5 cups (360 ml) dried apples, 1/2 cup (120 ml) water, 3 tbsp (45 ml) sorghum or brown sugar, 1 tsp (5 ml) cinnamon, 1/4 tsp (1 ml) allspice

Method

1. Make filling first: soak dried apples in water 1-2 hours. Cook with sorghum and spices over medium-low heat, stirring and mashing until a thick smooth paste forms. Cool completely.
2. Cake dough: cream lard and sugar. Beat in eggs. Add buttermilk. Add flour, baking soda, ginger, and cinnamon. Mix until soft dough forms.
3. Divide into 6-8 equal portions. Roll each thin, about 8 inches (20 cm) across, 1/4-inch (0.5 cm) thick.
4. Bake each layer on a greased cast iron skillet or 350°F (175°C) oven 8-10 minutes until just cooked through.
5. Cool layers completely.
6. Assembly: place first layer on a plate. Spread generous apple filling. Top with next layer. Repeat.
7. Wrap assembled cake in a clean cloth. Rest overnight at room temperature.
8. Slice after 24 hours minimum.

Field Note: *A stack cake cut immediately after assembly falls apart. One cut after*

24 hours slices cleanly. The overnight rest is the step that transforms individual components into a cohesive cake.

TOMATO SOUP CAKE

"A can of condensed tomato soup. Nobody tastes the tomato. The result is an unusually moist spice cake that keeps for five days."

Serves: 8-10   Time: 50 min

History & Context

Condensed tomato soup in a spiced cake batter alongside eggs and butter. The tomato does not replace them, it supplements them, contributing liquid, acidity that activates the baking soda for leavening, and natural sugars that help the cake stay moist for days longer than a standard spice cake. The flavor disappears entirely behind cinnamon, nutmeg, and cloves. This is not a Depression-era substitution recipe where the soup stands in for missing ingredients, it is a recipe where the soup is a genuine ingredient that produces a result better than the conventional version. The tomato flavor is genuinely undetectable.

Ingredients

- 1 can (10.75 oz, 305 g) condensed tomato soup, undiluted
- 1 tsp (5 ml) baking soda
- 1/2 cup (120 ml) butter or lard, softened
- 1 cup (240 ml) granulated sugar
- 2 eggs
- 2 cups (480 ml) all-purpose flour
- 1 tsp (5 ml) cinnamon, 1/2 tsp (3 ml) nutmeg, 1/4 tsp (1 ml) cloves, 1/4 tsp (1 ml) salt
- Optional: 1/2 cup (120 ml) raisins or walnuts

Method

1. Preheat oven to 350°F (175°C). Grease and flour a 9x13 pan.
2. Stir baking soda directly into the can of tomato soup. It will foam immediately, stir through the foam.
3. Cream butter and sugar until pale and fluffy, 3 minutes.
4. Beat in eggs one at a time.
5. Whisk flour, cinnamon, nutmeg, cloves, and salt.
6. Add flour mixture to butter mixture in three additions, alternating with tomato soup in two. Begin and end with flour. Stir only until just combined.
7. Fold in raisins or walnuts if using.
8. Bake 35-40 minutes until a toothpick comes out clean.

9. Cool completely before cutting.

Field Note: Do not tell people there is tomato soup in it until after they have eaten a piece. The tomato flavor is genuinely undetectable. This cake keeps well for 4-5 days tightly covered.

SWEET POTATO PIE

"Baked sweet potatoes blended smooth with citrus, two sugars, condensed milk, and butter. Makes two pies from one batch."

Serves: two 9-inch pies (16 slices)   Time: 2.5 hours + overnight chilling

History & Context

Sweet potato pie is the Southern alternative to pumpkin pie, and by most honest accounts, the better one. Sweet potatoes are cheaper per pound than almost any other vegetable, store for months in a cool dry location, grow in poor soil, and deliver more vitamin A, potassium, and fiber than white potatoes. The pie itself is straightforward custard chemistry: roasted sweet potato provides the base, eggs set it, fat enriches it, sugar sweetens it, and citrus lifts the whole thing. The overnight chill is not optional, the filling needs the full rest to set cleanly and develop its full flavor.

Ingredients

- 4 large orange-flesh sweet potatoes (about 4 lbs (1.8 kg) total)
- Juice of 1 lemon
- Juice of 1 orange
- 1/2 cup (120 ml) Carnation evaporated milk (or any canned evaporated milk)
- 2 tbsp (30 ml) sweetened condensed milk
- 1 tsp (5 ml) vanilla bean paste, or 2 tsp (10 ml) pure vanilla extract
- 1 1/4 cups (300 ml) white granulated sugar
- 1 1/4 cups (300 ml) packed brown sugar
- 1 tsp (5 ml) ground cinnamon
- Dash of nutmeg
- 1 stick (1/2 cup, 120 ml) unsalted butter, melted and cooled slightly
- 2 large eggs
- 2 unbaked 9-inch (23 cm) pie crusts (see 8-13, or store-bought)

Method

1. Preheat oven to 400°F (205°C). Scrub sweet potatoes thoroughly. Poke each one all over with a fork, at least 8-10 holes per potato.
2. Place potatoes directly on the oven rack or on a foil-lined baking sheet. Bake at 400°F (205°C) for 60 minutes until completely soft, a knife should meet zero resistance through the thickest part.

3. Remove from oven and allow to cool until comfortable to handle, about 30 minutes. Reduce oven temperature to 350°F (175°C).

4. Peel off and discard the skins. Place the sweet potato flesh in a blender or food processor.

5. Blend or process until completely smooth with no strings or lumps. This step is important, a smooth puree produces a silky custard. A chunky one produces an uneven pie.

6. Add lemon juice, orange juice, evaporated milk, condensed milk, vanilla, white sugar, brown sugar, cinnamon, and nutmeg. Blend until fully combined.

7. Add melted butter. Blend again until smooth and uniform.

8. TASTE TEST NOW before adding eggs. Adjust sugar, cinnamon, or vanilla to your preference. This is your only opportunity to taste and correct.

9. Add eggs. Blend or mix until just combined, do not overbeat once eggs are in.

10. Divide filling evenly between the two unbaked pie crusts. Fill to about 1/2 inch (1.5 cm) from the top.

11. Bake at 350°F (175°C) for 45-50 minutes. The edges should be set and the center should have only a slight jiggle when the pan is gently shaken, like set gelatin, not liquid.

12. Remove from oven. Cool completely at room temperature, at least 1 hour.

13. Cover loosely and refrigerate overnight before slicing. The filling sets fully during the overnight chill and the flavor deepens significantly.

Field Note: The taste test before eggs is the most important step, once the eggs are in and the pie is baked, nothing can be adjusted. The citrus juice (both lemon and orange) is not just flavor, the acid brightens the sweetness and prevents the filling from reading as flat or one-dimensional. Do not skip it. Sweet potato pie improves on the second day.

POTATO CANDY

"Mashed potato completely disappears into powdered sugar. Nobody tastes potato. What remains is fudge-like candy that costs almost nothing."

Serves: 24-30 pieces   Time: 30 min + chilling

History & Context

A small amount of cold mashed potato mixed with powdered sugar produces a pliable, fudge-like dough with no detectable potato flavor whatsoever. The potato provides only moisture and starch, the sugar overwhelms everything else. Rolled thin, spread with peanut butter, rolled up like a jelly roll, chilled, and sliced, it looks and tastes like an expensive confection. This was Depression-era candy made from whatever was cheapest that week. Peanut butter provides protein and fat. The whole batch costs under a dollar. If you only have granulated sugar, blend or process it for 30 seconds, it becomes powdered sugar that works perfectly here.

Ingredients

- 1/3 cup (80 ml) cold mashed potatoes, plain, no butter, no salt, no milk added
- 3 to 3.5 cups (720 to 840 ml) powdered sugar (or granulated sugar processed 30 seconds in a blender)
- 1/2 cup (120 ml) creamy peanut butter
- 1/4 tsp (1 ml) vanilla extract
- Pinch of salt

Method

1. Use plain cold mashed potato with nothing added, no butter, no salt, no milk. Leftover plain boiled potato mashed smooth works perfectly.
2. Place cold mashed potato in a bowl. Add vanilla and pinch of salt.
3. Add powdered sugar one cup at a time, mixing after each addition. The mixture will look soupy at first, then suddenly come together into a firm pliable dough. Stop adding sugar when it no longer sticks to your hands.
4. Lightly dust a clean surface with powdered sugar. Roll the dough into a rectangle about 1/4-inch (0.5 cm) thick, roughly 8x10 inches (20x25 cm).
5. Spread peanut butter evenly across the entire surface, leaving a 1/2-inch (1.5 cm) border on one long edge.
6. Starting from the long edge with peanut butter closest to it, roll the dough tightly into a log, like a jelly roll.
7. Wrap tightly in wax paper or plastic wrap. Refrigerate at least 1 hour until firm.

8. Slice 1/2-inch (1.5 cm) thick with a sharp knife. Pieces will look like pinwheel candies.

IMPOSSIBLE PIE

"Everything goes in the blender. Pour it in a pie plate. It makes its own crust. This is not an exaggeration."

Serves: 6-8   Time: 65 min

History & Context

A custard pie that requires no crust-making, no rolling, no chilling dough, and no special technique. All ingredients go into a blender, get poured into a greased pie plate, and bake for an hour. During baking, the coconut floats to the top and forms a lightly toasted crust on its own. The flour settles and forms a thin bottom layer. The middle sets into a smooth, creamy custard. This recipe circulated widely in the 1970s, often printed on Bisquick boxes, and became a staple in households where baking felt intimidating. It is genuinely one of the easiest desserts that exists, and the result tastes far more impressive than the effort justifies. Sweetened shredded coconut is shelf-stable for months. Powdered milk reconstituted to normal strength works perfectly in place of fresh milk.

Ingredients

- 4 eggs
- 3/4 cup (180 ml) granulated sugar
- 1/2 cup (120 ml) all-purpose flour
- 1/4 cup (60 ml) butter (half a stick), cut into pieces, room temperature if possible
- 1 cup (240 ml) sweetened shredded coconut
- 2 cups (480 ml) whole milk or reconstituted powdered milk
- 1 tsp (5 ml) vanilla extract
- Dash of nutmeg

Method

1. Preheat oven to 350°F (175°C). Grease a deep-dish 9-inch (23 cm) pie plate generously with butter or lard.
2. Add all ingredients to a blender in this order: milk first, then eggs, sugar, flour, butter pieces, coconut, vanilla, and nutmeg.
3. Blend on medium speed for 2 full minutes. The batter will be thin and very liquid, this is correct.
4. Pour carefully into the greased pie plate. The batter will be nearly full to the rim, transfer to the oven rack slowly.

5. Bake at 350°F (175°C) for 45-60 minutes. Start checking at 45 minutes. Done when the top is golden brown, the edges are set, and the center has only a slight jiggle.

6. Convection or fan-bake ovens run hotter, check at 40 minutes.

7. Remove from oven. Cool completely before slicing, at least 1 hour. The custard continues to set as it cools.

8. Slice and serve at room temperature or slightly warm.

> ***Field Note:*** *The pie forms three distinct layers on its own: a thin flour layer on the bottom, a creamy custard middle, and a toasted coconut crust on top. Do not skip the 2-minute blend, it is what distributes the ingredients so the layers form correctly. If you do not have a blender, whisk everything vigorously by hand for 3-4 minutes. Sweetened shredded coconut keeps for months in a sealed bag and is worth stocking. Powdered whole milk reconstituted to normal strength (follow package directions) substitutes directly for fresh milk and produces an indistinguishable result.*

PRESERVATION & EMERGENCY RATIONS

Preservation techniques, emergency rations, two ways to grow fresh food from almost nothing, emergency food for your pets, and garlic confit

Every technique in this chapter is aimed at the same problem: extending the window between food and spoilage without refrigeration or electricity. The methods are old. They require nothing beyond what most kitchens already contain. They require time, attention, and the willingness to do work now that protects future meals. The Cold War survival crackers and the 2400-calorie emergency bars are purpose-built for conditions where cooking is not possible. They are not pleasant eating. They are designed to keep a person functional when nothing else can. Recipes 8-10 through 8-12 are production systems rather than preservation techniques. Bean sprouts grow fresh living food from dried beans already in your pantry in four days with no equipment beyond a jar and water. Oyster mushrooms grow from cardboard and coffee grounds in a basement or shed with no sunlight. Both provide nutrition that long-term stored food cannot: fresh vitamins, protein, and the psychological reality of eating something that is not from a can. The sprouts require nothing you do not already have. The mushrooms require spawn purchased and stored now, before it is needed. Plan accordingly. Recipe 8-13 is for your dogs and cats. Every preparedness book ever written was written for people. A prepared household accounts for every member of it. The final entry is Recipe 8-14: Garlic Confit. Garlic slow-cooked in oil until golden and soft, kept submerged in its infused oil for weeks in the refrigerator. The garlic is used throughout this book. The oil is as valuable as the garlic. It is also the base for Recipe 6-15, the garlic aioli in Chapter VI.

◆ ◆ ◆

POTATO STARTER, YOUR PERMANENT BAKING YEAST

"One boiled potato starts a living yeast culture that replaces every packet you will ever need to buy. Make it once. Keep it forever."

Serves: ongoing

Time: 5 days to establish, 10 min/week to maintain

History & Context

Commercial yeast in foil packets is a convenience product that has existed for less than 150 years. Before that, every household that baked bread maintained a living yeast culture, fed, kept warm, passed down through families for generations. The potato starter is the most reliable version of this. Boiled potato water is rich in sugars, potassium, phosphorus, and B vitamins, one of the most ideal natural environments for wild yeast to colonize and thrive. You will probably keep buying yeast packets out of habit. That is fine. But when the store shelf is empty, and supply chain disruptions have already proven that day can come without warning, this is what keeps you baking. It costs one potato to start. It costs a cup of water a week to maintain. Dehydrate a backup portion and store it in a sealed jar and you have baking yeast that will outlast any emergency.

Ingredients

- 1 medium russet or Yukon Gold potato
- 2 cups (480 ml) water, tap water left out overnight (so chlorine dissipates) or filtered water
- A clean glass jar, quart size or larger
- Cheesecloth, coffee filter, or a loose lid for covering

Method

1. Peel and chop the potato into rough chunks. Place in a small pot with 2 cups (480 ml) of water. No salt, no oil.
2. Boil until potato is completely soft, about 15-20 minutes.
3. Remove potato pieces. Reserve 2 tablespoons (30 ml) of cooked potato and mash smooth.
4. Let the starchy potato water cool to room temperature, it should feel just warm on your wrist, not hot.
5. Combine the cooled potato water and the mashed potato in your clean glass jar. Stir together.
6. Cover loosely, cheesecloth, a coffee filter, or a lid left slightly ajar. Wild yeast from the air needs to enter. Do not seal airtight.

7. Set in a warm location, 70 to 80°F (20 to 25°C). Top of the refrigerator, near the oven, a sunny counter.

8. Wait 24-72 hours. Bubbles will begin forming, small at first, then larger. This is wild yeast colonizing the starter.

9. Once bubbling actively: every 24 hours, discard half the starter and replace with fresh potato water (or plain unchlorinated water) plus a small spoonful of mashed potato. This feeds the colony.

10. By day 3-5 the starter will double in size within hours of feeding. It will smell slightly tangy and yeasty. It is ready to use.

11. TO USE: replace one packet of commercial yeast (2.25 tsp, 11 ml) with 1/4 cup (60 ml) of active starter. Bread will take 1-3 hours longer to rise than with commercial yeast, this is normal. See recipes 1-2, 1-10, and 1-17.

12. REFRIGERATOR STORAGE: once active, move to the refrigerator. Feed once per week. To bake, pull it out the night before, give it a feeding, let it warm up. It will be fully active in 8-12 hours.

13. DEHYDRATION BACKUP, do this now: spread a thin layer of active starter on parchment paper. Let dry completely at room temperature 24-48 hours. Break into flakes. Store in a sealed jar in a cool dark place. To revive: add warm potato water, feed twice. It wakes back up. Properly dehydrated starter keeps for years.

COLD WAR DOOMSDAY CRACKERS, BULGUR WHEAT

"Three ingredients. Thirty-seven cents per person per day. The United States government spent four million dollars and five years arriving at this."

Serves: about 18 crackers   Time: 75 min

History & Context

In 1958, the Eisenhower administration tasked the USDA with developing the ideal survival ration for post-nuclear America. Requirements: lightweight, no cooking required, shelf-stable for years, reproducible at mass scale, cheap enough to stockpile for fifty million people. Bulgur wheat, a parboiled cracked whole grain with twice the fiber of brown rice, was chosen. By 1964, over twenty billion crackers had been sealed in airtight tins and distributed to fallout shelters across the country. They were never used for their intended purpose. In the 1970s they were distributed in famine relief programs instead. The recipe is three ingredients.

Ingredients

- 2 cups (480 ml) bulgur wheat flour (grind bulgur wheat in a blender until fine, or buy bulgur flour directly)
- 2 tsp (10 ml) salt
- 1 cup (240 ml) water

Method

1. Preheat oven to 375°F (190°C).
2. Combine bulgur flour and salt. Stir to distribute evenly.
3. Add water gradually while mixing. Work into a dough, it will be sticky initially.
4. Knead until smooth and no longer sticky. Add small amounts of additional flour if needed.
5. Roll out to no more than 1/2-inch (1.5 cm) thick. Thicker than this will not bake through evenly.
6. Cut into 2-inch (5 cm) squares or rectangles.
7. Use a nail, straw, or skewer to punch a grid of 5 holes through each cracker.
8. Place on an ungreased baking sheet. Bake 30 minutes at 375°F (190°C).
9. Flip each cracker. Bake another 30 minutes.
10. Turn the oven off. Leave crackers in the cooling oven for at least one more hour.
11. Remove only when completely hard. No flex at all.

Field Note: The cooling-oven step removes residual moisture that active baking

2400-CALORIE EMERGENCY BARS

"One day of calories. No cooking required to eat them. Made in under an hour."

Serves: 4 bars (approx. 600 cal each)   Time: 45 min + cooling

History & Context

Emergency calorie ration bars, compact, dense, shelf-stable, requiring no preparation to consume, are the logical endpoint of survival food thinking. Commercial versions have been produced for military and maritime use since the 1970s. They are Coast Guard-approved survival rations carried on life rafts. Making them at home is straightforward and costs a fraction of commercial alternatives. The format: a hot syrup poured over dense dry ingredients, pressed into a pan, baked to set, cut into bars.

Ingredients

- 3 tbsp (45 ml) olive oil or any neutral cooking oil
- 2 cups (480 ml) maple syrup or sorghum syrup
- 4 tbsp (60 ml) honey
- 2 tbsp (30 ml) peanut butter
- 3 cups (720 ml) old-fashioned rolled oats
- 1 cup (240 ml) additional rolled oats (in place of frosted flakes, cheaper, better shelf life)
- 1 cup (240 ml) powdered whole milk (better shelf life and lower cost than protein powder)
- 1 cup (240 ml) almonds, peanuts, or any available nuts
- 1 cup (240 ml) raisins or any dried fruit

Method

1. Preheat oven to 375°F (190°C).
2. Combine oil, syrup, and honey in a small saucepan over medium heat. Stir frequently until simmering.
3. Add peanut butter. Stir until fully melted. Remove from heat. Caution: this syrup is extremely hot.
4. Combine all dry ingredients in a large bowl: oats, powdered milk, nuts, and dried fruit. Mix well.
5. Pour hot syrup mixture over dry ingredients immediately. Stir vigorously until every ingredient is coated and has a uniform sheen. Work quickly, the mixture sets as it cools.
6. Press firmly and evenly into a 2-inch (5 cm)-deep baking pan. Pack tightly.

7. Bake at 375°F (190°C) for 20 minutes until edges begin to brown.

8. Cool completely in the pan, at least 30 minutes. Do not cut while warm.

9. Cut into 4 equal bars.

LEATHER BRITCHES, DRIED GREEN BEANS

"Thread, a needle, and moving air. The simplest vegetable preservation method that exists."

Serves: 4-6   Time: 2-4 weeks drying + 3 hours cooking

History & Context

Green beans threaded whole on string and hung to dry in moving air for 2-4 weeks. No salt, no vinegar, no canning equipment, no refrigeration. The dried beans packed in cloth sacks keep through an entire winter. Cooked slowly with fatback and water, they reconstitute into something more intensely flavored than fresh beans. This requires nothing beyond needle, thread, and a place with good air circulation.

Ingredients

- 1 lb (455 g) fresh green beans (pole beans are traditional, flat pods work best)
- Heavy thread and a large needle
- Cooking: 1/4 lb (115 g) salt pork or fatback, water to cover, salt and pepper

Method

1. Thread a large needle with about 18 inches (46 cm) of heavy thread. Push the needle through the center of each bean pod, leaving a small space between each bean.
2. Hang the strung beans in a warm, dry, well-ventilated location. Good air circulation is required.
3. Dry 2-4 weeks until beans have shriveled dark brown and leathery and rattle when shaken.
4. To cook: break off a large handful. Rinse briefly.
5. Place in a heavy pot with salt pork or fatback. Cover with water by 2 inches (5 cm).
6. Bring to a boil, reduce to low simmer. Cook 2-3 hours until completely tender.
7. Season with salt and pepper. Serve with their cooking liquid.

Field Note: The concentrated flavor that develops during drying is not achievable by any other preservation method. This technique requires nothing except needle, thread, and time, among the simplest possible long-term vegetable preservation methods.

BRINE-PRESERVED VEGETABLES

"Apple cider vinegar, water, salt, and a jar. The acid environment prevents bacterial growth. This works on almost any firm vegetable."

Serves: 1 quart per batch   Time: 30 min + resting

History & Context

Vinegar brine preservation is among the oldest and most reliable food preservation methods. The acid environment of vinegar brine at sufficient concentration prevents virtually all pathogenic bacterial growth. Cucumbers, green beans, ramps, onions, peppers, okra, and green tomatoes all respond well. The critical variables: at least 5% acidity vinegar, enough salt, and complete submersion.

Ingredients

- Any firm vegetable: cucumbers, green beans, onions, peppers, green tomatoes, okra
- Per quart jar brine: 2 cups (480 ml) apple cider vinegar (5% acidity minimum)
- 1 cup (240 ml) water
- 1 tbsp (15 ml) pickling salt (not iodized table salt)
- Optional per jar: 1 garlic clove, 1 tsp (5 ml) dill seed, 1/2 tsp (3 ml) mustard seed, dried chili

Method

1. Wash and prepare vegetables. Remove blossom ends from cucumbers.
2. Pack vegetables tightly into sterilized quart jars. Add any desired spices.
3. Combine vinegar, water, and salt in a saucepan. Bring to a boil until salt dissolves.
4. Pour hot brine over packed vegetables, leaving 1/2-inch (1.5 cm) headspace. All vegetables must be fully submerged.
5. Seal jars.
6. Refrigerator pickles: seal and refrigerate immediately. Ready in 24-48 hours. Keeps 2-3 months.
7. Shelf-stable: process in a boiling water bath 10 minutes. Keeps 1 year in a cool dark location.

Field Note: The minimum acidity for safety is 5%, check the label on your vinegar. Most commercial vinegar is 5%. The salt inhibits unwanted microorganisms during the initial brining process. Complete submersion is mandatory, any vegetable sticking above the brine can harbor mold.

WATERMELON RIND PICKLES

"One watermelon fed a family in three rounds. The rind was the last thing eaten and frequently the best."

Serves: makes 4-5 pints   Time: 2 hours + overnight

History & Context

The white rind of a watermelon, which most modern households discard without a second thought, becomes a sweet-tart condiment when cubed and preserved in a spiced brine of vinegar, sugar, cinnamon, and cloves. It keeps for months on a cool shelf. The same product appears in specialty food stores as a Southern delicacy. Depression families arrived at it through the straightforward refusal to throw away something that still had use.

Ingredients

- Rind from 1 large watermelon, white portion only, all pink flesh and dark green outer skin removed
- 1/4 cup (60 ml) pickling salt
- 4 cups (960 ml) water for brine soak
- Pickling syrup: 4 cups (960 ml) white sugar, 2 cups (480 ml) white vinegar, 2 cups (480 ml) water, 2 cinnamon sticks, 1 tsp (5 ml) whole cloves, 1 tsp (5 ml) whole allspice

Method

1. Trim rind: remove all pink flesh and dark green outer skin. Cut white portion into 1-inch (2.5 cm) cubes.
2. Dissolve salt in 4 cups (960 ml) water in a large bowl. Add rind and soak overnight (8 hours minimum). This firms the texture.
3. Drain and rinse rind thoroughly.
4. Place rind in a pot, cover with fresh cold water, bring to a boil. Simmer 5 minutes until just tender but still firm. Drain.
5. Combine sugar, vinegar, 2 cups (480 ml) water, and whole spices in the pot. Bring to a boil until sugar dissolves.
6. Add drained rind. Return to a boil, reduce to simmer. Cook 20-25 minutes until rind turns slightly translucent.
7. Pack hot rind into sterilized pint jars. Ladle hot syrup over, leaving 1/2-inch (1.5 cm) headspace.
8. Process in a boiling water bath 10 minutes. Or refrigerate, ready in 24 hours, keeps 2 months.

SALT-CURED PORK

"Salt, fat, and time. The oldest meat preservation method that exists and still the most reliable without refrigeration."

Serves: makes 1-2 lbs cured pork   Time: 10 min active + 7 days curing

---

History & Context

Before refrigeration, salt was the primary reason meat lasted more than a few days. A dry salt cure draws moisture out of the meat through osmosis, creating an environment where spoilage bacteria cannot thrive. Fatback, salt pork, and salt belly were staple ingredients in American cooking for three hundred years, not as a survival novelty but as the everyday cooking fat and flavoring used in beans, greens, soups, and cornbread across the South and Appalachia. Fatback costs almost nothing at any grocery store, pork belly is available at most grocery stores and every butcher, and coarse salt is already in the pantry. The cure takes seven days of doing nothing.

Ingredients

- 1-2 lbs (455 to 905 g) pork fatback or pork belly, available at any grocery store meat counter or butcher, very inexpensive
- 1/4 cup (60 ml) coarse kosher salt or pickling salt per pound of meat, do not use iodized table salt, iodine inhibits the cure
- Optional: 1 tsp (5 ml) black pepper, 1/2 tsp (3 ml) cayenne per pound

Method

1. Pat the pork completely dry with a cloth. Any surface moisture dilutes the cure.
2. Combine salt and optional spices. Rub every surface of the meat thoroughly, top, bottom, and all sides. Do not miss any surface.
3. Place the salted meat in a glass jar, ceramic crock, or food-safe plastic container. It will fit tightly.
4. Cover and refrigerate, OR store in the coolest location available, a basement, root cellar, or cool pantry works if the temperature stays below 50°F (10°C).
5. After 24 hours, liquid will have pooled in the bottom of the container. This is the brine drawn out of the meat by the salt. Do not pour it out, flip the meat and return it to the brine.
6. Flip the meat once per day for 7 days. The brine level will increase each day as more moisture is drawn out.
7. After 7 days the meat is cured. It will feel firmer and slightly drier than fresh pork. Rinse briefly under cold water and pat dry.

8. To use: slice off what you need and fry in a dry pan over medium heat. The fat renders out and the cured pork provides both cooking fat and intense salty flavor for beans, greens, soups, or cornbread.

9. Store the remaining cured pork submerged in its brine in the refrigerator for up to 3 months, or in a very cool location below 50°F (10°C).

Field Note: Non-iodized salt only, coarse kosher salt or pickling salt. Iodized table salt contains iodine that interferes with the curing process and can produce off flavors. The brine that accumulates is not waste, it is the preservation medium. Keep the meat submerged in it. A piece of cured salt pork dropped into a pot of beans or a pot of greens is the single most effective flavor addition this book contains.

USE NON-IODIZED SALT ONLY, IODIZED TABLE SALT INTERFERES WITH THE CURE AND CAN ALLOW SPOILAGE WHILE THE MEAT APPEARS SAFE. KEEP MEAT FULLY SUBMERGED IN BRINE AT ALL TIMES. IF THE MEAT DEVELOPS AN OFF SMELL, UNUSUAL COLOR, OR SLIME THAT IS NOT THE NORMAL BRINE, DISCARD IT ENTIRELY. DO NOT TASTE TEST MEAT YOU ARE UNCERTAIN ABOUT. WHEN IN DOUBT, THROW IT OUT.

SALT-PACKED VEGETABLES

"Cabbage, green beans, or carrots packed in coarse salt keep for months without refrigeration, canning equipment, or vinegar."

Serves: makes 1 quart   Time: 20 min active + 1 week

History & Context

Salting vegetables for long-term storage predates canning by thousands of years. The technique is identical in principle to salt-curing meat: coarse salt draws moisture from the vegetable cells, the released liquid creates a brine, and that brine, salty enough to prevent spoilage bacteria, preserves the vegetables for months. Sauerkraut is the most familiar version but the method works on cabbage, green beans, carrots, and most other firm vegetables. No canning equipment, no boiling, no vinegar, no special jars. A head of cabbage, a pound of salt, and a clean container is the entire supply list.

Ingredients

- 1 medium head green cabbage (about 2 lbs, 905 g), OR 1 lb (455 g) green beans, OR 1 lb (455 g) carrots
- 1 tbsp (15 ml) coarse kosher or pickling salt per pound of vegetable, non-iodized only
- A clean wide-mouth quart jar or any food-safe container with a lid
- Something to weight the vegetables down: a zip-lock bag filled with brine, a smaller jar filled with water, or a clean stone

Method

1. For cabbage: remove outer leaves. Shred finely, 1/8 inch (0.5 cm) or thinner. For green beans: trim ends, leave whole or cut in half. For carrots: peel and cut into coins or sticks.
2. Weigh your prepared vegetable. Calculate salt: 1 tablespoon (15 ml) per pound.
3. Combine vegetable and salt in a large bowl. Toss thoroughly to coat every surface.
4. Let sit 10 minutes. Then squeeze and massage the vegetable with your hands firmly for 3-5 minutes. Liquid will begin to release, this is the brine forming.
5. Pack the vegetable very tightly into your jar, pressing down hard after each handful. The liquid should rise above the vegetable surface as you pack. If it does not rise fully above the vegetables after 24 hours, dissolve 1 tsp (5 ml) salt in 1 cup (240 ml) water and add just enough to cover.
6. Weight the vegetables down so they stay submerged below the brine. Vegetables exposed to air above the brine will mold.

7. Cover loosely, not airtight. Gas will release during the first few days and needs to escape.
8. Store at room temperature for the first 3-7 days, then move to a cool location. Taste after 5 days, it will be salty and slightly tangy. Ready to eat at any point but keeps improving for weeks.
9. To use: rinse a portion under cold water to reduce saltiness, then use as you would any cooked vegetable, in soups, alongside beans, or on its own.

Field Note: The single rule that cannot be broken: vegetables must stay submerged below the brine at all times. Anything above the brine surface will develop mold. The mold does not necessarily ruin the batch, scrape it off and push the vegetables back down, but preventing it is better. A zip-lock bag filled with brine laid on top of the vegetables is the most reliable weight because it conforms to the jar shape and leaves no gaps. Cabbage produces the most brine of any vegetable and is the easiest starting point.

WATER BATH CANNING, TOMATOES AND HIGH-ACID FOODS

"A $30 starter kit and one afternoon turns a summer surplus into a year of shelf-stable food."

Serves: makes 7 quart jars   Time: 2-3 hours

History & Context

Water bath canning, submerging sealed jars in boiling water long enough to kill spoilage organisms and create a vacuum seal, has been the standard home food preservation method in the United States since the 1850s. A water bath canner costs about $25. A set of mason jars costs about $12 for a dozen. The lids cost about $3 for a box of twelve. The total starter investment is under $40 and the equipment lasts decades. Canned tomatoes, fruit, pickles, and jams made at home are shelf-stable for a year or more and cost a fraction of commercial equivalents. This is the single most practical food preservation skill a household can acquire, and it is not difficult, it requires following the procedure correctly, which is entirely learnable in one afternoon.

Ingredients

- Equipment: water bath canner or any large pot deep enough to submerge jars by 1 inch (2.5 cm), jar rack or folded cloth in pot bottom, jar lifter or tongs, mason jars with new lids and bands
- 21 lbs (9.5 kg) fresh tomatoes for 7 quart (6.6 L) jars, about 3 lbs (1.4 kg) per quart
- Bottled lemon juice, 2 tbsp (30 ml) per quart jar (do not substitute fresh, acidity varies)
- Canning salt, 1 tsp (5 ml) per quart (optional but recommended)
- Water for blanching and canning pot

Method

1. Sterilize jars: wash jars, lids, and bands in hot soapy water. Keep jars hot until filling, place in simmering water or a low oven.
2. Blanch and peel tomatoes: score an X in the bottom of each tomato. Drop into boiling water 30-60 seconds until skin splits. Transfer immediately to ice water. Peel, skin slips off easily.
3. Core tomatoes. Quarter or crush into a large pot. Bring to a boil, stirring. Simmer 5 minutes.
4. Fill each hot jar: add 2 tbsp (30 ml) bottled lemon juice and 1 tsp (5 ml) salt to each quart jar first.

5. Ladle hot tomatoes into jars, pressing down to eliminate air pockets. Leave 1/2-inch (1.5 cm) headspace, the gap between the food and the lid rim.
6. Wipe jar rims with a clean damp cloth. Any residue on the rim will prevent a proper seal.
7. Place lids on jars. Screw bands on fingertip-tight, snug but not cranked down hard.
8. Lower jars into the canner. Water must cover jars by at least 1 inch (2.5 cm). Bring to a full rolling boil.
9. Process at a full boil: 45 minutes for quart jars, 35 minutes for pint jars.
10. Turn off heat. Remove lid. Wait 5 minutes, then lift jars straight up without tilting. Place on a towel 1 inch (2.5 cm) apart.
11. Do not touch or move jars for 12-24 hours. You will hear the lids pop as they seal, this is correct.
12. After 24 hours: press the center of each lid. It should be concave and firm, not flex up and down. Any jar that did not seal must be refrigerated and used within a week.
13. Label with contents and date. Store in a cool dark location.

Field Note: The lemon juice addition is not optional for tomatoes, modern tomatoes have lower natural acidity than older varieties, and the added acid is required for safe water bath processing. Bottled lemon juice specifically because its acidity is standardized; fresh lemon juice varies. Only water bath can HIGH-ACID foods: tomatoes, pickles, fruit, and jams. Low-acid foods, vegetables, beans, meat, require a pressure canner for safety. This is the firm line. Water bath canning low-acid foods is how people get botulism.

WATER BATH CANNING IS SAFE ONLY FOR HIGH-ACID FOODS: TOMATOES WITH ADDED LEMON JUICE, PICKLES, FRUIT, AND JAMS. NEVER WATER BATH CAN VEGETABLES, BEANS, MEAT, OR ANY OTHER LOW-ACID FOOD. BOTULISM TOXIN IS ODORLESS, TASTELESS, COLORLESS, AND LETHAL. A JAR THAT LOOKS AND SMELLS FINE CAN STILL KILL YOU. LOW-ACID FOODS REQUIRE A PRESSURE CANNER. THIS LINE DOES NOT MOVE.

BEAN SPROUTS, FRESH FOOD FROM YOUR STORED BEANS

"Two tablespoons of dried lentils. A mason jar. Water. Four days. Fresh living food from ingredients you already have."

Serves: 2-4 as supplement   Time: 4-5 days, 2 min active per day

---

History & Context

Any dried bean, lentil, or grain in your pantry can be sprouted into fresh living food without soil, sunlight, or any special equipment. The sprout is the seed in the process of becoming a plant, and in those first few days it converts its stored starch into vitamins and living protein. This matters most in a long-term situation because dried and canned food contains almost no vitamin C. Without vitamin C over a period of weeks, scurvy develops, fatigue, joint pain, bleeding gums, eventually worse. Sprouting is the only way to produce fresh vitamin C from shelf-stable stores with no electricity, no grow lights, and no garden. A rotating system of four jars staggered one day apart produces roughly one pound of fresh sprouts every day from a shoebox-sized space on any shelf or countertop. Lentils are the easiest to start with. Any dried bean works. Wheat berries, if you have them, produce sweet nutritious sprouts in three days.

Ingredients

- 2 tbsp (30 ml) dried lentils, mung beans, or any small dried bean per quart mason jar
- Water for soaking and rinsing
- Cheesecloth, mesh, or any breathable fabric for the jar lid
- Rubber band or canning band to secure the cover
- 4 quart (3.8 L) mason jars for a continuous daily harvest rotation

Method

1. Rinse 2 tablespoons (30 ml) of dried lentils. Place in a quart mason jar. Cover with 1 cup (240 ml) of water.
2. Cover the jar mouth with cheesecloth or mesh secured with a rubber band. Soak 8-12 hours or overnight.
3. After soaking, drain completely by inverting the jar over a bowl. The mesh holds the beans while water drains out.
4. Rinse with fresh water, drain completely again, then lay the jar on its side at a slight angle so any remaining water drains and air circulates. A dish rack or folded towel works.

5. Rinse and drain twice daily, morning and evening. This takes about 30 seconds per jar.
6. After 3-5 days the sprouts will fill the jar. They are ready when the sprout tail is roughly the length of the bean itself.
7. Optional: set the jar in indirect light for a few hours on the last day. The sprouts turn slightly green and produce additional nutrients.
8. Eat immediately or rinse and store in the refrigerator if power is available. At room temperature, eat within a day of harvest.
9. To maintain continuous production: start a new jar every day. With four jars staggered one day apart, one jar reaches harvest every single day.

Field Note: *Lentils are the easiest starting point because they sprout reliably and quickly with no soaking failures. Mung beans are the classic sprout used in Asian cooking and are equally reliable. Large beans like kidney or pinto work but take longer and need more rinsing. The only way to fail is to let water pool in the jar, the sprouts need drainage and air, not submersion. If sprouts smell sour or rotten, the jar was not draining properly. Dump it, rinse the jar, and start again. The rotation system is the key: do not grow one large batch. Grow four small staggered batches so something is always ready. SCALING PER PERSON: One person needs 4 jars and roughly 8 tablespoons (120 ml) of dried lentils per week to maintain a daily harvest. Two people need 8 jars and about 1 cup (240 ml) of dried lentils per week. Four people need 16 jars and about 2 cups (480 ml) per week. Multiply straight across for any household size. MAKING IT PERPETUAL: A pound of dried lentils runs out in roughly three weeks at one-person consumption. The system only continues if you treat a portion of every batch as seed stock, not food. The rule is the 80/20 rule: eat 80 percent of every harvest. Let the remaining 20 percent grow on past sprout stage into small seedlings, tiny plants with roots and a first set of leaves. Those seedlings, planted into any container with soil, will grow into full lentil plants in about 90 days and produce seed pods containing 1-3 new lentils each. One mature lentil plant produces roughly 15-20 pods. A row of 20 plants in containers on a sunny windowsill or porch produces approximately 400-600 seeds per cycle, enough to restock several weeks of sprouting. The system requires light for the seed production stage, not the sprouting stage. A south-facing window is sufficient. Sprout in the dark on any shelf. Grow your seed stock plants in whatever light you have. The two operations run simultaneously and feed each other. This is not a theoretical system. It is how subsistence farmers have maintained seed stock for thousands of years. The only difference is that you are doing it in containers instead of a field. Do not ever sprout your last cup of dried lentils. That cup is your restart supply if the system breaks down. Treat it like the last match in a matchbook.*

OYSTER MUSHROOMS, CONTINUOUS INDOOR CULTIVATION

"The one food you can grow indefinitely indoors from waste materials when every other fresh food source is gone."

Serves: ongoing   Time: 2-3 weeks to first harvest, then continuous

---

History & Context

Oyster mushrooms grow on dead organic material in nature and on cardboard, straw, or used coffee grounds indoors. They require no sunlight, no soil, and no special equipment. Room temperature is sufficient. A single fruiting block produces multiple harvests over six to eight weeks before it is spent, and a rotation of blocks started two weeks apart produces a continuous ongoing supply. This is not a hobbyist project. It is a genuine food production system operable in a basement, shed, spare room, or any enclosed space with temperatures between 55 and 75 degrees. The honest limitation is that mushroom spawn, the living culture used to seed the substrate, must be sourced before it is needed. Dried oyster mushroom spawn stores for six months to a year in a sealed bag in a cool location. Buying several pounds now and storing it is the preparedness step. Once spawn is on hand, the substrate is free: cardboard boxes broken down and soaked in water, or straw, or used coffee grounds saved from your daily brewing. The nutritional value is real. Oyster mushrooms provide meaningful protein, B vitamins including B12, and minerals largely absent from grain and bean based diets. They also taste like actual food, which matters more than most preparedness guides acknowledge.

Ingredients

- Oyster mushroom spawn, available online, stock 2-4 lbs (0.9 to 1.8 kg) sealed in cool storage
- Substrate: broken down cardboard soaked in water, or straw, or used coffee grounds, all free waste materials
- A plastic bin, bucket, or large zip-lock bag with small holes poked in the sides for air exchange
- A spray bottle filled with clean water
- A shelf or surface in a cool shaded space between 55 and 75 degrees F (25°C)

Method

1. Prepare substrate: tear cardboard into pieces and soak in water for 1-2 hours, then squeeze out excess water until damp but not dripping. Coffee grounds can be

used directly as they come from brewing. Straw should be soaked and drained the same way as cardboard.

2. Layer substrate and spawn in your container, alternating: a 2-inch (5 cm) layer of damp substrate, then a thin layer of spawn scattered across it, then another layer of substrate, then spawn, repeating until the container is full. Finish with a layer of substrate on top.

3. Seal or close the container loosely. Poke 6-8 small holes in the sides about the diameter of a pencil to allow air exchange.

4. Place in a cool shaded location. No light is needed during this colonization phase.

5. Over the next 10-14 days white fuzzy mycelium will spread through the substrate. This is correct and healthy. The block is ready to fruit when white growth is visible throughout.

6. When fully colonized, open the container or cut larger holes in the sides. Begin misting the exposed surface twice daily with clean water.

7. Within 5-10 days small mushroom pins will appear at the holes or open surfaces. They grow quickly.

8. Harvest by gripping the cluster at the base and twisting gently. Harvest before the edges of the caps begin to curl upward, this is peak flavor and nutrition.

9. After harvesting, continue misting. A second and third flush will follow at roughly two-week intervals.

10. Start a new block every two weeks to maintain continuous production. A space with three or four blocks at staggered stages produces a steady ongoing harvest.

Field Note: The two most common failures are too much water (substrate soggy and pooling, which causes rot) and too little air exchange (not enough holes, which causes the mycelium to suffocate). Both are fixable. Soggy substrate: add more holes and let it dry slightly before misting again. Poor colonization: add more holes. The white fuzzy growth is healthy mycelium. Green or black patches are mold contamination, cut out the affected section and continue if contamination is minor, discard and start over if it spreads. Oyster mushrooms are aggressive colonizers and usually outcompete mold if the spawn is healthy and the substrate was properly prepared. For two people eating mushrooms as a regular supplement, plan on running four blocks simultaneously at staggered two-week start dates. That footprint fits on a single wire shelf unit roughly four feet wide.

SURVIVAL LENTIL BREAD, FROM ALMOST NOTHING

"Soaked lentils and water. That is the whole recipe. Everything else makes it better but nothing else makes it possible."

Serves: 1 small loaf, 6-8 slices   Time: Overnight soak + 50 min baking

---

History & Context

Lentil bread has been made in various forms across the Middle East, India, and Africa for centuries, long before wheat flour was widely available or affordable. The technique is simple: soak dried lentils until soft, blend or mash them smooth, and bake the resulting batter. The lentils contain enough natural starch to bind, enough protein to build structure, and enough moisture to produce a loaf that slices and toasts. No flour. No yeast. No eggs. No dairy. The version in this recipe is written for someone who may have very little left in their pantry. It starts from the absolute minimum that produces edible bread and adds ingredients in order of what improves it most. Read the ingredient ladder below before you start. Make the best version your pantry allows.

Ingredients

- MINIMUM VERSION (requires nothing else): 2 cups (480 ml) dried lentils soaked overnight in water, then drained, red lentils work best but any lentil works, 1/2 to 3/4 cup (120 to 180 ml) fresh water for blending, pinch of salt if available
- ADD IF YOU HAVE IT (each improves the result): 1 tbsp (15 ml) any cooking fat, oil, lard, bacon drippings, or butter adds moisture and helps the bread release from the pan
- ADD IF YOU HAVE IT: 1 tsp (5 ml) baking powder helps the loaf rise slightly and produces a lighter texture
- ADD IF YOU HAVE IT: 1 tsp (5 ml) vinegar or squeeze of lemon juice dramatically cuts the beany flavor and makes the bread taste more like actual bread
- ADD IF YOU HAVE IT: any spice you have, garlic powder, onion powder, cumin, or mixed herbs stirred into the batter adds real flavor
- ADD IF YOU HAVE IT: sesame seeds, oats, or flax seeds sprinkled on top before baking add texture and nutrition

Method

1. The night before: put your dried lentils in a bowl and cover with water by at least two inches. Leave overnight or for at least eight hours. They will double in size. This is the only time-sensitive preparation step.
2. When ready to bake: drain the soaked lentils completely and rinse them with fresh water.

3. If you have a blender: add the drained lentils and half a cup of fresh water. Blend on high until completely smooth, scraping the sides down as needed. The batter should pour slowly from a spoon like thick pancake batter. Add water a tablespoon at a time if it is too thick to blend.

4. If you do not have a blender: mash the drained lentils as smooth as possible with a fork or potato masher. This takes effort and will not be perfectly smooth, but it works. Add water a little at a time and keep mashing until you have a thick paste. The bread will be slightly more dense and rustic but entirely edible.

5. Add salt, fat, baking powder, vinegar, and any spices you are using. Stir until combined.

6. Grease your baking pan with whatever fat you have. If you have parchment paper, line the pan with it. If you have neither, grease the pan well and dust it lightly with any flour or cornmeal you have. This prevents sticking.

7. Pour the batter into the pan. Smooth the top. Sprinkle any toppings on now.

8. NO OVEN METHOD: If you have no oven, pour the batter into a greased skillet or pot with a tight lid. Cook on the lowest heat possible for 30 to 40 minutes until the top is set and a knife inserted in the center comes out clean. This produces a denser, flatter result but it works over any heat source including a camp stove or open fire.

9. OVEN METHOD: Bake at 350 degrees F (175°C) for 45 to 55 minutes until the top is golden brown and a toothpick or knife inserted in the center comes out clean.

10. This is important: do not cut into the bread for at least one hour after it comes out of the oven or off the heat. Lentil bread is very moist inside while hot. Cutting it too early produces a gummy, falling-apart result. Wait. It will be worth it.

11. Once fully cooled, slice with a sharp knife using a gentle sawing motion. Toast slices in a dry pan over any heat for two to three minutes per side to improve the texture and flavor significantly.

Field Note: The flavor of plain lentil bread is mild and slightly earthy. It is honest food, not exciting food. Three things improve it dramatically and all three are cheap or free: salt in the batter (use more than you think you need), vinegar or lemon juice in the batter (even a small amount cuts the beany edge completely), and toasting the slices before eating (transforms the texture from soft and dense to crispy outside with a chewy center). If your bread turns out gummy even after cooling fully, your oven temperature was too low or the bread needed more time. Put it back in for another ten minutes. If it falls apart when sliced, the batter was too wet. Next time reduce the water by a few tablespoons. Both problems are fixable. Neither means you failed. Lentil bread is forgiving. Keep trying until you get the version that works with your equipment and your ingredients. Once you have it right, you have a bread recipe that requires nothing you have to buy, nothing that expires, and nothing that depends on a supply chain. That is worth knowing how to make.

EMERGENCY PET FOOD, DOGS AND CATS

"They are family. Feed them like it."

Serves: Varies, see method   Time: 20 min

History & Context

Every preparedness book ever written was written for people. None of them mentioned the dog sleeping at the foot of the bed or the cat on the windowsill. That was an oversight. Anyone who has animals understands that watching a pet go hungry is not a secondary concern. For many people it is the thing they could least endure. A prepared household accounts for every member of it, including the ones who cannot ask for food themselves. This recipe uses ingredients already on the survival pantry list. It is not balanced long-term pet nutrition. It is emergency food designed to keep your animals alive, functional, and out of distress while you stabilize the larger situation. Here is the math so you can work it out for your own animals. A cat needs approximately 4 to 6 grams of protein per kilogram of body weight per day to maintain basic function. An average house cat weighs 8 to 10 pounds, which is 3.5 to 4.5 kilograms. Multiply: 4.5 kg times 5 grams equals roughly 22 grams of protein per day as a working target. One large egg contains about 6 grams of protein. One standard 3.75 oz can of sardines contains about 23 grams. So one egg gets you roughly one quarter of a cat's daily protein needs. Two eggs gets you just over half. Two eggs plus a portion of any canned fish gets you there. For a dog, the same formula applies but dogs are heavier. A 40-pound dog is about 18 kilograms. At 4 grams of protein per kilogram, that is 72 grams of protein per day. A dog is harder to feed from pantry staples alone, but dogs can digest carbohydrates effectively unlike cats, so rice, oats, and beans all contribute meaningful calories and some protein to a dog's emergency ration even if they do not fully meet protein needs.

Ingredients

- PROTEIN, use whatever you have, in this priority order:
- Best: any canned fish in water, sardines, tuna, salmon, or mackerel. Do not drain. Include the liquid. Include soft bones if present. A standard 3.75 oz can contains roughly 23 grams of protein.
- Good: eggs, hard boiled and chopped. One large egg contains approximately 6 grams of protein. Both dogs and cats digest eggs well.
- Acceptable for dogs, marginal for cats: cooked dried beans or lentils. One cup of cooked lentils contains about 18 grams of protein. Dogs extract nutrition from this reasonably well. Cats do not, use only if nothing else exists.
- CARBOHYDRATE BASE, for dogs only:

- 1 cup cooked white rice or oats per medium dog per meal. Provides bulk calories and helps the dog feel full. Cats get little nutritional benefit from grains, give cats a small spoonful at most, or none.
- FAT: 1 teaspoon cooking fat, lard, bacon drippings, or vegetable oil. Adds calories and palatability.
- Water as needed to adjust texture to a soft mash.

NEVER USE: ONIONS, GARLIC, GRAPES, RAISINS, XYLITOL, CHOCOLATE, MACADAMIA NUTS, OR AVOCADO. THESE ARE TOXIC TO DOGS AND CATS, SOME OF THEM FATALLY SO, EVEN IN SMALL AMOUNTS.

Method

1. Calculate your target. Weigh your cat or estimate: most house cats are 8 to 10 pounds (3.5 to 4.5 kg). Multiply their weight in kilograms by 5 to get their daily protein target in grams. For a 9-pound cat that is 4 kg times 5 equals 20 grams of protein per day. For a dog, multiply their weight in kilograms by 4. A 40-pound dog needs roughly 72 grams of protein per day.
2. Identify your protein source from the priority list in the ingredients above. Add up what you have. Two eggs plus half a can of sardines provides roughly 12 plus 11 equals 23 grams of protein, a full day for one average cat.
3. Hard boil the eggs if using. Cool completely, peel, and chop into small pieces.
4. Open the canned fish if using. Do not drain. Break into small pieces with a fork. The liquid contains protein and the soft bones are safe and provide calcium.
5. Cook beans or lentils until very soft and mashable if using those as the protein source.
6. FOR CATS: combine your protein sources in a bowl. Add a teaspoon of fat. Add a small splash of water if needed to make a soft mash. Add no more than a tablespoon or two of rice or oats. Cats are obligate carnivores, their digestive systems are not designed for carbohydrates and they extract almost no nutrition from grains. The protein is what keeps the cat alive.
7. FOR DOGS: combine your protein sources in a bowl. Add the cooked rice or oats. Add a teaspoon of fat. Mix well. Add water if needed. Dogs are omnivores and digest carbohydrates well, the rice provides real calories and bulk that helps the dog feel satisfied.
8. Serve at room temperature or slightly warmed. Do not serve hot.
9. Store unused portions covered in a cool location for up to 24 hours, or refrigerated for up to 2 days.

Field Note: The taurine problem: cats cannot synthesize taurine, an amino acid essential for heart and eye function. Taurine deficiency causes blindness and heart failure, and it develops over weeks, not months. Canned fish is the best taurine source in a survival pantry. Eggs contain some taurine but not enough alone for long-term cat health. Cooked meat scraps contain taurine. Beans and rice contain essentially none. If your only protein source is eggs and you have a cat, that cat is buying time, not thriving, a few weeks is likely safe, longer than that and taurine deficiency becomes a real risk. The practical rule: if you have one can of fish and both a dog and a cat, the fish goes to the cat. The dog will manage on eggs and rice far better than the cat will. Feed the cat every scrap of animal protein available before feeding it anything grain-based. A cat getting even small daily amounts of any cooked meat, fish, or egg alongside grain filler is in a dramatically better position than a cat eating only grain-based food.

GARLIC CONFIT, PRESERVED GARLIC IN OIL

"Garlic slow-cooked in oil until golden and soft. The garlic keeps for weeks. The oil is as valuable as the garlic."

Serves: 2 heads garlic + infused oil   Time: 45 min active, then cool

History & Context

Confit is a French preservation technique, cooking something gently submerged in fat at low temperature. For garlic, the result is dramatic: the raw bite disappears completely, replaced by something sweet, nutty, and spreadable. The slow heat caramelizes the sugars in the garlic and drives off the sharp sulfur compounds that give raw garlic its harshness. What remains is mellow, rich, and deeply flavored. More importantly, the oil itself becomes infused with garlic flavor and is arguably the more valuable product of the two. Garlic confit stored submerged in its oil in a sealed jar in the refrigerator keeps for three to four weeks. The infused oil keeps for the same period. Both are used throughout this book, the garlic in soups, gravies, bean dishes, and spread directly on bread, the oil as a finishing fat for anything that needs flavor. This recipe also forms the base for garlic aioli, see Recipe 6-15.

Ingredients

- 2 heads garlic, cloves separated and peeled
- 1 cup (240 ml) neutral oil, vegetable oil, light olive oil, or any refined oil. Do not use extra-virgin olive oil which has a low smoke point and can turn bitter
- Optional: 1-2 sprigs fresh rosemary or thyme, 1 bay leaf, a few black peppercorns
- A small heavy saucepan, the garlic should fit in a single layer with oil covering it by at least half an inch

Method

1. Peel all garlic cloves. The fastest method: separate cloves, place in a jar with a tight lid, shake vigorously for 30 seconds. The skins loosen and fall away.
2. Place peeled cloves in a small heavy saucepan. Add optional herbs and aromatics.
3. Pour oil over garlic until completely submerged. The cloves should be covered by at least half an inch of oil.
4. Set over the lowest possible heat. The oil should barely move, small occasional bubbles at the surface are correct. A rolling simmer is too hot and will fry rather than confit the garlic.
5. Cook on this very low heat for 35-45 minutes, checking every 10 minutes. The cloves are done when they are golden on the outside, completely soft when pierced with a knife, and sweet-smelling rather than sharp.

6. Remove from heat. Let cool completely in the oil before transferring.

7. Transfer garlic and all oil into a clean glass jar with a tight lid. Tap the jar gently to release any air bubbles.

8. Refrigerate. Use within 3-4 weeks. Always use a clean dry spoon to remove garlic and oil, moisture in the jar shortens shelf life significantly.

9. To use the garlic: mash cloves into soups and gravies, spread directly on bread, stir into bean dishes, or use as the base for aioli (Recipe 6-15).

10. To use the oil: drizzle over any cooked food as a finishing fat, use in place of plain oil in any recipe that would benefit from garlic flavor, or use as the oil base for aioli.

Field Note: The single most important thing: low heat. Garlic that cooks too fast turns bitter and grainy. If you see active bubbling, the heat is too high. The oil should look almost still with only occasional lazy bubbles. The finished garlic cloves should be golden, not brown, and should mash effortlessly under gentle pressure. Store in the refrigerator only, garlic stored in oil at room temperature can support the growth of Clostridium botulinum. This is not a shelf-stable product. Refrigerate immediately and use within 3-4 weeks.

GARLIC IN OIL MUST BE REFRIGERATED AT ALL TIMES. NEVER STORE GARLIC CONFIT AT ROOM TEMPERATURE. GARLIC SUBMERGED IN OIL AT ROOM TEMPERATURE CAN PRODUCE BOTULISM TOXIN WITH NO VISIBLE SIGNS OF SPOILAGE. REFRIGERATE IMMEDIATELY AFTER COOLING. USE WITHIN 3-4 WEEKS.

CHAPTER IX

WHAT TO DO WHEN YOUR RESERVES HAVE ALMOST RUN OUT

READ THIS NOW

This chapter is for two situations. The first is right now, today, when money is critically short and you need to know how to feed yourself and your family as efficiently as possible. The second is the harder situation: when food itself is becoming scarce and your reserves are running low. Both situations are addressed here, in plain language, step by step.

If your food supply is critically low and you have two weeks or less of reserves remaining, go directly to Section 5 of this chapter. Do not wait. That section tells you exactly what to do starting today to extend your food supply, begin growing fresh food from what you already have, and keep your household fed when stored food runs out. It was written specifically for that moment.

If you are in a difficult financial stretch but still have access to stores, start at Section 1. Everything in this chapter points back to recipes already in this book. The chapter is a planning layer: it tells you what to buy, in what order, and how to make it last. The recipes tell you what to do with it.

SECTION 1: How to Think About Buying When Money Is Critical

When money is seriously short, grocery shopping cannot be done the way most people shop, browsing for what sounds good, picking up extras, choosing convenience items. It has to be done the way a field engineer approaches a problem: identify the highest-value options available, acquire them in the right order, and waste nothing.

Buy calories first.

Calories keep people alive and functional. When money is critical, your first purchasing priority is the most calories per dollar available. In any grocery store, discount store, or dollar store, that list looks something like this, roughly in order of calorie density per dollar:

• Dried beans and lentils: among the highest calorie-per-dollar foods available, they also provide protein. A two-pound bag of dried pinto beans typically costs under two dollars and produces ten to twelve generous servings. Red lentils require no soaking and are ready in twelve minutes.

• White rice: cheap, stores well, and provides a dense calorie base. It does almost nothing nutritionally on its own, which is why it must be combined with beans or another protein source. Together, rice and beans form a complete protein. See Recipes 4-1 and 4-2.

• Rolled oats: oatmeal at the dollar store is frequently the best calorie-per-dollar purchase in the building. A large bag produces weeks of breakfasts or suppers. See Recipe 4-3.

• All-purpose flour: the base for bread, biscuits, flatbreads, pancakes, and gravy. A five-pound bag goes a long way. See Chapter I.

• Vegetable shortening (Crisco) or store-brand equivalent: fat is the most calorie-dense macro you can buy. A pound of shortening contains over 3,500 calories and costs very little. It is also essential for biscuits, pie crust, and frying.

• Eggs: the fastest, cheapest complete protein in any store. A dozen eggs is multiple days of protein at a price almost nothing else can match.

• Peanut butter: extremely calorie-dense, requires no cooking, stores well, and is available at every price tier from discount to full retail.

• Canned beans: more expensive per serving than dried, but require no soaking time and can be eaten straight from the can if cooking is not possible.

• Cabbage: the cheapest fresh vegetable almost anywhere, and one of the most nutritionally complete. A whole head lasts days in a cool location without refrigeration and makes multiple meals.

• Onions: cheap, keep without refrigeration for weeks in a cool spot, and make almost everything taste better. An onion in a pot of beans is the difference between something you merely eat and something you actually want to eat.

• Sweet potatoes: filling, calorie-dense, nutritious, and cheap. They provide vitamins that rice and beans do not.

• Canned fish (sardines, tuna): complete protein, long shelf life, and available in single-serving tins for under two dollars.

Buy nutrition second.

Once your calorie base is secured, spend what remains on nutrition, primarily whatever fresh or canned vegetables are cheapest that week, and whatever provides vitamins your staples do not. Cabbage, carrots, sweet potatoes, and canned tomatoes are reliable choices. A single head of cabbage, one bag of carrots, and one onion will cover the vegetable side of a week's meals for very little money.

Buy convenience last, or not at all.

Convenience foods (boxed meals, frozen dinners, individual serving packages, flavored instant anything) cost dramatically more per calorie than their plain equivalents. A box of flavored instant oatmeal costs three to four times what a bag of plain rolled oats costs for the same number of servings. The plain version is the correct purchase when money is short. If you know how to cook the plain version, and this book will show you how, you never need the convenience version.

SECTION 2: The Bulk-Cook Strategy

Bulk cooking is the single most effective strategy for stretching a limited food budget. The logic is simple: cooking one large batch takes approximately the same time and fuel as cooking one small serving. The large batch produces six to eight meals. The small serving produces one. The ratio of effort to output is radically better at scale.

For someone who is working, job-hunting, managing children, or simply exhausted by a hard stretch, this matters in a second way: when the food is already cooked, you eat it. When you have to cook from scratch every time you are hungry, there is a real risk that you will spend money on something fast and expensive instead, not because you want to, but because you are tired and the food is not ready. Pre-cooked bulk food is ready. That reliability has real value.

A basic bulk-cook week

The following is a framework, not a rigid plan. Adjust the recipes based on what you have and what is cheapest at your store this week. Every item listed points to a specific recipe in this book.

• One large pot of beans: cook a full pound of dried beans at once (Recipe 4-1). A pound of dried beans produces eight to ten cups of cooked beans. That is four to five days of protein for one person, or two to three days for two people. Season simply with salt, a half onion, and a bay leaf if you have it. Eat as a side, mash some into bread soup (Recipe 2-4), use the rest as a base for other meals.

• A large batch of rice: cook two to three cups of dry rice at once. Store covered in the refrigerator. Reheat one portion at a time in a skillet with a little fat and a splash of water. Combined with your beans, this is the core of multiple meals.

• A pot of soup: if you have any vegetables, any scrap ends, any bones, or any canned tomatoes, make a large pot of soup at the start of the week. See Recipe 2-1 (Water

Soup), Recipe 2-16 (Simple Vegetable Soup), or Recipe 2-5 (Bean and Ham Bone Soup). A large pot of soup will hold in a cool location for three to four days and feeds people quickly at any meal.

• A batch of bread or biscuits: Recipe 1-7 (Buttermilk Biscuits) or Recipe 1-3 (Skillet Cornbread) takes under thirty minutes and produces enough bread for a day or two. Bread turns soup into a meal. It turns beans into a meal. It is also a meal by itself with a little fat.

• Hard-boiled eggs: if you have eggs, hard boil six to eight at the start of the week. Hard-boiled eggs keep unpeeled in a cool location for a week. They are ready instantly, no cooking required when you need a fast protein.

Field Note: Refrigeration is helpful but not required for the bulk-cook strategy to work. In cool weather, a covered pot of beans or soup on a counter in a cool room is safe for 24 hours. In warm weather, if refrigeration is unavailable, cook smaller batches more frequently, or bring the pot to a full rolling boil once a day to reset its safety window. The boil method is discussed in the perpetual soup pot entry in Chapter II.

SECTION 3: A Sample One-Week Meal Rotation

The following rotation is built from the cheapest staples available: beans, rice, oats, eggs, flour, and whatever vegetables are cheapest this week. Every recipe referenced is in this book. The rotation is deliberately simple and repetitive. In a genuine crisis, repetition is not a failure of creativity. It is efficiency. A person who is fed the same nourishing meal three days in a row is in a substantially better position than a person who is not fed.

This rotation assumes one or two people. Scale up proportionally for larger households.

Breakfast, same all week:

Oatmeal with salt and whatever fat you have. See Recipe 4-5. A half cup of dry oats per person, one cup of water. Takes five minutes. If you have sugar, add a spoonful. If you have a banana or any fruit, slice it on top. This is a real breakfast. It is filling. It costs almost nothing.

Lunch, rotating:

• Day 1–2: Rice and beans from your bulk batch. Salt, a little fat if you have it, hot sauce or vinegar if you have it. See Recipe 4-19 (Beans & Rice).

• Day 3–4: Bean cooking liquid soup with a biscuit or cornbread. Use the liquid from your bean pot plus whatever vegetables you have. See Recipe 2-4 (Bread Soup) and Recipe 1-7 or 1-3.

• Day 5–7: Hard-boiled egg with leftover rice, or a biscuit with whatever spread is available. If bread is gone, flatbread takes ten minutes on a dry skillet. See Recipe 1-4 (Pandampo Flatbread).

Dinner, rotating:

• Day 1: Beans and rice with sautéed onion and whatever vegetables are available. Recipe 4-19 (Beans & Rice).

• Day 2: Vegetable soup with bread. Use whatever is on hand. Recipe 2-16 (Simple Vegetable Soup).

• Day 3: Vegetable fried rice. Leftover cold rice, one or two eggs scrambled in, soy sauce if you have it, whatever vegetables are available. Recipe 5-17 (Vegetable Fried Rice).

• Day 4: Bean and rice skillet. Beans, rice, diced onion, whatever canned tomatoes or seasoning you have, cooked together in one pan until slightly crispy on the bottom. No specific recipe number. This is improvised from your staples.

• Day 5: Egg and potato hash if you have potatoes. See Recipe 5-18. Otherwise, oatmeal for supper is a legitimate meal. See the supper application in Recipe 4-5.

• Day 6: Soup from whatever remains. End-of-week water soup, Recipe 2-1, using any remaining vegetables, bean liquid, and bread ends.

• Day 7: Cook a fresh batch of beans to start the next week's rotation. Eat from what remains of this week.

On boredom.

Yes, this rotation is repetitive. Rice and beans every day is not exciting. It is also what much of the world eats every day and has eaten every day for centuries, not because people lack creativity, but because it works. It is filling, it is nutritionally adequate when varied with whatever vegetables and eggs are available, and it is affordable at almost any price level. When things are genuinely hard, the bar is not excitement. The bar is fed. This rotation clears that bar.

That said, flavor is free or nearly free. Salt does most of the work. A little vinegar brightens a pot of beans. A bay leaf costs a few cents for a whole jar. Garlic powder, cayenne, and soy sauce (all on the pantry list in the front of this book) each cost a dollar or two for a supply that lasts months and transforms bland staples into something worth eating. If you can afford one condiment, make it something that adds flavor to everything: hot sauce, vinegar, soy sauce, or mustard. The food will taste better and you will sustain the rotation longer.

SECTION 4: If the Situation Gets Worse

This chapter has addressed short-term crisis budgeting: the situation where money is very tight but food is still available for purchase. The rest of this book addresses the scenario where purchasing food becomes difficult or impossible, either because money is completely gone, supply chains have failed, or both.

If that scenario appears to be developing, the transition point is simple: stop spending money on anything that is not a shelf-stable calorie. Every dollar available should go toward dried beans, white rice, rolled oats, flour, salt, sugar, and cooking fat, in that priority order. These are the ingredients that appear throughout every chapter of this book. They store for years when properly packaged. They form the base of a genuine food reserve that can carry a household through an extended disruption.

The Survival Pantry list at the front of this book details specific quantities and storage methods. If you have not read it, read it now. It is the bridge between the crisis-budgeting situation covered in earlier sections of this chapter and the longer-term resilience the rest of the book is designed to build.

The window to build that reserve is before you need it, not after. If you are reading this chapter because things are already hard, that window may be narrowing. Whatever you can set aside, even a five-pound bag of rice and a bag of dried beans this week, added to week after week, is meaningfully better than nothing. Start with what you can. Add to it when you can. The pantry does not have to be complete to be useful.

One More Thing: Rehydration

If someone in your household is sick with vomiting or diarrhea, or has been working hard in heat without enough fluids, plain water may not be enough to rehydrate them. The body loses salt and other minerals along with water when it sweats or purges, and water alone does not replace those. A person who is dehydrated from illness or heat and drinking only plain water may stay dehydrated even while drinking.

The solution is simple and uses ingredients already in your pantry. Oral rehydration solution can be made from one liter of water, six level teaspoons of sugar, and half a level teaspoon of salt. Stir until dissolved. That is the complete formula, the same one used by the World Health Organization for treating dehydration in field conditions worldwide. It does not taste good. It does not have to. Have the person drink it slowly and steadily, not all at once.

> *Field Note: This formula works because the small amount of sugar helps the gut absorb the sodium, which in turn pulls water into the bloodstream. Plain water skips that mechanism. If someone is seriously dehydrated and not improving after a few*

hours of plain water, switch to this mixture. The ingredients cost almost nothing and the difference can be significant.

SECTION 5: When Two Weeks of Food Remains: A Step-by-Step Survival Plan

This section is for a specific situation. You have looked at what you have left and done the math. You have roughly two weeks of food. You do not know when or if you will be able to get more. You may be scared. That is a normal response to a genuinely difficult situation.

This section will tell you exactly what to do, in order, starting today. Every step is written for someone who has never done any of this before. Nothing here requires experience. Nothing requires special equipment. Nothing requires electricity. Read the whole section once before you start so you understand where it is going. Then go back to Step 1 and begin.

You are not out of options. You are not out of time. But the steps you take in the next 24 hours matter more than almost anything else you can do. Let us start.

Step 1: Take a Complete Inventory. Do This Today.

Before anything else, you need to know exactly what you have. Get a piece of paper and a pen. Go through every cabinet, drawer, shelf, and storage space in your home. Write down everything that is food. Everything. Include things you forgot about. Include the baking soda, the cornstarch, the half-empty bag of flour, the can of beans in the back of the cabinet, the jar of peanut butter that is almost gone. Write the quantity next to each item.

Do not skip this step. People consistently underestimate what they have because they have not looked carefully. You may have more than you think. You also need to know exactly what you have in order to plan how long it will last. You cannot plan without this information.

When your list is done, sort it into three groups: things that provide calories and keep you full (beans, rice, flour, oats, pasta, oil, peanut butter), things that add nutrition and flavor (canned vegetables, spices, salt, vinegar, sugar), and things that are perishable and need to be eaten first (anything fresh, anything opened, anything that will not last).

Step 2: Ration What You Have. Do This Today.

Take the calorie-dense items from your inventory: your beans, rice, flour, oats, pasta, oil, peanut butter. These are your survival food. You need to understand roughly how many days they will last.

A very rough guide: one cup of dry rice produces about two servings. One cup of dry lentils or beans produces about three servings. One cup of dry oats produces about two servings. A serving here means a filling bowl of food, not a small portion.

Count your servings. Divide by the number of people in your household. That tells you roughly how many days of food you have at one meal per person per day. Write that number down. That is your planning window.

Now divide your stores into daily portions. Physically set aside what you will eat each day if that helps you visualize it. The goal is to stretch your two weeks of food to three weeks or more by being intentional about portions, while simultaneously starting the food production steps below that will begin feeding you before those stores run out.

Step 3: Start Your Sprout Jars. Do This Today. Right Now.

This is the most important immediate action you can take. Your sprout jars will produce fresh food in four to five days. That is this week. Every day you delay starting them is a day of fresh food you will not have.

Find every mason jar, jar with a wide mouth, or any container you can drain water through. A plastic bottle with holes poked in the lid works. A colander works. A bowl with cheesecloth over it works. Use what you have.

Find your dried lentils, mung beans, or any small dried bean. If you only have large beans like kidney or pinto, use them anyway. They take a day or two longer but they work.

For each jar: put in two tablespoons of dried beans. Cover with water. Put a piece of cloth, a paper towel, a coffee filter, or anything breathable over the top. Secure it with a rubber band or the jar ring. That is the complete setup.

Soak overnight. Tomorrow morning, drain the water out by tipping the jar upside down through the cloth. Rinse with fresh water, drain again, then lay the jar on its side at a slight angle so water drains and air gets in. A dish rack works. A folded towel works. The jar just needs to not be sitting in water.

Rinse and drain every jar twice a day. Morning and evening. This takes about thirty seconds per jar. In four to five days you will have a full jar of sprouts ready to eat.

Start as many jars as you can find today. If you have eight jars, fill all eight, starting them one day apart so they do not all finish at the same time. With eight jars staggered one day apart, you will have two jars reaching harvest every day once the system is running.

Step 4: Set Up Your Mushroom Blocks If You Have Spawn.

If you purchased oyster mushroom spawn as part of your preparedness supplies (see Recipe 8-11), now is the time to use it. Mushroom blocks take ten to fourteen days to colonize before they produce food, so starting today means your first harvest arrives in about two weeks, right as your other food reserves are getting critical.

Find a plastic bin, a bucket, a cardboard box, or any container. Tear up cardboard boxes into pieces and soak them in water for an hour, then squeeze out the excess water until the cardboard is damp but not dripping. If you have used coffee grounds, use those instead or in addition. Layer damp cardboard and spawn alternately until the container is full. Poke holes in the sides with a pencil. Set it in a cool shaded spot and leave it alone for ten to fourteen days.

If you do not have mushroom spawn, skip this step. Do not worry about it. The sprout system will carry you.

Step 5: Cook Simply and Stretch Everything.

While your sprouts are growing, you are still eating from your stored food. The goal now is to make every ingredient go as far as possible without leaving anyone so hungry they cannot function. Here is how to do that.

Eat one hot meal a day. It does not have to be large. It has to be real. A bowl of cooked beans over rice with salt is a real meal. A pot of oatmeal with peanut butter stirred in is a real meal. A flatbread cooked in a dry skillet with a bowl of bean soup is a real meal. You are not eating for pleasure right now. You are eating to stay functional. These meals accomplish that.

Stretch your beans by turning them into soup. When you cook beans, use more water than usual and add whatever vegetables you have, even just an onion and some salt. A pot of bean soup feeds more people per cup of beans than a pot of plain beans does, because the liquid is filling. Do not pour the cooking liquid out. It is food. Eat it.

Stretch your flour by making flatbread instead of biscuits. Flatbread uses less fat, takes ten minutes on a dry skillet, and produces more bread per cup of flour than any other method. See Recipe 1-4. When flour is limited, flatbread is how you make it last.

Stretch your rice by cooking it in more water than the package says. Congee, which is rice cooked in four to six times the normal amount of water until it becomes a thick porridge, turns one cup of rice into four large bowls of filling food. It is eaten across Asia as a staple meal. Add salt and whatever you have available on top. It is a real meal.

Stretch your oats the same way. Cook them long and slow with extra water. They become thick, dense, and filling. A half cup of dry oats cooked in two cups of water for twenty minutes produces a bowl that will hold a person for four to five hours.

Step 6: Protect Your Seed Stock. This Is How You Do Not Run Out.

This step is what separates a temporary food crisis from a permanent one. Every handful of dried beans you eat is gone. Every handful you protect and grow into a plant produces new beans. This is not complicated. It is just something most people in a modern context have never had to think about.

Keep back one cup of dried lentils and one cup of any other dried bean you have. Do not eat these. Do not sprout these. These are your seed stock.

Find any container that can hold soil. A five-gallon bucket. A large pot. A plastic storage bin. A wooden box. A bucket with holes poked in the bottom for drainage works perfectly. Fill it with any soil you can find. Garden soil, potting mix, soil dug from outside, anything. Lentils and beans are not picky.

Plant your seed stock beans one inch deep and about three inches apart. Water them. Put the container in the sunniest spot you have access to. A south-facing window. A porch. A rooftop. Any outdoor space. Even a cloudy window will work, though plants in more light will grow faster.

Water when the top inch of soil feels dry. That is the complete care requirement.

In about ten days, green shoots will appear. In about three to four weeks, the plants will be several inches tall. In about ninety days, the plants will produce seed pods. Each pod contains one to three new beans or lentils. A container with twenty plants produces roughly four hundred to six hundred seeds. Those seeds go back into your sprout rotation and your seed stock simultaneously.

You are now in a loop. Sprouts feed you now. Plants restock your seeds for later. As long as you protect a portion of every harvest as seed stock and keep plants growing, you do not run out. The system is self-sustaining.

> *Field Note: The single most important rule of this system: never plant or eat your last seeds. Always keep a reserve. If something kills your plants, if a frost hits, if something goes wrong, that reserve is how you restart. Treat your seed stock like the most valuable thing in your home, because in this situation, it is.*

Step 7: Add Sprouts to Everything.

By day five your first jars of sprouts will be ready. Here is how to use them to maximum effect.

Eat them raw on top of anything. A bowl of rice with a pile of fresh sprouts on top is now a nutritionally complete meal. The rice provides calories. The sprouts provide protein, vitamins, and the fresh food your body needs. This combination, plain rice with raw lentil sprouts, has kept people alive and functional for centuries across Asia and the Middle East. It works.

Cook them for more calories. Raw sprouts are mostly water. Boiled sprouts are dense and filling. Add a jar of sprouts to any soup or bean pot in the last five minutes of cooking. They absorb the flavor and become a substantial part of the meal. A pot of plain bean soup with a full jar of cooked sprouts added becomes a thick stew.

Use the sprout liquid. The water you rinse your sprouts with contains nutrients. Do not pour it down the drain. Use it to cook your rice or oats. Use it as the base for soup. It is free nutrition.

Keep your jars going every single day without exception. Rinse them morning and evening. Start a new jar every day to replace the one you harvest. The system only works if it never stops. A jar you forget to rinse for a day smells sour and has to be thrown out. Thirty seconds twice a day is all it takes to keep the system running.

A Realistic Picture of What One Day of Food Looks Like at This Stage.

This is what a day of eating looks like when you are running low on stored food but your sprout and mushroom systems are producing. This is not abundance. It is survival. It is enough.

Morning: a bowl of congee. One quarter cup of dry rice cooked in two cups of water for twenty minutes with salt. Top with a small handful of raw sprouts. This is breakfast. It is warm, filling, and will hold you for several hours.

Midday: a cup of bean soup from your pot, with a piece of flatbread if you have flour. If the soup runs out, a handful of raw sprouts and a spoonful of peanut butter is a meal. It does not feel like one. It is one.

Evening: your main meal. Whatever you are cooking today from your stores, stretched as far as it will go. A small serving of beans and rice with a full jar of cooked sprouts added. If your mushroom blocks are producing, a handful of oyster mushrooms cooked in a dry pan until golden and added on top. This is a real meal. It has protein, carbohydrates, vitamins, and flavor. A person can function on this.

This is approximately 1,000 to 1,400 calories per day depending on portions. That is below the normal daily requirement. It is above the minimum required to avoid organ damage in a healthy adult. It is enough to keep you thinking clearly, moving, and functional while you work toward a more stable situation.

Children need proportionally similar calories to adults and should not be put on reduced rations except as a last resort. If food is critically short and children are in the household, adults eat less first.

One Final Word.

If you are reading this section because you are in this situation right now, understand that the system described above has kept human beings alive through famines, wars, sieges, and collapses for thousands of years. Sprouted beans and cooked grains are not a desperate improvisation. They are the foundation of human survival across most of recorded history. The people who came before you did not have grocery stores. They had seeds, water, and the knowledge of what to do with them.

You now have that knowledge. Start today.

Now Make Something With It.

Raw sprouts eaten straight from a jar will keep you alive. But making something, even something simple, changes the experience from enduring to surviving with dignity. That distinction matters more than most people expect. Here are three things you can make from your sprouts right now, listed from the absolute minimum of ingredients to slightly more if you have them. No special equipment is required for any of these. A pot, a pan, and heat are enough.

Sprout Porridge: Water and Heat Only.

This requires nothing but sprouts, water, and a pot. It is the most basic preparation and the one that works when everything else is gone.

Put two cups of sprouted lentils and one cup of water in a pot. Cook over medium heat, stirring occasionally, for about ten minutes until the lentils are completely soft. Mash them against the side of the pot with a spoon as they soften. Keep cooking and stirring until the mixture thickens into a rough porridge. Add more water if it gets too thick to stir. Add salt if you have it. Eat it hot.

This is dense, filling, and high in protein. It does not taste exciting. It tastes like cooked lentils, which is what it is. It will hold a person for four to five hours. That is what it is designed to do.

Sprout Pancakes: Add Any Fat and Salt.

If you have any fat at all, even a small amount of oil, lard, bacon drippings, or butter, you can make something that feels genuinely like a meal rather than a survival ration.

Mash two cups of cooked sprouted lentils as smooth as you can get them. Add enough water to make a thick batter that just pours from a spoon, roughly half a cup. Add a pinch of salt. If you have baking powder, add half a teaspoon and the pancakes will puff slightly. If you have any spice at all, garlic powder, onion powder, cumin, anything, add a pinch. Heat a skillet over medium heat with just enough fat to coat the bottom. Pour small rounds of batter into the pan, about three inches across. Cook two to three minutes until the bottom is firm and edges look dry. Flip once. Cook two more minutes.

These are not fluffy breakfast pancakes. They are dense savory cakes with a slightly crispy outside and a soft center. They are real food. Eat them hot with salt. If you have any sauce, broth, or liquid left in a can, use it for dipping.

Sprout Bread: The Best Thing You Can Make.

If you have a blender or can mash lentils very smooth, and you have an oven or a covered pan that can hold heat, you can make actual bread from nothing but soaked lentils and water. This is not a compromise. It is bread. People have been making versions of it for thousands of years.

The full recipe with every variation based on what ingredients you have available is Recipe 8-12 in Chapter VIII of this book. Turn to it when your sprouts are ready. Read the ingredient ladder at the top of that recipe first. It tells you exactly which version to make based on what you have on hand. Even the most stripped-down version, lentils, water, salt, and heat, produces something you can slice, toast in a dry pan, and eat like bread. It will not taste like a bakery loaf. It will taste like food made by someone who refused to give up. That is exactly what it is.

> *Field Note: The single most important flavor improvement available for almost no cost: salt. If you have salt, use it generously in everything you make from sprouts. Salt does not just add flavor. It suppresses the naturally bitter edge that cooked lentils have on their own and makes everything more palatable. A meal you can eat willingly is more valuable than a meal you have to force down. Season your food even now. Especially now.*

Key Recipes Referenced in This Appendix

Recipe 1-3: Skillet Cornbread | Recipe 1-4: Pandampo Flatbread | Recipe 1-7: Buttermilk Biscuits

Recipe 2-1: Water Soup | Recipe 2-4: Bread Soup | Recipe 2-16: Simple Vegetable Soup

Recipe 4-1: Just Beans | Recipe 4-5: Oatmeal with Fat and Salt | Recipe 4-19: Beans & Rice

Recipe 5-17: Vegetable Fried Rice | Recipe 5-18: Egg and Potato Hash | Recipe 8-12: Survival Lentil Bread

Recipe 8-10: Bean Sprouts, Fresh Food From Your Stored Beans | Recipe 8-11: Oyster Mushrooms, Continuous Indoor Cultivation

See also: The Survival Pantry, front of this book

CHAPTER X

PROTECTING YOUR FOOD SUPPLY IN NUCLEAR FALLOUT

What actually contaminates food, what does not, and what to do about it

---

This chapter addresses a specific and important problem: a well-stocked pantry is a false sense of security if you do not understand which foods in it are safe to eat after nuclear fallout has occurred.

The practical answer is reassuring but requires understanding the mechanisms. The key distinction is between external contamination, radioactive fallout particles on the outside of your food, and internal contamination, where radioactive material has been incorporated into the food itself. These are different problems requiring different responses. External contamination is largely manageable. Internal contamination in stored food is largely not a problem, because the packaging is the protection.

Everything in this chapter comes from FEMA, CDC, WHO, and the civil defense research conducted at Oak Ridge National Laboratory under Cresson Kearny, whose Nuclear War Survival Skills, published in 1979 and updated through the 1980s, remains the most practical publicly available civil defense reference produced by the United States government. Nothing here is speculation.

SECTION 1: How Fallout Actually Works

Fallout is not invisible radiation in the air. It is physical material, pulverized earth and debris that was sucked up into a nuclear fireball, made radioactive by neutron activation, and then returned to the ground as particles. These particles range from fine dust to gravel-size. They are the source of the ongoing radiation danger after a nuclear detonation.

The critical fact: fallout particles sit on top of surfaces. They do not penetrate sealed containers. They do not pass through glass, metal, cardboard, or plastic packaging. A can of beans sitting outside in fallout will have radioactive particles on its surface. The beans inside will not be contaminated.

This is not a simplified version of the science, it is the actual mechanism, confirmed by the 1955 Nevada nuclear weapons tests and documented in the civil defense literature. Food packaging stops fallout contamination. The handling protocol follows directly from this fact.

The 7-10 Rule: How Radiation Decays

Fallout radiation decays rapidly in the hours and days after detonation. The rule of thumb used by civil defense planners is called the 7-10 rule: for every sevenfold increase in time after the explosion, the radiation intensity decreases by a factor of 10.

In practical terms: if the radiation level is 1,000 roentgens per hour at one hour after detonation, it will be approximately 100 r/hr at 7 hours, approximately 10 r/hr at 49 hours (two days), and approximately 1 r/hr at 343 hours (about two weeks). This is why the standard civil defense guidance is to shelter in place for at least two weeks, by that point, the immediate fallout danger has dropped dramatically.

For food safety purposes, this means that food in sealed containers that survived the initial two weeks is safe to handle and eat, assuming you decontaminate the outside of the container before opening it. The radioactive particles on the outside will not have penetrated inside. The radiation level has dropped enough that brief handling of the outside of a container does not constitute significant exposure.

> *__Field Note:__ The two-week shelter period is not arbitrary. Radioactive iodine-131, the most immediately dangerous fallout component for thyroid cancer, has a half-life of approximately 8 days. After two weeks it has decayed to a small fraction of its initial level. The longer-lived isotopes, cesium-137, strontium-90, remain a concern for food production in contaminated soil for years, but do not penetrate sealed food containers.*

SECTION 2: What Is Safe to Eat: The Decision Framework

The following guidance comes directly from FEMA, CDC, and WHO. The framework is consistent across all three agencies and is grounded in the same underlying physics.

SAFE: Food Already Inside a Building

Any food that was inside a building when fallout arrived is safe to eat. The building's walls, roof, and floors blocked the fallout particles from reaching it. This includes food in open bowls or on countertops, as long as it was inside. Internal household radiation does not contaminate food on a shelf.

This is the CDC's explicit guidance: 'Food in a pantry or drawer away from radioactive material is safe to eat.'

SAFE: Sealed Containers That Were Outside

Canned goods, glass jars, sealed plastic containers, Mylar bags, and any other sealed food packaging that was outside during fallout is safe to eat after the outside surface is decontaminated. The fallout particles are on the surface of the container, not inside it.

Decontamination procedure: wipe the outside of the container thoroughly with a damp cloth. Seal that cloth in a plastic bag. Keep the bag away from people and do not handle it again without gloves. Then open and eat the contents normally.

FEMA's guidance: 'It is safe to eat food in sealed containers that were outside as long as you wipe off the container with a damp towel or cloth before using.'

SAFE: Refrigerated and Frozen Food

Food in a refrigerator or freezer is safe to eat. The refrigerator walls block fallout contamination. Standard food spoilage rules apply, if you lose power, a closed refrigerator keeps food safe for about four hours, a closed full freezer for about 48 hours. Radiation is not the concern here; normal spoilage is.

NOT SAFE: Uncovered Food That Was Outside

Any food that was outside and uncovered during fallout should not be eaten. This includes garden produce, food left on outdoor tables, open water containers, and anything that had direct contact with fallout particles.

Do not eat food from your garden after fallout until official authorities confirm that the area's radiation levels are acceptable. Root vegetables are higher risk than above-ground produce because they absorb soil contaminants. Above-ground produce can sometimes be made safer by removing outer leaves and washing the edible portions thoroughly, but this should not be attempted without guidance.

NOT SAFE: Open Water Sources

Surface water, streams, ponds, lakes, rainwater collected in open containers, should not be consumed after fallout without testing or filtration. Fallout particles settle on water surfaces and into shallow well water.

Water safety guidance: bottled water in sealed containers is safe. Water in your home's hot water heater and toilet tank (not bowl) is safe, it was inside. If tap water must be used, the CDC notes that tap water is still safe for decontamination and cleaning even when its safety for drinking is uncertain. Boiling tap water does NOT remove radioactive contamination, this is a common misconception. Boiling removes biological contamination. It has no effect on radioactive material.

> *Field Note: The single most important misconception to correct: boiling does not remove radioactive contamination from water. It removes bacteria and viruses. Radioactive material dissolved in water remains dissolved at any temperature. Bottled water in sealed containers is your primary safe water source. Deep well water (from wells cased to prevent surface contamination from entering) may be safe, wait for official guidance specific to your area.*

SECTION 3: Underground Storage and the Basement Advantage

Underground storage provides two separate benefits: physical shielding from gamma radiation during the shelter period, and complete protection from fallout particle deposition.

A root cellar, basement pantry, or underground storage area is the ideal location for a long-term food reserve for exactly this reason. Food stored several feet underground or within a concrete basement was not exposed to fallout particles at all, the ground above intercepted them. The radiation dose received by food stored in a basement during the two-week shelter period is negligible.

This is one of the strongest arguments for a basement or underground pantry that exists independently of nuclear concerns: it is also cooler, more temperature-stable, and darker than above-ground storage, all of which extend shelf life. The nuclear survival benefit comes as an addition to an already optimal storage environment.

Mylar and Sealed Bucket Storage

Food sealed in Mylar bags with oxygen absorbers inside food-grade 5-gallon (18.9 L) buckets is among the most fallout-resistant food storage available. The Mylar bag blocks oxygen and light for shelf life purposes. It also provides a continuous sealed barrier against fallout particles. A bucket sealed with a gamma-seal or snap-on lid adds another physical layer. Food stored this way in a basement before an event is protected by: the ground above, the basement walls, the bucket, and the Mylar bag.

The oxygen absorber that extends shelf life also means the interior of the bag is an inert environment that fallout particles, even if they somehow reached the bag exterior, could not penetrate.

SECTION 4: Meat, Animals, and the Organ Meat Warning

Animals that grazed outdoors during fallout will have ingested fallout particles along with their feed. Radioactive materials concentrate in specific organs, particularly the thyroid gland, kidneys, and liver. The muscle meat of an animal that received a moderate radiation dose may be safe, but its organs are not.

The guidance from Kearny's Nuclear War Survival Skills, based on Oak Ridge National Laboratory research: do not eat the thyroid, kidneys, or liver of animals that were grazing outdoors during fallout. Muscle meat from the same animals, cooked extremely well done (cut into pieces less than 1/2-inch (1.5 cm) thick and cooked to an internal temperature above boiling throughout), may be safe, but carries higher risk than stored food. If an animal appears sick or has died from unknown causes, do not eat it under any circumstances, radiation damage compromises immune function and can allow bacterial contamination that cooking does not reliably neutralize.

In areas where fallout was light enough that animals survived without symptoms, their meat is likely safe by normal standards. The concern is proportional to the fallout intensity the animal received.

The practical upshot: your stored canned protein, sardines, salmon, tuna, Spam, is vastly safer and simpler than attempting to process an animal whose radiation exposure history you do not know. The pre-positioned pantry is the better food source in this scenario.

> *Field Note:* Never eat the liver, kidneys, or thyroid of animals that were outside during heavy fallout. These organs concentrate radioactive material. Muscle meat from the same animal, thoroughly cooked, carries lower but not zero risk. Your stored canned protein carries essentially no contamination risk by comparison.

After the immediate fallout danger passes, two radioactive isotopes present longer-term food production concerns: cesium-137 (half-life approximately 30 years) and strontium-90 (half-life approximately 29 years). These can be taken up by plant roots from contaminated soil and incorporated into food crops grown in affected areas.

The practical guidance for home food production in the post-fallout period: do not plant in or eat from gardens in confirmed fallout zones without radiation monitoring that shows acceptable levels. Above-ground crops (tomatoes, squash, beans) that are washed thoroughly are lower risk than root vegetables (carrots, potatoes, beets) which absorb more soil contamination. Leafy greens are higher risk because their large surface area catches both external fallout particles and absorbs ground-deposited contamination through their roots.

The WHO guidance: 'Avoid consumption of locally produced milk or vegetables' and 'avoid consumption and harvesting of aquatic animals and plants including fish, shellfish, and algae' in areas of confirmed serious contamination. These restrictions apply to the ongoing food production situation in the contaminated zone, not to pre-positioned sealed stored food.

The lesson for pre-positioning: one year's worth of sealed stored food in a basement gives you the time needed to wait for radiation levels to drop and for official guidance on local food production to become available. Without that buffer, you are forced to make immediate decisions about food sources that are difficult to assess without monitoring equipment.

SECTION 6: Practical Decontamination Procedures for Food Containers

The following procedures apply when you need to handle food containers that were outside during fallout, or that came from an area with confirmed contamination. These procedures are from FEMA and CDC guidance.

For Canned Goods and Sealed Jars

1. Do not touch your face during this procedure.
2. Put on rubber or latex gloves if available. If not, improvise with plastic bags over your hands.
3. Take the container outside or to a decontamination area, not your food preparation space.
4. Using a damp cloth, wipe down the entire exterior surface of the container thoroughly, top, sides, and bottom.
5. Seal the used cloth in a plastic bag immediately.
6. Inspect the container for damage. Dented cans where the seal may be compromised should not be used.
7. Bring the wiped container into your food preparation area.
8. Wash your hands thoroughly with soap and water.
9. Open and use contents normally.
10. Place used gloves in the same bag as the contaminated cloth. Seal and keep away from people.

For Mylar Bags and Sealed Buckets

Wipe down the exterior of the bucket with a damp cloth before opening. When opening the bucket lid, do so in a ventilated area if possible, any fallout dust that settled on the lid surface should not be inhaled. The Mylar bag inside should be clean. If it shows any breach or damage to the seal, treat its contents with the same caution as outdoor exposed food.

For Water Containers

Sealed bottled water: wipe outside, open normally. Safe to drink.

Open water containers that were outside: do not drink. Use for washing and decontamination only.

Water in your hot water heater: safe. Turn the heater off and drain from the bottom valve.

Toilet tank water (not bowl): safe. The tank is sealed from outside air under normal conditions.

Well water: if from a deep drilled well with a sealed casing, likely safe, wait for official guidance. Shallow wells and hand-dug wells are higher risk for surface contamination infiltration.

SECTION 7: The Priority List: What to Do First

If you are reading this after a nuclear detonation has occurred or appears imminent, the priorities in order are:

11. GET INSIDE. A substantial building, concrete, brick, basement, reduces your radiation exposure by factors of 10 to 100 compared to being outdoors. Get inside immediately and stay inside.
12. STAY INSIDE for at least 24 hours, ideally 48-72 hours for the most dangerous initial fallout period. Two weeks substantially completes the decay of the most dangerous isotopes.
13. EAT YOUR STORED FOOD. Food sealed inside your home before the event is safe. Open and eat it normally.
14. DO NOT GO OUTSIDE for food in the first 24-72 hours. No food source outside is worth the radiation exposure during the initial fallout period when levels are highest.
15. DRINK SEALED BEVERAGES ONLY. Bottled water, canned drinks, water from your water heater or toilet tank.
16. WIPE DOWN any sealed containers from outside before opening them. This takes 60 seconds and is the entire decontamination procedure.
17. DO NOT BOIL WATER to remove radiation. It does not work. Boiling removes biological contamination only.
18. DO NOT EAT organ meats from animals that were outside in heavy fallout.
19. DO NOT EAT garden produce or outdoor crops until official guidance confirms the area's contamination status.
20. WHEN IN DOUBT ABOUT A FOOD SOURCE: use your stored pantry instead. That is what it is there for.

Sources

FEMA: Ready.gov, Radiation Emergencies; Nuclear Detonation Safety: Food, Drinking Water and Medicine (2020)

CDC: Food, Drinking Water and Medicine Safety in a Radiation Emergency

WHO: Radioactivity in food after a nuclear emergency (2023)

Cresson H. Kearny: Nuclear War Survival Skills, Ch. 9, Food (Oak Ridge National Laboratory, updated 1987, public domain)

OSTI/USDA: Civil Defense in the Food Industry, Radiological Hazards in Processed Foods Resulting from Nuclear Warfare

U.S. Government civil defense pamphlets: Protection Against Nuclear Attack; Family Food Stockpile for Survival